Dispatches From Calabria

Eating My Way through Culinary School in Italy

Gary J. Mihalik

Copyright © 2024 by Gary J. Mihalik

All rights reserved. Published in the United States of America. No part of this book may be reproduced or transmitted in any form or by any means, graphic, electronic or mechanical, including photocopying, recording, taping or by any information storage or retrieval system, without permission in writing from the publisher.

This edition published by Highpoint Life Books
For information, write to info@highpointpubs.com.

First Edition
ISBN: 979-8-9897773-7-2

Library of Congress Cataloging-in-Publication Data

Mihalik

Dispatches from Cambria: Eating My Way Through Culinary School in Italy

Summary: "This is a day-by-day culinary adventure in one of Italy's top cooking schools, situated amid natural beauty and cultural richness – including scores of amazing recipes and beautiful photos." – Provided by publisher.

ISBN: 979-8-9897773-7-2 (Paperback)
1. Cooking 2. Italy

Library of Congress Control Number: 2024909410

Cover and Interior Design by Sarah M. Clarehart
Photos by the author.

Manufactured in the United States of America

Contents

Recipe Index vi

Acknowledgments x

Preface xi

Introduction xv

1 And So It Begins... 1

Pollo Arrosto / Roast Chicken ❧ Cavolfiore Gratinato con Besciamella / Roast Cauliflower with Bechamel ❧ Pan di Spagna / Sponge Cake ❧ Torta con la Frutta e Panna Montata / Sponge Cake with Cream and Fruit ❧ Peperoncini Sott'Olio / Chile Peppers in Oil

2 Making It to the First Day of Class 11

Brodo di Pollo / Chicken Broth ❧ Cotechino con le Lenticchie / Cotechino Sausage with Lentils ❧ Polpette con Formaggio Pecorino / Meatballs with Pecorino Cheese ❧ Strozzapreti al Ragù di Vitello / "Priest-Strangler" Pasta with Veal Ragù ❧ Supplì / Roman Rice Balls

3 Bureaucracy and Bourbon 25

Pasta alle Acciughe e Aglio / Anchovy Garlic Paste ❧ Lupara / Lupara ❧ Pasta alla Puttanesca / Pasta alla Puttanesca ❧ Pollo alla Romana / Roman-Style Chicken ❧ Pasta al Profumo di Mare / "Perfume of the Sea" Pasta ❧ Brodo di Pesce / Fish Stock

4 Pasta and Bread 39

Lasagne con Agnello e Carciofi / Lamb and Artichoke Lasagna ❧ Pasta Fresca all'Uovo / Fresh Egg Pasta ❧ Ragù di Agnello / Lamb Ragù ❧ Linguine allo Scoglio / Linguine "From the Reef" ❧ Ragù di Molluschi / Mollusk Ragù

5 Pizza Tre Volte 53

Olio all'Aglio / Garlic Oil ❧ Mafalde con i Broccoli / Mafalde Pasta with Broccoli ❧ Orecchiette con Cime di Rapa e Salsiccia / Orecchiette Pasta with Broccoli Rabe and Sausage ❧ Pasta per Pizza / Pizza Dough ❧ Salsa per Pizza / Pizza Sauce ❧ Ricotta Infornata / Baked Ricotta ❧ Risotto al Parmigiano / Parmesan Cheese Risotto

6 Beyond Satiety 67

Spritz / Aperol Spritz ❦ Arancini di Riso / Arancini ❦ Cannoli Siciliani / Cannoli ❦ Pasta alla Norma / Pasta alla Norma ❦ Olive Arrostite / Roasted Olives ❦ Tiramisù / Tiramisù

7 Horses Galloping through Fields of Clover 79

Brodo Concentrato di Pollo / Concentrated Chicken Stock ❦ Paninetti / Little Bread Rolls ❦ Pasta Integrale con Ragù di Coniglio / Whole Wheat Pasta with Rabbit Ragù ❦ Scaloppine di Maiale al Marsala / Pork Cutlets with Marsala ❦ Spaghetti Aglio e Olio / Spaghetti with Garlic and Oil ❦ Pasta Integrale / Whole Wheat Pasta

8 Pig Week 93

Pancetta Tesa / Flat Pancetta ❦ Porchetta / Slow-Roasted Pork ❦ Salsiccia Calabrese / Calabrian Sausage ❦ Salsiccia Toscana / Tuscan Sausage ❦ Tonno del Chianti / Tuna of Chianti (Pork Confit)

9 The Barber Makes House Calls 109

Fettine di Manzo in Umido con Olive Nere / Thinly Sliced Beef Braised in Tomato Sauce with Black Olives ❦ Fiori di Zucca Fritti / Fried Zucchini Blossoms ❦ Fusilloni con Sugo di 'Nduja e Pomodoro / Fusilloni Pasta with 'Nduja and Tomato Sauce ❦ Brodo di Funghi / Mushroom Broth ❦ Pere Affogate nel Vino Rosso / Red-Wine Poached Pears ❦ Risotto ai Funghi / Mushroom Risotto

10 Dead Vegetable Week 125

Salsa di Pomodoro / Basic Tomato Sauce ❦ Cacio e Pepe / Cacio e Pepe ❦ Arancia Candita / Candied Orange Peel ❦ Pasta all'Amatriciana / Pasta all'Amatriciana ❦ Pasta alla Gricia / Pasta alla Gricia

11 If It Doesn't Taste Yummy, It's Worthless 139

Fagioli e Verdure / Beans and Greens ❦ Bomba Calabrese / Calabrian Preserved Spicy Eggplant ❦ Melanzane Imbottite / Stuffed Eggplant Rolls ❦ Olio Santo / Hot Chile Oil ❦ Crostata di Ricotta / Ricotta Tart ❦ Pasta Frolla / Shortcrust Pastry

12 How Far Over the Top Can We Go? 151

Antipasto di Burrata e Cime di Rapa / Burrata and Broccoli Rabe Antipasto ❦ Ceci con Olio Infuso / Chickpeas with Infused Oil ❦ Maltagliati con Ragù di Code di Bue / Maltagliati Pasta with Oxtail Ragù ❦ Brodo di Verdure / Vegetable Broth

13 Italy Is Blessed with Poor Distribution 163

Focaccia / Focaccia ❦ Pasta alle Vongole / Pasta with Clams ❦ Polpo alla Sous-Vide / Octopus Sous-Vide ❦ Carpaccio di Polpo / Octopus Carpaccio ❦ Pasta alla Chitarra con Cozze e Pomodorini / Pasta Cut on the "Chitarra" with Mussels and Cherry Tomatoes ❦ Zuppa di Pomodoro / Tomato Soup

14 Gelato and Meatballs 177

Crostata di Marmellata / Jam Tart ❦ *Gelato al Fiordilatte / Milk and Cream Gelato* ❦ *Polpette e Peperoni Dolci / Meatballs and Sweet Peppers* ❦ *Pasta e Fagioli / Pasta and Beans* ❦ *Sbriciolata al Cioccolato Bianco Caramellato / Caramelized White Chocolate Crumble*

15 Butter and Sugar and Lard, Oh My! 191

Babà / Babà ❦ *Fraguni / Savory Ricotta-Filled Tarts from Calabria* ❦ *Pane Arabo / "Arab" Bread* ❦ *Piadina / Italian Flatbread* ❦ *Pizzette / "Cocktail" Pizza*

16 An Execution at the Italian Culinary Institute 207

Biga / Italian "Pre-Dough" ❦ *Cantucci / Tuscan Almond Biscotti* ❦ *Caponata / Caponata* ❦ *Ciabatta / Ciabatta* ❦ *Fregola con Vongole e Pomodorini / Fregola Pasta with Clams and Cherry Tomatoes* ❦ *Pane Carasau / Crispy Sardinian Flatbread*

17 A Cat Named Pancetta and a Pizza Called Amnesia 223

Fileja con Gamberi e Funghi / Fileja Pasta with Shrimp and Mushrooms ❦ *Frittata di Pasta / Pasta Frittata* ❦ *Limoncello / Limoncello* ❦ *Minestra di Fagioli di Zia Fidalma / Aunt Fidalma's Bean Soup* ❦ *Rigatoni ai Piselli / Rigatoni with Peas*

18 We Herd You Were Making Cheese 237

Pasta al Ragù Calabrese di Agnello / Pasta with Calabrian Lamb Ragù ❦ *Polenta Concia / Polenta with Cheese and Butter* ❦ *Ricotta di Vacca / Ricotta* ❦ *Formaggio Tomino / Tomino Cheese* ❦ *Funghi Trifolati / Braised Mushrooms*

19 And So It Ends (for Now!) 251

Besciamella / Béchamel Sauce ❦ *Lasagne alla Bolognese / Lasagne Bolognese* ❦ *Crescia di Formaggio Pasqualina alla Romana / Roman Easter Cheese Bread* ❦ *Ragù Bolognese / Ragù Bolognese* ❦ *Olio Profumato al Rosmarino / Rosemary Oil*

Index 264

Recipe Index

Appetizers / Antipasti

Arancini / Arancini di Riso 71
Baked Ricotta / Ricotta Infornata 63
Burrata and Broccoli Rabe Antipasto / Antipasto di Burrata e Cime di Rapa 157
"Cocktail" Pizza / Pizzette 202
Fried Zucchini Blossoms / Fiori di Zucca Fritti 115
Octopus Carpaccio / Carpaccio di Polpo 172
Roman Rice Balls / Supplì 21

Pasta and Sauces / Pasta e Salse

Basic Tomato Sauce / Salsa di Pomodoro 131
Béchamel Sauce / Besciamella 256
Cacio e Pepe / Cacio e Pepe 132
Fileja Pasta with Shrimp and Mushrooms / Fileja con Gamberi e Funghi 228
Fregola Pasta with Clams and Cherry Tomatoes / Fregola con Vongole e Pomodorini 219
Fresh Egg Pasta / Pasta Fresca all'Uovo 45
*Fusilloni Pasta with 'Nduja and Tomato Sauce / Fusilloni con Sugo di 'Nduja e
   Pomodoro* 116
Lamb and Artichoke Lasagna / Lasagne con Agnello e Carciofi 44
Lamb Ragù / Ragù di Agnello 46
Lasagna Bolognese / Lasagne alla Bolognese 257
Linguine "from the Reef" / Linguine allo Scoglio 48
Lupara / Lupara 30
Mafalde Pasta with Broccoli / Mafalde con i Broccoli 58
Maltagliati Pasta with Oxtail Ragù / Maltagliati con Ragù di Code di Bue 159
Mollusk Ragù / Ragù di Molluschi 50
*Orecchiette Pasta with Broccoli Rabe and Sausage / Orecchiette con Cime di
   Rapa e Salsiccia* 59
Pasta all'Amatriciana / Pasta all'Amatriciana 135
Pasta alla Gricia / Pasta alla Gricia 136
Pasta alla Norma / Pasta alla Norma 75
Pasta alla Puttanesca / Pasta alla Puttanesca 32
Pasta and Beans / Pasta e Fagioli 187
*Pasta Cut on the "Chitarra" with Mussels and Cherry Tomatoes / Pasta alla Chitarra
   con Cozze e Pomodorini* 173
Pasta with Calabrian Lamb Ragù / Pasta al Ragù Calabrese di Agnello 243
Pasta with Clams / Pasta alle Vongole 169
"Perfume of the Sea" Pasta / Pasta al Profumo di Mare 34
"Priest-Strangler" Pasta with Veal Ragù / Strozzapreti al Ragù di Vitello 19
Ragù Bolognese / Ragù Bolognese 260
Rigatoni with Peas / Rigatoni ai Piselli 234
Spaghetti with Garlic and Oil / Spaghetti Aglio e Olio 89
Whole Wheat Pasta / Pasta Integrale 90
Whole Wheat Pasta with Rabbit Ragù / Pasta Integrale con Ragù di Coniglio 86

Rice, Polenta, Soup, and Broth / Riso, Polenta, Zuppa e Brodo

Aunt Fidalma's Bean Soup / Minestra di Fagioli di Zia Fidalma 233
Chicken Broth / Brodo di Pollo 15
Concentrated Chicken Stock / Brodo Concentrato di Pollo 83
Fish Stock / Brodo di Pesce 36
Mushroom Broth / Brodo di Funghi 118
Mushroom Risotto / Risotto ai Funghi 120
Parmesan Cheese Risotto / Risotto al Parmigiano 64
Polenta with Cheese and Butter / Polenta Concia 245
Vegetable Broth / Brodo di Verdure 161

Meat, Poultry, Eggs, and Seafood / Carne, Pollame, Uova e Frutti di Mare

Cotechino Sausage with Lentils / Cotechino con le Lenticchie 16
Meatballs and Sweet Peppers / Polpette e Peperoni Dolci 185
Meatballs with Pecorino Cheese / Polpette con Formaggio Pecorino 17
Octopus Sous-Vide / Polpo alla Sous-Vide 171
Pasta Frittata / Frittata di Pasta 230
Pork Cutlets with Marsala / Scaloppine di Maiale al Marsala 88
Roast Chicken / Pollo Arrosto 4
Roman-Style Chicken / Pollo alla Romana 33
Slow-Roasted Pork / Porchetta 101
Thinly Sliced Beef Braised in Tomato Sauce with Black Olives / Fettine di Manzo in Umido con Olive Nere 114

Side Dishes / Contorni

Beans and Greens / Fagioli e Verdure 143
Braised Mushrooms / Funghi Trifolati 248
Chickpeas with Infused Oil / Ceci con Olio Infuso 158
Roast Cauliflower with Bechamel / Cavolfiore Gratinato con Besciamella 5
Stuffed Eggplant Rolls / Melanzane Imbottite 146

Pizza and Bread / Pizza e Pane

"Arab" Bread / Pane Arabo 199
Ciabatta / Ciabatta 217
Crispy Sardinian Flatbread / Pane Carasau 220
Focaccia / Focaccia 167
Italian Flatbread / Piadina 201
Italian "Pre-Dough" / Biga 213
Little Bread Rolls / Paninetti 84
Pizza Dough / Pasta per Pizza 61
Pizza Sauce / Salsa per Pizza 62
Roman Easter Cheese Bread / Crescia di Formaggio Pasqualina alla Romana 259
Savory Ricotta-Filled Tarts from Calabria / Fraguni 198

Desserts / Dolci

Babà / Babà	196
Cannoli / Cannoli Siciliani	73
Caramelized White Chocolate Crumble / Sbriciolata al Cioccolato Bianco Caramellato	188
Jam Tart / Crostata di Marmellata	182
Milk and Cream Gelato / Gelato al Fiordilatte	183
Red-Wine Poached Pears / Pere Affogate nel Vino Rosso	119
Ricotta Tart / Crostata di Ricotta	148
Shortcrust Pastry / Pasta Frolla	149
Sponge Cake / Pan di Spagna	6
Sponge Cake with Cream and Fruit / Torta con la Frutta e Panna Montata	7
Tiramisù / Tiramisù	76
Tuscan Almond Biscotti / Cantucci	214

Preserving, Cheese, and Cured Meat / Conserve, Formaggio, e Salumi

Anchovy Garlic Paste / Pasta alle Acciughe e Aglio	29
Calabrian Preserved Spicy Eggplant / Bomba Calabrese	145
Calabrian Sausage / Salsiccia Calabrese	103
Candied Orange Peel / Arancia Candita	133
Caponata / Caponata	216
Chile Peppers in Oil / Peperoncini Sott'Olio	8
Flat Pancetta / Pancetta Tesa	99
Garlic Oil / Olio all'Aglio	57
Hot Chile Oil / Olio Santo	147
Ricotta / Ricotta di Vacca	246
Roasted Olives / Olive Arrostite	76
Rosemary Oil / Olio Profumato al Rosmarino	262
Tomino Cheese / Formaggio Tomino	247
Tuna of Chianti (Pork Confit) / Tonno del Chianti	106
Tuscan Sausage / Salsiccia Toscana	104

Beverages / Bevande

Aperol Spritz / Spritz	71
Limoncello / Limoncello	232

To my husband, Frank, who encouraged me to go to culinary school. He managed everything stateside during the five months I spent in Italy, and he continues to manage everything during my frequent return visits. He provided unending support to me during the process of testing recipes and writing this book. He ate almost everything I made, though he drew the line at sea creatures with suckers.

Acknowledgments

I am deeply grateful to Chef John Nocita, Chef Juan Penzini, and the faculty and staff of the Istituto Culinario Italiano (Italian Culinary Institute) for providing me with a life-changing experience.

Family and friends were my official tasters during the years I spent testing the recipes for this book. Prominent among them are Frank Pieri, my husband; Frank and Marisa Pieri, my father- and mother-in-law; Robert Reddington, John O'Malley, Frank Watson, and Michael Riordan, members of our weekly dinner group in Palm Springs; Rich DePippo, Doug Howe, Patricia Assimakis, and Becky Gould, members of Santa Fe Ate, our dinner group in Santa Fe. Whether they knew it or not other taste testers included Mike Abramson, Gay Nathan, Julie Paradise, and Gregg Hartnett.

Cristiana Skelmba, my Italian tutor, read the manuscript to try to prevent me from being embarrassed with my imperfect Italian.

And finally, I owe a debt of gratitude to all those many friends who encouraged me to turn my blog posts into a book. Without their perseverance, I would never have considered publishing this collection.

PREFACE

I have been cooking since I was seventeen years of age, when I went away to college at the University of Pennsylvania.

I was part of the largest entering freshman class in Penn's history, and there was not enough lodging in the dorms that traditionally housed the entering class. Therefore, freshmen were offered lodging in upperclassmen dorms. I applied and was accepted into a hastily established college house that occupied two floors of High Rise East housing both freshmen and upperclassmen.

Penn's high rises—East, North, and South, which were collectively known as the "Superblock"—contained apartments that each housed two to four students. Upperclassmen apartment living meant not having to walk down the hallway to a communal bathroom or kitchen (for those few dorms that even had communal kitchens).

As a freshman I was required to have a meal contract. The most limited contract offered was ten meals per week. That's the one I took. I certainly didn't need a meal contract for seven cereal-and-milk breakfasts that I could whip up in my own kitchen. The same was true for weekend lunches, which were mostly sandwich-based affairs. Thus, out of the nominal twenty-one meals each week, a ten-meal-per-week contract really only left out two dinners on Saturday and Sunday.

Saturdays often saw groups of my fellow freshmen going out for dinner. That's when I had my first taste of Indian food at Maharaja Restaurant, located just beyond Superblock. It's also when I had my first taste of Chinese food in Philadelphia's Chinatown with Dennis and Martha Law, graduate students from Hong Kong who were resident advisors in the college house.

I often cooked on Sundays. Up until this point in my life I hadn't really spent time cooking (other than baking, which I had started doing around the age of twelve). Sundays quickly became established as the time for me to call home (after my breakfast of a half dozen glazed doughnuts eaten while reading *The New York Times*), when my mom I would talk about food. Specifically we talked about how to cook whatever it was that I was planning on making for dinner that evening. That's how I learned to cook: instructions over the telephone from my mother.

By the end of the year I was a credible cook. So much so that the brother of one of my high school classmates, who was a year or two ahead of me at Penn, asked me if I wanted to room with him in High Rise South (upperclassmen were offered the ability to keep their dorm-apartments from year to year). The arrangement was that I would cook dinner and he would clean up. It seemed like a good deal to me! He had a one-bedroom two-person apartment, which meant I wouldn't have to share the kitchen with anybody!

I was technically a much better cook by the end of the year, though I still wasn't cooking much that was adventurous. That spring, I applied to enter the International Residence Project, another college house arrangement (but not for freshmen) back in High Rise East. I was accepted and was introduced to my future roommate, Ray Hugh from Guyana, later in the spring semester.

Ray was second-generation Guyanese of Chinese ancestry. He liked to cook and opened up a whole new world of flavors for me, preparing Chinese, East Indian (51 percent of the population of Guyana was of East Indian descent at the time), and West Indian food.

While staying in the International Residence Project college house, my exposure to foods from around the world exploded: Filipino from Jose Eduardo Delgado, Persian from Azadeh Ali Mohammed, Jamaican from Valrie Tracey, Bangladeshi from Najma Davis, and, most significantly, Sri Lankan from Reggie and Nanacy Rajapakse, to name just a few.

Despite my love of cooking, however, it never took center stage in my life. I went to medical school, completed a residency in psychiatry, and got two graduate degrees, one in anthropology and one in business. I opened a psychiatric practice, taught medical students and residents, taught graduate students, and went on to become the chief medical officer of a psychiatric hospital and then at a second, much larger, psychiatric hospital. I became the associate director of standards at the Joint Commission (called the Joint Commission on the Accreditation of Healthcare Organizations at the time) while also working as the chief medical officer of a behavioral health plan. I started a healthcare consulting company, became the chief medical officer of a much larger behavioral health plan, and then opened a consulting company in Dubai when my company landed a contract with the Ministry of Health of the United Arab Emirates. I eventually sold my consulting company in the middle of 2016, agreeing to stay on for a year to facilitate a smooth transition. With nothing better to do, I stayed on for a second year. When the second year was up, I didn't make any move toward leaving.

All the while, I kept cooking.

I cooked for Kitchen Angels in Santa Fe, New Mexico. I cooked for celebrity chefs at the annual Palm Desert Food and Wine Festival in California. I cooked for family and friends.

During this time, I had been considering delving deeper into Italian cuisine. I kept researching schools online. I decided the best place to learn about Italian food was in Italy.

My next decision was that the course could not be longer than six months and that was already pushing the limits of how long I wanted to be away. I also didn't want to spend time on the basics of how to cook. I wanted the school to jump right into Italian cuisine with no time spent on teaching knife skills or how to sauté. Finally, the school had to provide a credible education on food from all of Italy, not from just one region.

As much research as I did—and I did a lot—only one school met my criteria. This was the Italian Culinary Institute (ICI) in Calabria. One early morning in July 2018 while vacationing on Fire Island, I repeated my search. Again, the ICI—and in particular its Master of Italian Cuisine program—was the only institution that met my requirements. Two years after selling my company, something in me had changed. I pulled up the online application form and filled it out. I clicked "submit" and then immediately began to wonder if I had done the right thing.

I calmed myself down by acknowledging that even if I were to be accepted, I wouldn't be obligated to attend. Two days later my acceptance notification arrived by email, setting off another round of angst. I agonized for a day and then submitted my deposit. Come January, I would be going to Italy for three months!

Upon my return it was clear to me that my life had changed. This thing that I loved and that had always been relegated to the sidelines in my life was now about to take center stage.

Come with me to the Italian Culinary Institute.

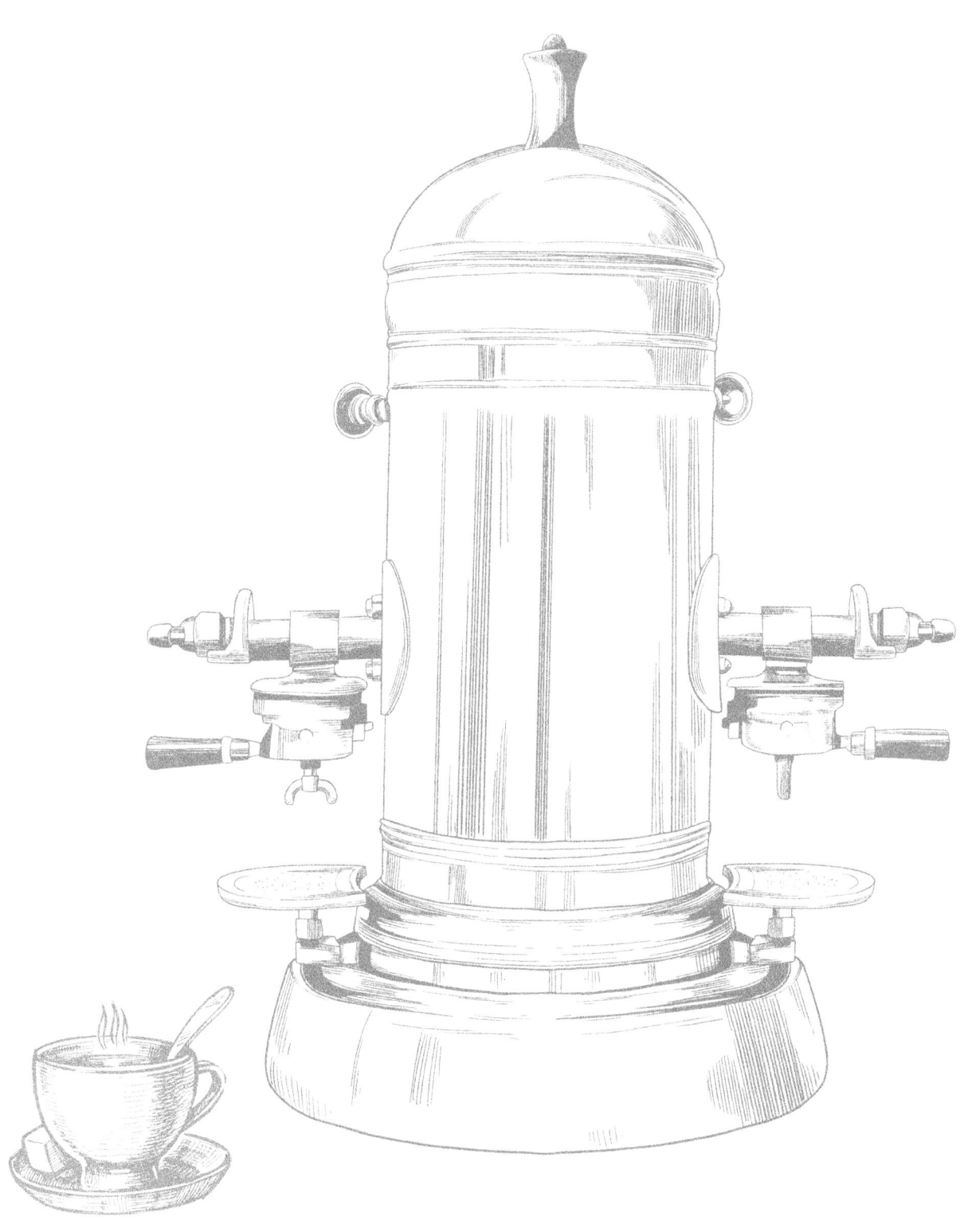

INTRODUCTION

This book is based on a series of blog posts I wrote in 2019 while I was in culinary school at the Italian Culinary Institute in Calabria, Italy. Except for minor editing for clarity, they are as I originally posted them. Each chapter is paired with five or six recipes related to the blog post. These were selected from the hundreds of dishes that we made and tasted throughout the course.

At the ICI, all recipes are in metric measures, as is common in almost the entire world except for the United States. In professional kitchens in Europe, most ingredients are weighed, including liquids. In home kitchens in Europe, liquids are usually measured by volume as they are in the United States, but solid ingredients are weighed. When I was cooking with Zia Fidalma in Tuscany, she would pull out her (very accurate) scale the same way an American would pull out a measuring cup.

For the recipes in this book, I have mostly converted liquids to volume measures and include both metric and American measures. In some instances when I thought the recipe demanded it, I provide the liquid measures by weight only. Weighing liquids is especially important for canning, preserving, meat curing, and cheesemaking. If you do a significant amount of cooking and you start to weigh everything, you will quickly learn that it is a much faster method for measuring ingredients. Highly accurate digital scales are quite inexpensive.

I have included American measures for all the recipes. As much as possible I provide these in the customary volume format: teaspoons, tablespoons, cups, etc. However, for some ingredients, volume is just too inaccurate so I provide the ingredient quantity by weight. For example, when grating cheese, the volume of a given weight of cheese is substantially dependent on the size of the pieces.

In most instances, the American measures are equivalent to the metric measures, but occasionally there are minor differences. For example, when cooking pasta, the difference between three liters and three quarts is not significant, so I didn't upsize the American measure to three quarts and two-thirds cup. For this reason, please use only one set of measures or the other when preparing a recipe. The two most common sizes for packages of pasta are 500 grams and 1 pound (454 grams). These can be used interchangeably unless a recipe specifies otherwise. For this reason, measures for pasta and a few other ingredients are noted as ~1 pound.

Using the metric system makes scaling recipes up and down much easier. It also makes it easier to calculate formulas. So although I have provided both metric and American measures, I encourage you to use the metric ones.

Notes on Key Ingredients for Italian Cuisine

There are many exhaustive references on ingredients for Italian cuisine. My intent in this section is to provide information on a few critical foodstuffs that will aid you in selecting the best ingredients for cooking.

Italian Common Wheat Flour

There is much misconception about Italian flour in the United States. Most cooks have heard about 00 (double-zero) flour but don't really understand what it is. Double zero (doppio zero in Italian) refers to the fineness of the grind, nothing more. With 00 being the finest, the next slightly coarser grind is 0, after that is 1, and, although you'll rarely see it, 2. Fineness of grind says nothing about how the flour will perform when making pastry or bread.

The second characteristic to understand about how Italian flour is categorized is its W-value. The W-value is a measure of how extensible the dough is. The W-value roughly correlates with gluten content, similar to the range from low-gluten cake flour to all-purpose flour to high-gluten bread flour, but is a much more precise measure because instead of just measuring protein content, it measures how the flour reacts when moistened. Higher W-values make more extensible (stretchy) doughs. Roughly, W-values run from 90 (which is difficult to find) to 400. Flour in the W-350 to W-400 range is often referred to as Manitoba flour in reference to where the grain was originally grown. No recipe in this book calls for flour with a W-value lower than 180. One of the helpful things about W-value is that you can create a flour with a new W-value by combining two different flours. If you combine equal parts of W-180 flour and W-320 flour, you will end up with a flour with a W-value of 250.

I tend to keep double-zero flour with three different W-values in my pantry: W-180, W-320, and W-400. From these I can create any W-value I want with just a little bit of arithmetic.

Italian Durum Wheat Flour

Durum is the hardest of all cultivated wheat. Durum is Latin for hard. Most dry pasta is made exclusively from durum wheat. As with common wheat flour, durum wheat flour comes in different grinds. For practical purposes there are three categories: semolino, semolina, and semola, which is sometimes referred to as semola rimacinata (reground). Semolino is the coarsest grind. Semolina is medium. Semola is the finest. These distinctions do not hold for durum wheat flour packaged for the American market. Most recipes in this book that call for durum wheat flour require semola. It is best to buy an Italian brand that is clearly labeled as semola rimacinata to get the correct grind.

Olive Oil

The best-quality olive oil is made from ripe olives by mechanical means: grinding, pressing, and centrifugation. The label often says "first cold pressing." Extra-virgin olive oil is the highest quality, and to be labeled as such the oil must be mechanically extracted, have excellent flavor, and have a free acid content of no more than 0.8 percent. Virgin olive oil is also extracted by mechanical means but can have a free acid content of up to 2 percent. It may also have slight defects in taste. Other types of mechanically extracted olive oil will not be encountered in the domestic market. The pomace (crushed olives) that remains after the mechanical extraction of oil can be processed by chemical means to produce other types of olive oil that have little flavor or taste. These are often referred to as olive oil, refined olive oil, light olive oil, and olive pomace oil, for example.

Despite common misconceptions, extra-virgin olive oil is a good oil for frying, though generally at temperatures not above 175°C (350°F). Because of its cost, extra-virgin olive oil is not commonly used for dishes that require deep-frying. While virgin olive oil would be good for applications where the oil is heated, it can be difficult to find. For this reason, I recommend that you use extra-virgin olive oil exclusively.

Extra-virgin olive oil can vary in color from yellow to deep green, and its taste can go from buttery to grassy to peppery. If you take the time to taste different extra-virgin olive oils, you will find that these characteristics mean that different extra-virgin olive oils will enhance dishes differently.

Pasta

Fresh pasta and dry pasta are really different foods and, with a few exceptions, not interchangeable. One is not better than the other. The intended use will dictate which is more appropriate. Most dry pasta is made from durum wheat (discussed previously). Two production steps that can greatly affect the quality of the finished pasta are extrusion and drying. The best-quality pasta is extruded through brass molds that create a slightly irregular surface that is good for gripping sauce. Less expensive pasta is often extruded through non-stick (e.g., Teflon) molds. Drying is also important to the texture of the pasta. Slow-drying produces the best, toothy texture. Less expensive pasta is often dried rapidly with heat, which can cook up soft, even when not over-boiled. I suggest you only buy pasta made in Italy that has been extruded from bronze molds and slow-dried. Not all pasta sold in the United States from Italian companies is actually made in Italy. Read the package carefully.

Tomato Products

Tomatoes are integral to Italian cuisine. Other than cherry and grape tomatoes, good tomatoes are generally available for a very short time each year and even then, whether or not you can get excellent vine-ripened tomatoes depends on where you live. Most recipes in this book call for canned tomato products. I have chosen to not include dishes that require fresh tomatoes except for cherry and grape tomatoes (pomodorini) that are available year-round. I recommend you stock three types of tomato products: Italian double-concentrated tomato paste in a tube, canned peeled tomatoes packed in tomato puree (preferably San Marzano tomatoes), and Italian tomato puree (passata). In the American domestic market, canned peeled tomatoes come in three sizes: 992 grams (35 ounces), 794 grams (28 ounces), and 397 to 411 grams (14 to 14½ ounces). Italian tomato puree generally comes in jars and cartons. I prefer jars. These are usually 690 grams to 700 grams (24 to 24½ ounces) in size. Recipes specify which size is the most appropriate.

Rice for Risotto

Three types of rice are commonly used for risotto: arborio, carnaroli, and vialone nano. Of these, arborio is the least preferred (though generally the easiest to source) because it does not have much holding time after it is cooked. Carnaroli and vialone nano maintain their texture for 5 to 7 minutes, making them just a bit easier to work with. (I suggest you have everyone seated at the table a few minutes before you anticipate plating the risotto so that it is eaten at the pinnacle of culinary perfection.) Vialone nano is available but not as common as carnaroli. I use carnaroli almost exclusively for risotto, though any of these three types of rice will produce a good product.

Sausage Casing

Only two recipes call for stuffing sausage into casing. Both of the sausage recipes call for 32 to 35 millimeter hog casing. That is exactly how you will see it described when buying it. Hog casing is a natural product preserved in salt or salt solution. I suggest buying it preserved in salt as it will last nearly indefinitely under refrigeration. Loosen the bundle and free up one length of casing. Submerge it in cool water and swish it around to remove excess salt. When you are sure there are no knots or kinks, place one end of the casing over a faucet and slowly run cool water through the casing to flush out any salt. Be careful not to burst the casing. Leave the cleaned casing soaking in cool water while preparing as many as you will need.

When you are ready to stuff the sausage, thread the casing over the sausage stuffer attachment. It looks like a long, thin funnel. Leave about 5 centimeters (2 inches) of casing not threaded on the stuffer attachment. Begin to press the sausage out of the stuffer. It should grab the casing and begin to move it off the stuffer. Guide the process with your hand. If visible air pockets appear, use a sausage pricker to puncture the casing where the air pocket is and squeeze out the air.

Kitchen Equipment

Most of the recipes in this book do not use any special equipment, but there are a few items you may not have.

Scales

Except for liquids, weighing ingredients produces more consistent results than volume measurements. The weight of 4 cups of flour will vary from cook to cook and from time to time, even for the same cook. One pound of flour will always be 1 pound of flour. In professional settings, it is common to weigh liquids, too. It's easier, faster, and potentially more accurate than using volume. I strongly encourage you to buy a scale—actually, two scales. The first should be one that can weigh up to about 8 kilograms (about 17½ pounds) in 1 gram increments. (Even if you use the option of American weights, buy based on the specifications given in the metric system.) Very reliable models can be found for about $15. Some recipes require small amounts of ingredients. Included among these are recipes for sausage, preserving, and gelato. For these recipes I suggest a second scale that can weigh in increments of one hundredth of a gram up to about 200 grams (about 7 ounces). Slightly more expensive than the first, these can be had for about $25. Virtually every digital scale on the market will weigh in metric as well as in pounds and ounces.

Pasta Sauté Pan

Almost every pasta recipe in this book requires finishing the pasta in the sauce. The pasta is par-cooked by boiling and then added to the sauce in a large sauté pan and finished with additional liquid, usually pasta-cooking water, while being stirred and flipped to emulsify the sauce. Pasta sauté pans are wide, aluminum affairs with a gentle 90-degree curve. They are wide to accommodate lots of pasta. The aluminum makes the pans light enough to maneuver easily. The curve facilitates flipping the pasta. You can make do with other wide, shallow pans, but if you make a lot of pasta, a pasta sauté pan is a good investment. I have two. My smallest is 36 centimeters (14 inches). It easily accommodates 500 grams (about 1 pound) of pasta. This is the size I suggest you get unless you plan on regularly making twice this amount of pasta.

Pasta Machine

While there is a mystique to having someone's grandmother roll out pasta by hand with a rolling pin, it's just not a practical place for most cooks to start unless they do so from a young age with lots of guidance from a skilled pasta maker. A pasta machine makes it easy to roll every sheet of pasta to the same thickness. Most pasta machines come with blades to cut two widths: spaghetti and fettuccine. I am not at all suggesting that you not learn how to roll pasta with a rolling pin, but unless you have a teacher who is skilled at rolling pasta, it is best to start with a pasta machine. For example, with a pasta machine you can get an appreciation for the differences in thickness that would be difficult to learn by rolling your own. The settings on older pasta machines were geared to Italian pasta traditions. Newer machines usually have several additional settings that produce much thinner pasta and are targeted to non-Italian production. Although there is no official standard, setting #7 is about as thin as you want to go on most pasta machines.

Vegetable Press

Just a few recipes in this book call for a vegetable press, and even those suggest alternatives. However, I find my press an indispensable aid in the kitchen. A vegetable press consists of a perforated metal basket that sits inside a larger, solid-metal sleeve with a spout. There is a chaser that screws down to compress what is in the basket. The liquid comes out of the spout. A vegetable press makes quick work out of squeezing the liquid from vegetables.

AND SO IT BEGINS...

JANUARY 12

I arrived in Italy on January 8. It was twenty-nine hours door-to-door: Santa Fe to Albuquerque to Dallas to London to Rome to Lamezia Terme to Località Caminia in the town of Stalettì.

The trip was uneventful except for a few moments of anxiety near the end. Although the flight from Rome to Lamezia Terme was full, there were only about ten of us who checked bags. Standing around the baggage carousel, one by one the others peeled off. I was the lone passenger left standing in an empty terminal except for the very concerned airport official who only spoke Italian. She kept disappearing, apparently to see if other bags were being unloaded. Each time she came back she looked ever more dire.

The view from my terrace at Baia dell'Est. Just down the hall and across a small lobby is the Italian Culinary Institute.

Finally my bags appeared. I was relieved. So, obviously, was the airport official! She smiled and her face relaxed. With a sincere "Ciao e grazie!" I was off.

I exited baggage claim prepared to discover that my driver had left, thinking I hadn't made the flight. Luckily, he was there and I breathed a sigh of relief.

The ride to the hotel, Baia dell'Est, was just under forty-five minutes. I arrived at 7:20 p.m. and was met by Mariana, who manages logistics for the Italian Culinary Institute. She took me to my room, showed me the bottles of water and wine the school had left for me in case I needed reviving after my journey, and told me that she was taking the current group of students, who were attending a five-day course on making salumi, to dinner at 7:50 p.m. if I wanted to join them.

I tore through my suitcases, flinging clothes everywhere, to find the bits I needed to make a coherent outfit. I jumped in the shower, dressed, and was ready to go at 7:45. I'm not quite sure how I managed that.

We (the current group of students, Mariana, Chef Juan, and I) piled into a minibus and went to Il Ghittone, a local pizzeria. Chef Juan, Mariana's husband and second-in-command chef at the Institute, said that the local tradition was to order beer, fried potatoes, and pizza. Absorbing the flavors of Italy is a big part of the total immersion experience of this three-month culinary expedition, so I was not about to argue with tradition even if beer isn't one of my favorite beverages. Fried potatoes and pizza, on the other hand, are a completely different story!

A sign on the wall of the pizzeria, Il Ghittone, in Montepaone Lido, indicating there is an automatic external defibrillator (DAE) on the premises. This is the first location with a defibrillator in the province of Catanzaro. Should one be comforted or concerned?

The menu consisted of four pages of Calabrian-style pizza, plus two pages of other stuff I didn't bother reviewing. We were here to eat pizza, after all! In addition, there was a separate menu of Roman-style pizza that Chef Juan suggested we not order simply because he thought we should taste the hyperlocal food. I was more than happy to oblige, ordering pizza Calabrese with tomato sauce, mozzarella, schiacciata, 'nduja, and black olives (with pits).

Schiacciata (meaning "squashed") is similar to sopressata but weighed down during curing to flatten it a bit. 'Nduja, a spreadable salame that has been a favorite of mine since I discovered it several years ago, is made with a large amount of Calabrian chile peppers—sometimes up to 50 percent of its total weight, although more commonly it is around 30 percent.

I also requested peperoncino, hoping to get the minced, salted, and oil-packed Calabrian peppers that I had on my last visit to Calabria. The waiter, clearly pleased that someone had asked for peperoncino, brought two bowls. He brought sliced fresh peperoncini, however, and they were fiery hot. Nonetheless, I made a substantial dent in them.

Pizza Calabrese at Il Ghittone: tomato sauce, mozzarella cheese, schiacciata, 'nduja, and black olives (with pits).

We lingered at the restaurant for more than two hours. Getting back to the hotel around 10:30 p.m., I had no choice but to put everything away since my clothes were strewn on the bed and all around the room from my frantic predinner quest for sartorial appropriateness. Sleep came at about 12:30 a.m.

At 7:30 the next morning, I was at La Tavernetta, the restaurant at Baia dell'Est, for breakfast. Orlando, the barista, revived me with four double espressos! While talking to Orlando several months later, I learned that he was so concerned about my caffeine intake that day that he went to Mariana to ask if I was okay.

Peperoncini freschi (fresh very hot peppers) to add to pizza.

With my class not scheduled to start for a few more days, I spent the morning responding to email and completing other tasks. I had lunch with the "Salumi Students" at the school. The Salumi Students are sometimes called the "Pig People," a nickname that went along with the "Gelato People," the "Pastry People," and the "Cheese People," who arrived in weeks to come.

The afternoon became a jet-lagged blur after the effects of Orlando's espresso wore off. I think I napped, but I know I appeared at the school for a simple dinner of roast chicken, roasted cauliflower with besciamella (white sauce), and salad. The meal was topped off with a torta di frutta made with layers of sponge cake (pan di Spagna), whipped cream, and fresh fruit (mandarin oranges and kiwi), and drizzled with raspberry sauce.

Wine! Did I mention wine? Bottomless bottles accompany all meals. (Well, not really breakfast, though I think if one asked, it would appear!)

On January 10, the Salumi Students went on an outing to a local mercatino (small outdoor market) in Catanzaro Lido, followed by a trip to a kitchen and restaurant supply store. I was invited to accompany them. Afterward we had lunch at the "Panino Lab," where one designs one's own sandwich that is then made to order. I liked my choice (semolina ciabatta, schiacciata, pecorino fresco, 'nduja, and arugula) so much that I can't wait to go back!

My sandwich creation from the Panino Lab: semolina ciabatta bread, schiacciata, 'nduja, and arugula.

We arrived back at the school at 1:30 p.m. and convened in the kitchen at 2. Chef John Nocita, who runs the school, invited me to participate in that day's lessons, much to my surprise and delight.

 ### Pollo Arrosto
Roast Chicken

The Italians and the French could not be further apart in their usual methods for roasting chicken. The French opt for a high temperature and short cooking time. The Italians, however, go for a low temperature and a long time. Italian roast chicken often resembles the texture of pulled pork. If you've never had chicken this way, give it a try. If you want to substitute dried rosemary for fresh, use about 2 teaspoons.

Metric Measure	Ingredient	American Measure
1.8 kilograms	Whole chicken (approximate weight)	4 pounds
To taste	Garlic powder	To taste
2 tablespoons	Rosemary, fresh, chopped	2 tablespoons
To taste	Salt, preferably fine sea salt	To taste
To taste	Freshly ground black pepper	To taste
125 milliliters	Dry white wine or water	½ cup

1. Pat the chicken dry. Remove excess fat.

2. Prop the chicken up and season the cavity generously with garlic powder, ½ of the rosemary, salt, and pepper.

3. Put the chicken in a roasting pan with a cover, preferably one that is just a little larger than the chicken, and season generously with garlic powder, the remaining rosemary, salt, and pepper.

4. Put the chicken, uncovered, in a 230°C (450°F) oven. After 20 minutes, pour the wine into the bottom of the roasting pan, cover the pan, and turn the oven temperature to 120°C (250°F).

5. Cook for 2½ hours, basting occasionally with the pan juices.

6. Uncover the chicken during the last 20 minutes or so to brown the skin and evaporate excess liquid from the pan juices, if necessary.

7. Gently divide the chicken and place it on a serving platter. (Carving it is not really an option if you've cooked it correctly!) Pour the defatted pan juices over the chicken.

Tip: I rarely use garlic powder, but for roast chicken and turkey I make an exception. Quite simply, I prefer the flavor.

 Cavolfiore Gratinato con Besciamella
Roast Cauliflower with Bechamel

Instead of garlic oil, you can sauté 1 clove of garlic, bruised with the side of a chef's knife, in extra-virgin olive oil until golden. Discard the garlic. If you don't mind the little black flecks, you can use black pepper instead of white pepper.

Metric Measure	Ingredient	American Measure
1 head	Cauliflower, cut in florets	1 head
2 tablespoons	Garlic Oil (page 57)	2 tablespoons
250 milliliters	Milk, 2% or whole	1 cup
19 grams	Unsalted butter	4 teaspoons
19 grams	All-purpose flour	2½ tablespoons
To taste	Nutmeg, freshly grated	To taste
20–25 grams	Freshly grated Parmigiano Reggiano cheese	Scant 1 ounce
To taste	Salt, preferably fine sea salt	To taste
To taste	Freshly ground white pepper	To taste

1. Toss the cauliflower with the garlic oil and salt and pepper to taste.

2. Roast the cauliflower in a shallow roasting pan at 200°C (400°F) until brown in places, tossing occasionally, approximately 30 minutes.

3. Meanwhile, use the milk, butter, flour, and nutmeg to make besciamella following the instructions on page 256. Add salt and pepper to taste.

4. Toss the cauliflower with the besciamella. Adjust the salt and pepper, if necessary. Put the cauliflower in a baking dish just large enough to hold it in a single layer. Sprinkle with the Parmigiano Reggiano cheese.

5. Cover the dish and bake at 180°C (350°F) until bubbling, approximately 35 minutes.

6. Uncover and move the baking dish to the upper third of the oven. Bake until golden on top, approximately 10 minutes more.

PAN DI SPAGNA
Sponge Cake

There are many techniques for making pan di Spagna ranging from this straightforward version to much more complicated ones. This is the recipe I turn to over and over. Vanilla and almond extracts are typical flavors to add, depending on the intended use of the cake. I like the combination of almond extract and lemon zest. Depending on your intended use, this batter can be baked in a 30-centimeter (12-inch) round cake pan or two 23-centimeter (9-inch) round cake pans.

Metric Measure	Ingredient	American Measure
160 grams	All-purpose flour	1⅓ cups, sifted before measuring
250 grams	Granulated sugar, divided	1¼ cups
8 large	Eggs, separated	8 large
2 tablespoons	Water	2 tablespoons
1½ teaspoons	Extract, if desired	1½ teaspoons
2 teaspoons	Freshly grated lemon or orange zest, if desired	2 teaspoons
¼ teaspoon	Fine salt	¼ teaspoon

1. Sift the flour with 100 grams (½ cup) of the sugar three times.

2. In a large bowl, beat the egg yolks, water, extract (if using), and zest (if using) with a whisk until combined.

3. Using a stand mixer with the whisk attachment, beat the egg whites until foamy. While continuing to beat the egg whites, add the salt and remaining sugar. Beat the egg whites until they are stiff but still glossy.

4. Meanwhile, add the flour and sugar mixture to the yolk mixture in five additions, mixing each time with a whisk until combined.

5. When the egg whites are stiff, add a large spoonful to the yolk mixture and fold to lighten the mixture. Afterward, fold in the remaining egg whites.

6. Pour the batter into a clean, dry, ungreased, and unfloured pan (or pans). Bake at 165°C (325°F) until the edge just begins to separate from the pan, approximately 45 to 50 minutes for a 30-centimeter (12-inch) pan and 35 to 40 minutes for two 23-centimeter (9-inch) pans.

7. Run a knife around the edge of the pan(s). Let cool 10 minutes then invert the pan(s) onto a wire rack.

8. When completely cool, remove the cake(s) from the pan(s).

Tip: Very few recipes in this book call for all-purpose flour. This recipe, the one that I grew up with, was standardized with American ingredients. I don't see any reason to change something that works well.

Torta con la Frutta e Panna Montata
Sponge Cake with Cream and Fruit

You can make this in one layer or two. If I am using some fruit that needs to be sweetened, like strawberries or cherries, I usually make two layers. I put the sweetened fruit and any collected juices on top of the bottom layer and then cover the fruit with whipped cream. I put more whipped cream directly on top of the second layer and then arrange fruit that does not have collected juices such as sliced peaches or nectarines or blueberries on top of the whipped cream. The fruit sauce is optional, but it adds another layer of flavor.

Metric Measure	Ingredient	American Measure
1 recipe	Pan di Spagna (page 6)	1 recipe
170 grams	Fresh raspberries	6 ounces
85 grams	Granulated sugar	½ cup less 1 tablespoon
600 milliliters	Heavy cream (36% fat)	2½ cups
90–100 grams	Confectioner's sugar	½ cup less 1 tablespoon
As needed	An array of fresh, in-season fruit	As needed
As needed	Granulated sugar for the fruit	As needed

1. Make the pan di Spagna using almond extract and lemon zest. Bake in one or two layers (see headnote) as desired. The cake can be prepared up to 2 days in advance. Wrap tightly and refrigerate. Bring to room temperature before proceeding.

2. Make the raspberry sauce by combining the raspberries with the granulated sugar. Lightly crush the berries and allow them to macerate for about 10 minutes to draw out some juices. Bring to a boil over low heat until there is sufficient liquid that the berries will not stick, then turn the heat to high and boil until syrupy. Refrigerate, uncovered, until cold.

3. Prepare the fruit by cutting it into bite-sized pieces, if necessary, and lightly sweetening, if necessary.

4. Whip the cream until frothy. Add the confectioner's sugar. Continue beating until soft peaks form.

5. Top the cake layer(s) with fruit and whipped cream (see headnote).

6. Put a puddle of fruit sauce on the bottom of each plate. Add a slice of cake and serve immediately.

PEPERONCINI SOTT'OLIO
Chile Peppers in Oil

Peperoncini sott'olio graces tables in homes and restaurants throughout Calabria. The Italian word for chile (hot pepper) is peperoncino. Long thin peppers, such as cayenne, are a good choice for preserving this way but you can also use cherry peppers, serrano peppers, or a combination. I would avoid exceedingly hot peppers such as habanero, Scotch bonnet, and ghost peppers.

Metric Measure	Ingredient	American Measure
200 grams	Chopped hot peppers (see headnote)	7 ounces
20 grams	Salt, preferably fine sea salt	4 teaspoons
750 milliliters	White wine vinegar, 6% acidity	3 cups
As needed	Extra-virgin olive oil	As needed

1. Combine the chopped peppers and salt in a nonreactive bowl (such as stainless steel). After 6 hours, scrape the mixture into a nonreactive sieve. Place the sieve over a bowl, cover loosely with plastic wrap, and allow the peppers to drain.

2. After 18 hours in the sieve, put the peppers in a clean bowl. Heat the vinegar to boiling and pour over the peppers. Swish for 1 minute. Pour the mixture through the sieve.

3. Squeeze excess liquid from the peppers by wrapping them in cheesecloth and pressing them in a potato ricer or by wrapping them in a clean kitchen towel and squeezing.

4. Spread the peppers on half-sheet pans lined with paper towels. Allow the peppers to dry until they just become leathery, 8 to 24 hours, depending on the humidity.

5. Pack the peppers in clean jars and fill the jars with olive oil. Use the blade of a knife to work out any air bubbles.

Close the jars and store in a cool, dark place for 1 month before using.

DISPATCH #2

MAKING IT TO THE FIRST DAY OF CLASS

JANUARY 13

It's close to 11:30 p.m. on Saturday, January 12 as I'm starting to write this dispatch. I finished my first Calabria dispatch a few hours ago. At the time, I planned to start Dispatch #2 after dinner with the goal of finishing and posting it on the thirteenth.

That's still the plan, but this evening has put a sharp turn in my planned storyline about massive food consumption. Stick with me and you'll see why.

In Dispatch #1, I stopped my tale at 2 p.m. on Thursday, January 10. We had just gotten back from lunch and started in the kitchen.

From 2 to 5 p.m. one cured meat product after another was inaugurated in the kitchen. These included three types of pancetta, prosciuttino, cotechino, zampone, duck prosciutto, rabbit and duck liver paté, cured rabbit leg, bratwurst and kielbasa (yes, I know this is a course on Italian cuisine), and on and on.

Salumi hanging in the Italian Culinary Institute's curing room.

Each of the ground meat products was subjected to testing, meaning a portion was cooked, divided up, and passed around the room for all to taste. We discussed what adjustments needed to be made to the seasonings. Often a second round of testing ensued before the mixture was declared perfect and put into casings.

Cotechino was among the most challenging to test because it contains about 30 percent pork skin. It requires hours of cooking to be palatable, even when ground finely. The texture of quickly cooked cotechino resembles ground-up hockey pucks. We knew this would be the case, but the point was to taste for the perfect balance of seasonings, not the texture of the finished product.

Half the cotechino mixture was made into a fat sausage (cotechino) and half was stuffed into a pig's trotter to make zampone. Zampone actually means trotter or foot. Zampa, a related word, means paw. Zampa also happens to be my mother-in-law's maiden name.

At 5 p.m. we took a break and were served platter upon platter of cured meat products. This included head cheese, which had been made in the previous few days, along with enough wine to wash it all down. For good measure, bowls of pasta alla carbonara were brought out. Round about this time, those folks who had succumbed to Mariana's encouragement to have two panini at the Panino Lab at lunchtime were regretting their decisions.

SMOKING WITH OLIVE BRANCHES

We resumed class around 5:30 p.m., marching down to the curing room, where the meats were hung to cure. It was absolutely fascinating to me to see Chef Juan light olive branches to lightly smoke all the meat products. He said that in Calabria it is traditional to smoke all aged and cured meat products for an hour or so twice a day for about four days. Never in my life had I heard of this. It certainly does not appear in any of the tomes on salumi that I have read! This is a topic that I need to explore further in the coming weeks.

Chef Juan lighting olive branches to lightly smoke the salumi in the curing room.

The research didn't take long. As the next few weeks went by, more and more families in the nearby towns and villages began to cure their own pigs. At sea level, the air was so thick with smoke that it became difficult to breathe with even modest exertion. Luckily, climbing the few hundred feet up to the school put one above the smoky haze that hung over the buildings that were closer to sea level!

In addition, though not strange to me, the ICI only uses salt to cure its meat products. In the States we would call these meat products "uncured" because we use the term "cured" to mean that preservatives such as sodium nitrate and sodium nitrite have been added as well, ignoring the fact that salt is itself a type of "cure." Curing with salt alone is generally believed to be too risky for the home cook.

Part of the never-ending meal at Al Fondaco.

Sodium nitrate and sodium nitrite are much more effective antibacterial agents than salt alone. They also help meat to maintain a more attractive reddish color. Though artisanal Italian salumi-makers often seem to achieve this same result without added nitrates and nitrates.

We went back to the kitchen and continued with meat production until shortly after 9 p.m., at which time we were told to prepare for dinner! Mind you, we had already had a stupid amount of food for the day. Dinner consisted of pounds and pounds of fresh sausages that had been prepared over the previous days, salad, and bread, all lubricated with the ever-present wine. We ended with gelato and cake.

The previous night, Chef Juan had announced at the end of dinner that if we had brought any "gastric protectant" with us—some sort of antacid or acid blocker—that we should start taking it that night in preparation for "massive eating" the next day. He did not exaggerate.

I've read many articles about chefs who travel to experience local cuisine to develop new ideas for their restaurants. The stories always involve eating the same ridiculous amount of food, if not more. There's really no way to taste food without swallowing it, and one bite is usually not enough to fully appreciate the taste and texture. In the cooking profession, eating is research, and the more research one does, the better. Periodic overindulging goes with the territory.

Friday the eleventh was a relatively mellow day. The few remaining outgoing students and the few incoming students who had arrived were invited to lunch at La Tavernetta, the restaurant at Baia dell'Est, the hotel at which we're staying. Lunch started with two gorgeous crustaceans—very large prawns I believe. They were wrapped in cooked angel hair pasta and flash-fried to crisp the pasta and cook the seafood. It was a brilliant preparation. There was also a portion of monkfish wrapped in seaweed and cooked. Next was seafood ravioli in a light tomato sauce. The meal ended with decon-

A deconstructed cannolo (singular of cannoli) at La Tavernetta restaurant at Baia dell'Est.

Making It To the First Day of Class

structed cannoli and Amaro del Capo, one of scores (probably really hundreds) of amaro liqueurs made throughout Italy.

For dinner, the ever-growing group of incoming students went to the pizzeria I went to my first night (the one with the automatic defibrillator). I had Pizza Diavola. Fresh hot peppers were sliced and strewn on the pizza before baking. I confirmed that the fat in cheese is a perfect vehicle for capsaicin. Every bite of pizza was searing in spiciness, even if that particular bite didn't contain an actual slice of hot pepper.

Saturday the twelfth was another easygoing day. Lunch again was at La Tavernetta. We started with an exquisite stew of minuscule octopus and tomato served with simple grilled bread. The dish reminded me of the way my family prepares baccalà, only more refined in taste. The next course was a fish fillet rolled in seasoned breadcrumbs and sautéed. It was served on a puddle of golden sauce made from pureed potatoes.

We were hypothesizing about the source of the yellow color in the potato puree: turmeric or saffron, perhaps. (When you're with a bunch of food-obsessed people, every dish gets dissected and analyzed.) We were assured by Orlando (our waiter and the morning barista) that the sauce contained neither and that the yellow color came from the potatoes and bread. The bread on the table did have a golden hue, but none of us could comprehend how the sauce could be so rich in color without the addition of some ingredient with a substantial depth of color. The mystery remains to be solved.

Dessert was gelato, or at least I think it was. My brain was starting to shut down at this point. We finished the meal with another local amaro, Amaro Silano.

I went for a long walk after lunch. That, coupled with not having eaten the last two bites of my fish, made me feel virtuous and ready for the official welcome dinner at Al Fondaco.

Feast at Al Fondaco

If Thursday was a day of stupidly "massive eating," I have no words to describe the meal we enjoyed that evening at Al Fondaco—a rustic restaurant but one of the most perfectly maintained facilities I've seen in Italy. The same attention to detail was lavished on the food, which was beyond compare…and all of it local.

We toasted with an Italian sparkling wine and then each of us got a plate of cured meats, cheeses, and pickled eggplant, all made in-house, accompanied by an onion jam and fruit conserve. Jugs of local red wine were put out and then the tables were littered with antipasti, so many that I can't remember them all. They included stuffed eggplant, stuffed zucchini, supplì, savory fried dough, meatballs with large amounts of pecorino cheese, stuffed tomatoes, braised individual artichoke leaves with a meat topping and cheese gratin, meat croquettes, and pork saltimbocca to, quite literally, name just a few. There was still silverware left on the table so we knew more was coming.

Two pasta courses followed. One similar to strozzapreti (referred to as fileja in Calabria) was served in a veal ragù. The other was zucchini and pecorino ravioli in a light tomato sauce. Next came porchetta with a salad to lighten things up! Dessert consisted of a fresh cheese with a sweet syrup, tiramisù, sliced fresh fruit, walnuts, local mandarin oranges, and interestingly enough, lupini. I've only ever had lupini served as an antipasto or as part of a casual lunch. These were not as salty as I am accustomed to and went quite well with the remainder of the dessert course. We ended with limoncello, Amaro del Capo, and espresso.

Al Fondaco is a truly superlative restaurant serving traditional Calabrian cuisine.

We were all subdued on the drive back to the hotel. Nearly comatose is probably a better description. Luckily I had continued to take my Pepcid after Chef Juan's injunction a few nights earlier.

I wish I could say that I would be able to forego food for a few days, but I know that won't be possible. We report to the kitchen at 9 a.m. on Sunday in chef's attire.

The first day of the master's program is about to begin!

Brodo di Pollo
Chicken Broth

I freeze chicken backs, wing tips, skin, and bones when I cut up chicken for different dishes for use in making broth. If I don't have enough of these parts, I buy legs or leg quarters to make up the difference. I also keep mushroom stems and rinds from Parmigiano Reggiano cheese in the freezer. Don't worry about chicken skin making the broth fatty. All the fat is removed after the broth is chilled. Skin has lots of flavor and adds body to the broth. Though not essential, I add 2 or 3 chicken feet to this recipe when I have them. There is no need to peel the onion or the garlic.

Metric Measure	Ingredient	American Measure
650–700 grams	Meaty chicken bones, backs, wing tips	1½ pounds
60 grams	Chopped mushroom stems and/or caps	2 ounces
125 grams	Chopped celery	4½ ounces
100 grams	Chopped carrot	3½ ounces
100 grams	Chopped onion	3½ ounces
2 cloves	Garlic, chopped	2 cloves
45 grams	Parmigiano Reggiano cheese rind	1½ ounces
3–4 sprigs	Parsley	3–4 sprigs
1 tablespoon	Tomato paste	1 tablespoon
100 milliliters	Dry white wine	6½ tablespoons
¾ teaspoon	Whole black peppercorns	¾ teaspoon
4 liters	Water	4 quarts plus 1 cup

1. Combine all ingredients in a pressure cooker or a large stock pot.

2. Cook for 65 minutes in a pressure cooker, or simmer on the stove for 5 to 6 hours, partially covered, stirring occasionally.

3. If using a pressure cooker, allow the pressure to release slowly.

4. Strain the broth. Refrigerate until the broth is cold and the fat has hardened, at least 12 hours. Remove the congealed fat.

5. There should be 4 liters (4 quarts plus 1 cup) of broth. If not, add water to reach this amount.

Tip: Unless I plan to use broth for a clear soup, I do not bother with skimming the broth as it cooks. Without the need to skim, a pressure cooker makes fast work of preparing broth. An electric pressure cooker, such as an Instant Pot makes the process hands-off.

COTECHINO CON LE LENTICCHIE
Cotechino Sausage with Lentils

Cotechino is a Northern Italian sausage that includes some pork skin along with meat and warm spices. It requires long cooking. Though some Italian specialty stores carry fresh cotechino, it is readily available online and in some shops precooked in shelf-stable packaging. It requires only a brief boil in its cooking bag.

Metric Measure	Ingredient	American Measure
500 grams	Brown lentils	~1 pound
60 milliliters	Extra-virgin olive oil	¼ cup
2	Medium carrots, finely diced	2
1	Large fennel bulb, in medium dice	1
1	Medium onion, finely diced	1
2 cloves	Garlic, minced	2 cloves
120 milliliters	Dry white wine	½ cup
2 liters	Chicken Broth (page 15) or Vegetable Broth (page 161)	8 cups
1	Bay leaf, preferably fresh	1
2½ teaspoons	Salt, preferably fine sea salt	2½ teaspoons
1 teaspoon	Freshly ground black pepper	1 teaspoon
1–2 as desired	Cotechino sausages	1–2 as desired

1. Rinse and drain the lentils. Reserve.

2. In a heavy-bottomed Dutch oven, sauté the carrot, fennel, onion, and garlic in the olive oil until the vegetables begin to soften.

3. Add the wine and boil gently until completely evaporated.

4. Add the broth and bay leaf. Simmer 15 minutes.

5. Add the lentils to the pot and simmer, partially covered, approximately 30 to 45 minutes or until cooked but not mushy. Add salt and pepper to taste after the first 15 minutes.

6. Meanwhile, cook the cotechino according to the package directions, which typically involves reheating it in the sealed bag. (If the cotechino is fresh, check with the butcher, but it will likely need at least 2 hours of gentle boiling.)

7. As the lentils are nearing completion, add the liquid from the cotechino boiling bag or 1 or 2 ladles of cooking liquid if the cotechino is fresh. Adjust the seasoning.

8. Pour the lentils into a serving platter with deep sides. Top with the sliced cotechino.

Polpette con Formaggio Pecorino
Meatballs with Pecorino Cheese

Although Americans think of spaghetti and meatballs as a classic combination, serving them together is completely contrary to the structure of an Italian meal. A typical meal in Italy consists of an antipasto followed by a primo piatto then a secondo piatto with contorni, and maybe a dolce (an appetizer followed by a first plate then a second plate with side dishes, and maybe dessert). The first plate is either pasta, rice (such as risotto), or soup. The second plate leans toward protein (meat or fish). So even if Italians make spaghetti and meatballs, the spaghetti would be served separately as the primo piatto and the meatballs afterward as the secondo piatto.

Metric Measure	Ingredient	American Measure
67 grams	Fine dry breadcrumbs	2 1/3 ounces
135 milliliters	Milk, 2% or whole	½ cup plus 1 tablespoon
675 grams	Ground beef, 85–90% lean	1½ pounds
67 grams	Freshly grated Pecorino Romano cheese	2 1/3 ounces
2 large	Eggs	2 large
2 sprigs	Rosemary, leaves only, minced	2 sprigs
2 leaves	Sage, minced	2 leaves
3 tablespoons	Minced parsley	3 tablespoons
1 clove	Garlic, minced	1 clove
2 teaspoons	Salt, preferably fine sea salt	2 teaspoons
To taste	Freshly ground black pepper	To taste
As needed	Neutral oil, such as corn or sunflower	As needed
½ recipe	Basic Tomato Sauce (page 131)	½ recipe

1. Combine the breadcrumbs and milk. Allow the breadcrumbs to completely absorb the milk and become tender.

2. Combine the beef, breadcrumb-milk mixture, cheese, eggs, rosemary, sage, parsley, garlic, salt, and pepper. Mix with your hand until the mixture is completely homogeneous.

3. Divide into portions of approximately 45 grams (1.6 ounces) each. A 33-milliliter portion scoop (#30) is a perfect size for this.

4. Roll each portion into a smooth ball, moistening your hands with water as needed.

5. Bring 7 centimeters (3 inches) of oil to 175°C (350°F) in a deep fryer or heavy pot. Fry the meatballs until deeply browned.

6. Drain the meatballs on paper towels.

7. Warm the tomato sauce in a shallow pan. Add the meatballs and simmer, partially covered for 30 to 40 minutes.

STROZZAPRETI AL RAGÙ DI VITELLO
"Priest-Strangler" Pasta with Veal Ragù

As with many of the tomato-based pasta sauces in this book, this recipe yields enough for 1 kilogram (2¼ pounds) of pasta. Extra ragù freezes well. If you don't want to use veal, you can substitute lean pork. In Italian home kitchens, jars and cans of tomato products often serve as unofficial measures to add water to a recipe. The advantage is that the water removes the last bit of tomato goodness from the can's hard-to-reach places.

Metric Measure	Ingredient	American Measure
1 kilogram	Veal leg or shoulder	2¼ pounds
75 milliliters	Extra-virgin olive oil	5 tablespoons
2 cloves	Garlic, bruised with a chef's knife	2 cloves
90 grams	Finely diced onion	3 ounces
50 grams	Finely shredded or minced carrot	1¾ ounces
75 milliliters	Dry white wine	5 tablespoons
55 grams	Tomato paste	4 tablespoons
125 milliliters	Dry red wine	½ cup
700 grams	Passata (tomato puree)	24½ ounces
1 teaspoon	Dried oregano	1 teaspoon
1	Bay leaf, preferably fresh	1
1 tablespoon plus more to taste	Salt, preferably fine sea salt	1 tablespoon plus more to taste
To taste	Freshly ground black pepper	To taste

1. Using a small, sharp knife, remove any silver skin and large pieces of fat from the veal. Cut the veal into 1-centimeter (½-inch) cubes.

2. In a heavy-bottomed saucepan, sauté the garlic in olive oil until golden brown. Remove and discard the garlic.

3. Add the veal to the garlic-flavored oil and sauté on medium-high heat until well browned.

4. Add the onion and carrots. Sauté until the onion has softened.

5. Add the white wine. Cover and boil gently until the liquid has evaporated.

6. Add the tomato paste and sauté on medium heat until the paste takes on a sweet aroma and darkens slightly, 2 to 3 minutes.

7. Add the red wine and boil gently to cook away most of the liquid.

8. Add the passata. Fill the passata jar with water, swish to loosen the last of the passata, and add to the saucepan along with the oregano, bay leaf, salt, and pepper.

9. Simmer, partially covered, for 3 hours, stirring occasionally, and adding water if the sauce becomes too thick.

10. Cool slightly and then use a potato masher to press on the meat, causing it to shred into the sauce.

Pasta and Assembly

This sauce works well with a variety of pasta shapes, but I prefer something a bit rustic, such as strozzapreti or casarecce to compliment the texture of the sauce.

Metric Measure	Ingredient	American Measure
½ recipe	Veal Ragù (page 19)	½ recipe
500 grams	Strozzapreti or other dry pasta	~1 pound
55 grams	Freshly grated Parmigiano Reggiano cheese	2 ounces
To taste	Salt, preferably fine sea salt	To taste
To taste	Freshly ground black pepper	To taste

1. Bring 3 liters (3 quarts) of water seasoned with 75 grams (¼ cup) of salt to a rolling boil.

2. Meanwhile, gently heat the veal ragù in a large sauté pan.

3. Add the pasta to the boiling salted water and cook at a rapid boil for approximately 2 minutes less than the minimum cooking time on the package for al dente pasta, stirring frequently to prevent sticking.

4. Drain the pasta, reserving the pasta-cooking water.

5. Add the par-cooked pasta to the ragù in the sauté pan and finish cooking at a moderate boil, adding the reserved pasta-cooking water 1 ladle at a time, shaking the pan and stirring the pasta, until the pasta is al dente, leaving the sauce liquid enough to just coat the pasta. Adjust the salt and pepper while finishing the pasta.

6. Off the heat, add the cheese and then flip and stir the pasta to emulsify the cheese and sauce. Add a bit more pasta-cooking water if the sauce has thickened too much.

7. Serve immediately, passing extra cheese at the table.

Supplì
Roman Rice Balls

Supplì al telefono is an Italian term that refers to overhead telephone lines. These Roman treats are filled with mozzarella that becomes stringy when hot and is thought to resemble these lines. Be sure to use partially aged mozzarella as you would for pizza rather than fresh mozzarella so that it stretches. For an alternate method of cooking the rice, see the recipe for Arancini on page 71. Use whichever you prefer.

Metric Measure	Ingredient	American Measure
2 liters	Water	2 quarts plus ½ cup
65 grams plus more	Salt, preferably fine sea salt	3½ tablespoons plus more
400 grams	Arborio or carnaroli rice	2 cups
60 grams	Freshly grated Parmigiano Reggiano cheese	⅔ cup
60 grams	Unsalted butter	4 tablespoons
To taste	Freshly ground black pepper	To taste
125 grams	Mozzarella	¼ pound
4 large	Eggs	4 large
1 tablespoon	Whole milk	1 tablespoon
300 grams	Fine dry breadcrumbs	2 cups
As needed	Neutral oil, such as corn or sunflower	As needed

1. Bring the water and 65 grams (3½ tablespoons) of salt to a boil. Add the rice and boil until just cooked. The rice should be al dente but not hard. Drain the rice in a fine sieve.

2. In a large bowl, mix the Parmigiano Reggiano cheese, butter, and black pepper into the hot rice. Taste and adjust the salt and pepper. Spread the rice in a half-sheet pan, cover, and allow it to cool to room temperature. Inverting another half-sheet pan on top is an easy way to cover the rice.

3. Meanwhile, cut the mozzarella into 1-centimeter (½-inch) cubes. Reserve.

4. When the rice is cool, lightly beat 2 of the eggs. Mix the eggs into the rice using your hand to mix thoroughly without compacting the rice.

5. Scoop up approximately 60 milliliters (¼ cup) of the rice and begin to form it into a ball. Press a cube of mozzarella into the center of the rice ball and enclose it with rice. Be sure each ball is smooth. Do not compress the rice heavily while forming the supplì. If necessary, moisten your hands with water before forming each ball to keep the rice from sticking. The supplì can be made one day ahead to this point and refrigerated, tightly covered.

6. Lightly beat the remaining 2 eggs with the milk. Season with salt and pepper. Coat each rice ball with egg then with the breadcrumbs. Let the supplì sit at room temperature for 1 hour before frying.

7. Bring at least 7 centimeters (3 inches) of oil to 175°C (350°F) in a heavy pot or deep fryer. Fry the supplì, a few at a time, turning occasionally, until brown. Be careful not to burn the breadcrumbs. Drain on paper towels. Serve immediately.

Porchetta and a light salad at Al Fondaco. (See page 101 for a recipe for porchetta.)

Clockwise from top: Men fishing in Pietragrande, a small town on the beach below the Italian Culinary Institute. An unusual private residence overlooking the sea, just down the hill from the Italian Culinary Institute. Zucchini and cheese ravioli at Al Fondaco.

Making It To the First Day of Class

ROMA
DISTRIBUZIONE
VISITATE
L'ITALIA
ROMA
FERROVIA

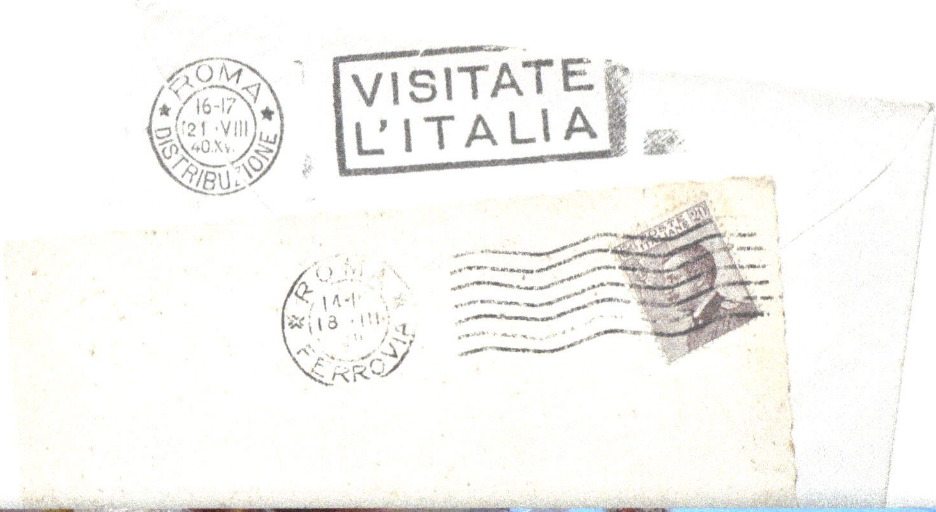

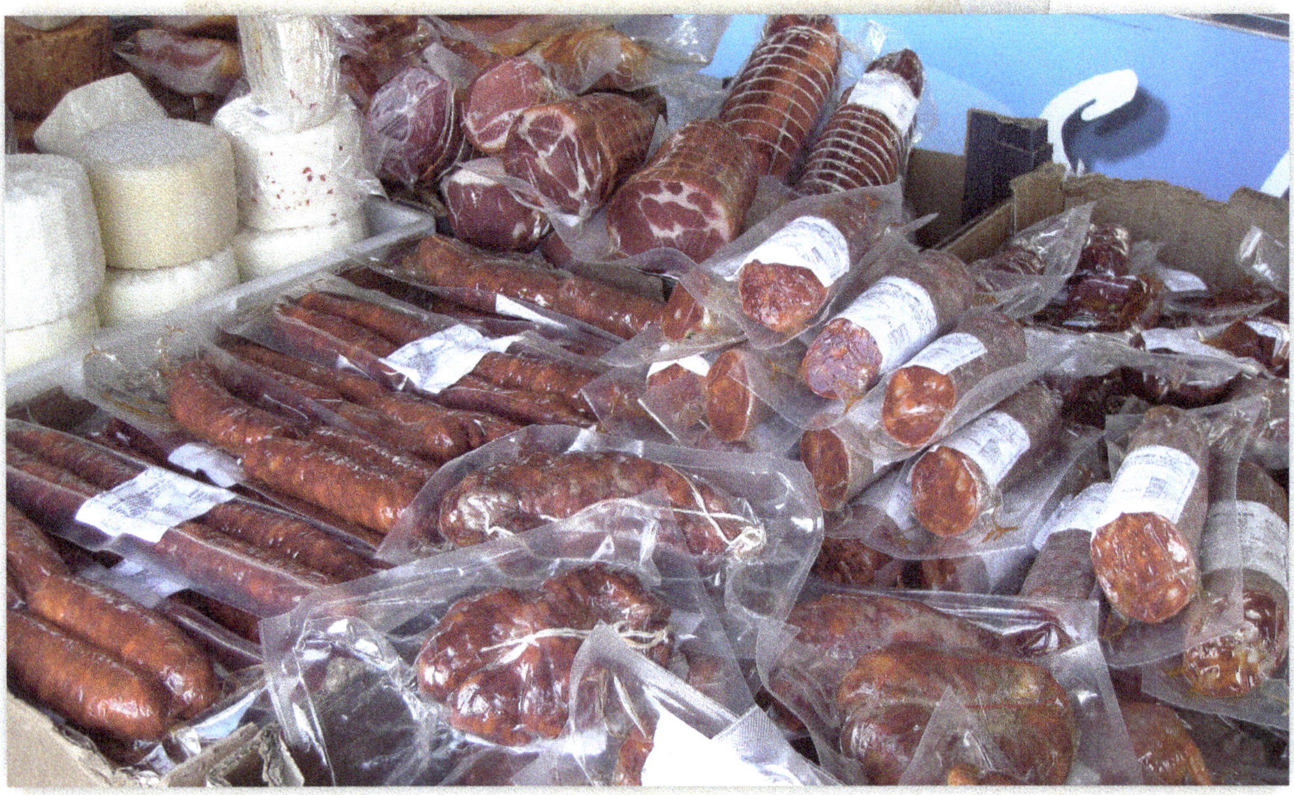

Bureaucracy and Bourbon

JANUARY 16

The average student gains five pounds (or is it five kilograms?) during the three-month Master of Italian Cuisine program. At least that's what I've been told.

It's not hard to believe.

Our first day in the classroom was Sunday, January 13, and I had barely digested the previous evening's meal from Al Fondaco. I was so wound up—and so overly full—from the meal that I couldn't even get into bed until 1:30 a.m.

I groaned when my alarm went off at 7:30 a.m. I groggily hauled myself out of bed and made what has become my daily pilgrimage to Orlando for espresso. After my second espresso doppio I felt a bit more revived. Class started at 9.

Spaghetti alla puttanesca.
(See page 32 for a recipe.)

Whereas the first day was lecture combined with tasting foundational components of regional Italian cuisine, the second day was spent in the kitchen watching Chef John prepare basic foods—and of course tasting them, with one exception. Because we ran out of time before tasting olive oils on the first day, we began the day by tasting eight Italian extra-virgin olive oils from Liguria, Veneto, Garda, Siena, Chianti, Puglia, and two from Sicily. To make a point, Chef John also had us taste "olive oil," a chemically extracted oil that had no olive flavor but a distinct chemical bite.

Here's what Chef John prepared on day two. Asterisks (*) mean that we tasted the dish as well! (Please excuse the English and Italian mash-up; it's kind of how it goes in the kitchen at ICI.)

- ★ Simple tomato sauce*
- ★ Anchovy-garlic paste
- ★ Cotechino on warm bread with a fried egg, spicy mayonnaise (maionese di bomba), and Taleggio cheese*
- ★ Risotto alla Parmigiana con tartufo bianco (risotto with Parmigiano cheese and white truffles)*
- ★ Salsa verde
- ★ Ragù di agnello (lamb ragù)
- ★ Salted egg yolks (tuorli di uova sotto sale)
- ★ Spaghetti alla puttanesca*
- ★ Ragù di seppia (cuttlefish sauce)
- ★ Garlic oil (this is also a component part of many dishes)*
- ★ Trifolata (mushroom sauce)
- ★ Lupara (rigatoni with sausage, tomato sauce, cream, and hot red pepper). This dish is from Naples. It contains rigatoni, which remind Italians of the short-barreled eight-gauge shotgun used in Naples. Enough said!*
- ★ Scaloppine di maiale (pork scallopine) with marsala, served with shaved lardo (salted and cured pork fat!)*
- ★ Peperonata
- ★ Bollito di maiale
- ★ Ragù Bolognese
- ★ Seared cubes of mortadella served with bruschetta topped with bomba alla Calabrese (spicy conserved vegetable spread) [Just in case we were hungry!]*
- ★ Trofie pasta with lemon, olives, shrimp, and bottarga. This dish is referred to as "profumo di mare"—perfume of the sea —by the staff.*
- ★ Vin Santo and cantucci (biscotti)*

The last task of the cooking day was to start dinner for the group. The main part of the meal was pollo alla Romana (chicken Roman style). It's a simple but delicious dish of chicken cooked with sweet peppers and tomato puree then finished in the oven with grated Pecorino Romano cheese on top. We prepared about fifty chicken thighs since they are the best cut for braising. I got to prepare half of them!

ICI's interpretation of Lupara, a Neapolitan dish named after a short-barreled eight-gauge shotgun because of the resemblance of rigatoni to the barrel of a gun. (See page 30 for a recipe).

THE PASSPORT PROJECT

After class Mariana and Chef Juan helped me complete the paperwork that I needed to submit in order to schedule an appointment to finalize my visa. The difficult part was completing the multipage 178-section questionnaire for which there were three separate instruction manuals! Luckily most of the 178 questions did not need to be answered, but it took Chef Juan (an attorney before he became a chef) to understand the nuances.

Mariana and I then went on a journey. The first stop was to a tobacco shop (seriously) to buy the €16 stamp that needed to be affixed to the paperwork. Then we went to a shop selling magazines and office supplies to have copies made of all the documents I had been given by the consulate general in Los Angeles in case the originals went missing on their way to the questura (local precinct), as well as my entire passport. The Italians are serious.

Every page of my passport needed to be photocopied including all the blank ones and the outside cover. The woman at the shop kept looking at me and indicating that it seemed foolish to photocopy blank pages. I couldn't really disagree, but those were the directions. Mariana just threw her hands up and the woman continued photocopying, making a very neat booklet with the pages all stapled together. This only cost €4, which was worth the amusement value of seeing an Italian criticize Italian government bureaucracy.

Once the photocopying was done, I was able to complete the question on the form that asked how many additional sheets I was submitting. Because the shopkeeper photocopied my passport double-sided, she and Mariana had a discussion about whether the correct number was the number of pages or the number of sheets. Both agreed it was physical sheets.

The next stop was to a local shop to get four passport photos. This was quick and efficient and only cost €7, about half the cost of two photos at Walgreens back in the States. Then we were off to the post office to submit the paperwork. Yep! The post office is the intermediary, but first I needed more euros since the fees could only be paid in cash.

Unfortunately, the ATM in the lobby of the post office was out of service, but there was one down the street. However, neither my ATM card nor Mariana's would get the automatic door to open. Luckily it only took a few minutes for someone to come by with an ATM card that would open the door.

With €200 in my pocket, we went to the post office. Once inside, Mariana said I could fill in the date on the application form. Juan had cautioned not to do this until I was certain that I would be submitting the documents. Apparently, any error invalidates the documents and requires a whole new packet to be completed.

A few minutes later, Mariana and I were in front of a clerk who set about reviewing everything. She calculated the fee to be €100.42. I handed her €101. She gave me back a few coins then handed me €30. Apparently, the fee is divided into two parts. €70.42 goes with the application, and €30 goes on the envelope as postage. Really? €30 for postage!

A few minutes later I handed her back the €30 for the postage. I'm not really sure why she couldn't have kept it in the first place, especially since she quoted me the full amount at the outset. Mariana was familiar with this process. When the €30 was put in front of me, Mariana said to "leave it" because I would be "giving it back" in a few moments.

Pasta al Profumo di Mare: trofie pasta with shrimp, mussels, cuttlefish, and taggiasche olives flavored with caramelized lemon slices. (See page 34 for a recipe.)

We walked out of the post office less than 15 minutes after we had entered and I had an appointment on February 4 at 9 a.m. to go to the police station to start the next step in the process. Mind you, I already have a visa in my passport from the consulate general in Los Angeles. All of this is just the process of "registering" with the questura!

That evening I walked down the hallway from my apartment to dinner at the school with a glass of bourbon in my hand, the first since getting to Italy, to celebrate having negotiated just a tiny bit of the Italian bureaucracy. One of these days I'll tell you the story of actually getting the visa in Los Angeles—a saga that stretched across several months and two continents!

Pasta alle Acciughe e Aglio
Anchovy Garlic Paste

When making this paste, I drain the oil from a 2-ounce can of oil-packed anchovies, then weigh the anchovies. I add garlic equal to half the weight of the anchovies. The amounts listed here should be modified based on the weight of the anchovies. Use this paste to add a punch of anchovy and garlic to a dish. Some examples include Pasta alla Puttanesca (page 32) and Burrata and Broccoli Rabe (page 157).

Metric Measure	Ingredient	American Measure
56 grams	Oil-cured anchovies, drained	2 ounces
28 grams	Chopped garlic	1 ounce
2–3 tablespoons	Extra-virgin olive oil	2–3 tablespoons

1. Put the anchovies, garlic, and 2 tablespoons of olive oil in a small blender jar or mini food processor.

2. Blend to make a smooth paste, adding more olive oil as needed to obtain a thick puree.

3. Store in the refrigerator for up to several weeks.

Lupara
Lupara

A lupara is a sawn-off shotgun that has associations with organized crime in Italy, especially around Naples. The resemblance between rigatoni and the barrel of a shotgun explains the unusual name for this dish. If fresh or frozen porcini are not available, use other mushrooms, such as portobello, cremini, or button mushrooms, plus 5 grams (⅙ ounce) dried porcini. Rehydrate the porcini in a little water, chop them finely, and add them with the other mushrooms. Add the porcini-soaking liquid to the pan before the wine. The sauce base makes enough for 1 kilogram (2¼ pounds) of rigatoni. It freezes well.

Lupara Sauce Base

Metric Measure	Ingredient	American Measure
150 grams	Italian sausage with fennel seed	5 ounces
25 milliliters	Extra-virgin olive oil	1⅔ tablespoons
150 grams	Fresh or frozen porcini mushrooms, sliced	5 ounces
20 grams	Unsalted butter	1½ tablespoons
To taste	Minced fresh hot chile	To taste
150 milliliters	Dry red wine	Scant ⅔ cup
150 milliliters	Chicken Broth (page 15) or Vegetable Broth (page 161)	Scant ⅔ cup
1 recipe	Basic Tomato Sauce (page 131)	1 recipe
4–5	Fresh basil leaves, chopped	4–5
To taste	Salt, preferably fine sea salt	To taste
To taste	Freshly ground black pepper	To taste

1. Sauté the sausage in the olive oil until lightly browned. Add the porcini mushrooms, butter, and fresh chile, if using, and sauté 5 to 7 minutes. During this time, the sausage should brown much more.

2. Add the wine and evaporate completely. Add the broth, partially cover, and simmer until completely evaporated.

3. Add the tomato sauce, basil, and salt and pepper to taste. Simmer about 10 minutes.

Pasta and Assembly

In place of the garlic oil, you can gently sauté 4 cloves of garlic, smashed with the side of a chef's knife, in 45 milliliters (3 tablespoons) of extra-virgin olive oil until golden. Discard the garlic. I like to garnish each portion of pasta with a drizzle of extra-virgin olive oil, a sprinkling of grated Pecorino Romano cheese, and chiffonade of fresh basil leaves.

Metric Measure	Ingredient	American Measure
½ recipe	Lupara Sauce Base (page 30)	½ recipe
To taste	Cayenne pepper	To taste
500 grams	Dry rigatoni	~1 pound
100 milliliters	Heavy whipping cream	6½ tablespoons
3 tablespoons	Garlic Oil (page 57)	3 tablespoons
40 grams	Freshly grated Parmigiano Reggiano cheese	Scant ½ cup
A drizzle	Extra-virgin olive oil	A drizzle
To garnish	Pecorino Romano cheese	To garnish
To garnish	Basil chiffonade	To garnish
To taste	Salt, preferably fine sea salt	To taste
To taste	Freshly ground black pepper	To taste

1. Bring 3 liters (3 quarts) of water seasoned with 75 grams (¼ cup) of salt to a rolling boil.
2. Meanwhile, warm the sauce base in a large sauté pan until gently bubbling. Add cayenne pepper to taste, if desired.
3. Add the pasta to the boiling salted water and cook at a rapid boil for approximately 2 minutes less than the minimum cooking time on the package for al dente pasta, stirring frequently to prevent sticking.
4. Drain the pasta, reserving the pasta-cooking water.
5. Add the par-cooked pasta to the sauce in the sauté pan and finish cooking at a moderate boil, adding the reserved pasta-cooking water 1 ladle at a time, shaking the pan and stirring the pasta, until the pasta is al dente, leaving the sauce liquid enough to just coat the pasta. Adjust the salt and pepper while finishing the pasta.
6. As the pasta nears completion, add the heavy cream.
7. Off the heat, add the garlic oil and cheese and then flip and stir the pasta to emulsify the cheese and sauce. Add a bit more cooking water if the sauce is too thick.
8. Garnish each serving with extra-virgin olive oil, grated Pecorino Romano cheese, and basil chiffonade, if desired.

Pasta alla Puttanesca
Pasta alla Puttanesca

Although penne is commonly used for this dish in the United States, spaghetti is the more common choice in Italy. Choose whichever you prefer. If you would rather bring a big bowl of pasta to the table instead of portioning it, add the garnishes to the pasta in the large bowl.

Metric Measure	Ingredient	American Measure
50 grams	Anchovy Garlic Paste (page 29)	1¾ ounces
2 tablespoons	Extra-virgin olive oil	2 tablespoons
½ recipe	Basic Tomato Sauce (page 131)	½ recipe
30 grams	Roasted Olives (page 76), pitted	1 ounce
To taste	Cayenne pepper	To taste
500 grams	Dry spaghetti	~1 pound
10 grams	Salt-packed capers, rinsed	2 tablespoons
1 teaspoon	Dried oregano	1 teaspoon
To taste	Salt, preferably fine sea salt	To taste
To taste	Freshly ground black pepper	To taste
50 grams plus more to garnish	Freshly grated Pecorino Romano cheese	1¾ ounces plus more to garnish
To garnish	Garlic Oil (page 57)	To garnish
To garnish	Minced parsley	To garnish

1. Put the anchovy-garlic paste and olive oil in a large sauté pan. Sauté on medium-low heat until the raw garlic smell is gone and the paste darkens a bit and looks curdled, stirring nearly constantly to avoid burning.

2. Add the tomato sauce, olives, and cayenne pepper. Simmer until thick, approximately 15 minutes.

3. Bring 3 liters (3 quarts) of water seasoned with 75 grams (¼ cup) of salt to a rolling boil.

4. Add the pasta to the boiling salted water and cook at a rapid boil for approximately 2 minutes less than the minimum cooking time on the package for al dente pasta, stirring frequently to prevent sticking.

5. Just before draining the pasta, add the capers and oregano to the simmering sauce.

6. Drain the pasta, reserving the pasta-cooking water.

7. Add the par-cooked pasta to the liquid in the sauté pan and finish cooking at a moderate boil, adding the reserved pasta-cooking water 1 ladle at a time, shaking the pan and stirring the pasta, until the pasta is al dente, leaving the sauce liquid enough to just coat the pasta. Adjust the salt, pepper, oregano, and cayenne pepper as the pasta cooks.

8. Off the heat, add the cheese and then flip and stir the pasta to emulsify the cheese and sauce. Add a bit more cooking water if the sauce is too thick.

9. Plate the pasta and top each portion with a drizzle of garlic oil, a large pinch of minced parsley, and a generous sprinkling of Pecorino Romano cheese.

POLLO ALLA ROMANA
Roman-Style Chicken

Red and yellow are the primary colors of the Roman flag, hence red and yellow peppers are traditionally used in this dish. I prefer to use imported Italian tomato puree (called passata in Italian) packed in jars rather than domestic tomato puree. These jars usually contain between 690 and 700 grams, which is just about 24½ ounces. As an alternative, you can pass a 28-ounce can of whole peeled tomatoes through a food mill instead of using puree.

Metric Measure	Ingredient	American Measure
3 medium	Red bell peppers	3 medium
3 medium	Yellow bell peppers	3 medium
4–5 cloves	Garlic, bruised with a chef's knife	4–5 cloves
60 milliliters	Extra-virgin olive oil	¼ cup
12	Skin-on, bone-in chicken thighs	12
180 milliliters	Dry white wine	¾ cup
240 milliliters	Chicken Broth (page 15)	1 cup
700 grams	Tomato puree (passata)	24½ ounces
2 teaspoons plus more	Salt, preferably fine sea salt	2 teaspoons plus more
1 teaspoon plus more	Freshly ground black pepper	1 teaspoon plus more
1 teaspoon	Dried oregano	1 teaspoon
90 grams	Freshly grated Pecorino Romano cheese	3 ounces

1. Cut the peppers into strips approximately 2½-centimeters (1-inch) wide. Cut each strip into 3 or 4 triangles. Reserve the peppers.

2. Using a wide, shallow, oven-safe pan with a lid, sauté the garlic in olive oil on medium-low heat until light brown. Remove and discard the garlic.

3. Season the chicken generously with salt and pepper. On medium-high heat, sauté the chicken in the garlic-flavored oil, starting skin side down and turning occasionally, until well browned. Remove and reserve the chicken.

4. Add the peppers to the pan used for the chicken, season with salt, and sauté briefly on medium-high heat to put a light char on some of the pieces. Remove and reserve the peppers.

5. Add the wine to the pan, bring to a boil, and scrape up any browned bits. After the wine evaporates, add the broth and tomato puree. Mix well and add the chicken, skin side down, along with any accumulated juices. Season with 2 teaspoons salt, 1 teaspoon pepper, and the oregano.

6. Simmer, partially covered, approximately 45 minutes. Turn chicken over and remove and discard the skin. Taste the sauce for seasoning and adjust as needed.

7. Add the peppers to the chicken and simmer approximately 1 hour, partially covered. The sauce should be thick.

8. Sprinkle the top with Pecorino Romano cheese and put under a broiler to lightly brown the cheese.

Pasta al Profumo di Mare
"Perfume of the Sea" Pasta

Trofie is a medium-length pasta that is rolled flat, cut into strips, and then rolled around a wire that is subsequently removed. You can find it dried in well-stocked Italian food stores. If you can't find trofie, I would opt for linguine or bavette. If you don't have garlic oil, you can use extra-virgin olive oil to garnish the pasta.

Metric Measure	Ingredient	American Measure
2	Lemons	2
300 grams	Small, headless, peel-on shrimp (51–60 count)	10 ounces
125 grams plus more	Salt, preferably fine sea salt, divided	7 tablespoons plus more
60 milliliters	Extra-virgin olive oil	¼ cup
4 cloves	Garlic, bruised with a chef's knife	4 cloves

Metric Measure	Ingredient	American Measure
375 milliliters	Fish Stock (page 36)	1½ cups
50 grams	Small olives, preferably taggiasche, pitted	⅓ cup
500 grams	Dry trofie pasta (see headnote)	~1 pound
To taste	Freshly ground black pepper	To taste
5 grams (6–8 sprigs) plus more to garnish	Fresh mint leaves	⅕ ounce (6–8 sprigs) plus more to garnish
60 grams	Shredded ricotta salata cheese	2 ounces
To garnish	Garlic Oil (page 57)	To garnish

1. Slice 1 lemon in ½-centimeter (just under ¼-inch) slices. Using a fine grater, remove the zest of the other lemon.

2. Bring 2 liters (2 quarts) of water seasoned with 50 grams (3 tablespoons) of salt to a boil. Add the shrimp, return to a boil. Cover the pot, remove it from the heat, and allow the shrimp to rest for 1 minute.

3. Drain and plunge the shrimp into ice water to stop cooking. Drain when cool. Peel and de-vein the shrimp.

4. In a sauté pan large enough to hold all the ingredients, sauté the garlic in the olive oil over medium-low heat. When the garlic turns golden, add the lemon slices in a single layer. Remove and discard the garlic as it turns from golden to light brown. Continue to sauté the lemon slices until they soften somewhat and get brown in places.

5. Add 250 milliliters (1 cup) of the fish stock and the olives. Boil gently until reduced by half. Remove and reserve the lemon slices.

6. When the lemon slices are cool, squeeze their juice into the liquid in the sauté pan. Discard the lemon slices.

7. Bring 3 liters (3 quarts) of water seasoned with 75 grams (¼ cup) of salt to a rolling boil.

8. Meanwhile, return the liquid in the sauté pan to a simmer.

9. Add the pasta to the boiling salted water and cook at a rapid boil for approximately 2 minutes less than the minimum cooking time on the package for al dente pasta, stirring frequently to prevent sticking.

10. Drain the pasta, reserving the pasta-cooking water.

11. Add the par-cooked pasta to the liquid in the sauté pan along with the remaining 125 milliliters (½ cup) of fish stock and finish cooking at a moderate boil, adding the reserved pasta-cooking water 1 ladle at a time, shaking the pan and stirring the pasta, until the pasta is al dente, leaving the sauce liquid enough to just coat the pasta. Adjust the salt and pepper while finishing the pasta.

12. Add the shrimp to the pasta along with the last ladle of pasta-cooking water.

13. Off heat, stir in the mint.

14. Garnish each portion with ricotta salata, additional mint leaves, and a drizzle of garlic oil.

BRODO DI PESCE
Fish Stock

Use very fresh, non-oily, white-fleshed fish to make fish stock. Do not use the gills, and do not use any pieces of fish that are obviously bloody. Use a light, dry white wine and specifically one that has not been oaked. Sauvignon blanc and pinot grigio are good choices. Unlike most fish stock, this one is designed to pack a powerful punch, adding savory fish-inflected goodness to an array of pasta and rice dishes.

Metric Measure	Ingredient	American Measure
1 kilogram	Fish scraps and bones	2¼ pounds
500 grams	Tomatoes	17½ ounces
60 milliliters	Extra-virgin olive oil	¼ cup
300 milliliters	Dry white wine	1¼ cup
1 medium	Onion, thinly sliced	1 medium
4 liters	Water	4 quarts plus 1 cup
To taste	Salt, preferably fine sea salt	To taste
To taste	Freshly ground black pepper	To taste

1. Cut the fish into pieces that are not bigger than 5 centimeters (2 inches).

2. Cut the tomatoes into slices 1 centimeter (just under ½ inch) thick.

3. In a large sauté pan, heat the olive oil. Add the fish, season with salt, and sauté until there is a good quantity of brown bits, but no very brown ones.

4. Add the tomatoes, season with pepper, and sauté until the tomatoes collapse. Cook off most of the liquid that develops.

5. Put the contents of the sauté pan in a stock pot.

6. Add the wine to the sauté pan and boil, scraping up any brown bits. Add to the stock pot with the fish.

7. Add the onion and water to the fish. Cook at a gentle boil until the liquid is reduced to just under 1 liter (about 1 quart). Strain well and refrigerate or freeze if not using immediately.

Chef Juan begins the preparation of Pollo alla Romana that ultimately included about fifty chicken thighs. (See page 33 for a recipe.)

Pasta and Bread

JANUARY 19

Tuesday was pasta day. Wednesday was bread day. This being Calabria, seafood was included on both days.

On Thursday, January 17, we did a bit of food production in the morning and then observed cooking demonstrations in the afternoon. (It appears that we will do much more hands-on cooking in the coming weeks.) We began by splitting into two groups. One group made pasta and the other made bread. Given the amount of bread and pasta we consume as a group, this is going to be a regular occurrence.

Although I feel that I have a lot to learn about making both pasta and bread, I chose pasta because I feel less confident in making it than I do bread. Jumping right in seemed like the best way to tackle my uncertainty.

Most people in the pasta group were told to make plain pasta. Two of us were told to make pasta with orange zest, and two others were told to make pasta with truffles.

Fluffy ciabatta is a delight to eat.
(See page 217 for a recipe.)

I made a batch (about 14 ounces) of plain egg pasta. It was supposed to be truffle pasta, but there were no directions given about when to put the truffles in. Besides, the truffles weren't even out. Before I could start making pasta, I had to cut a mess of carrots into brunoise—about 1/8 inch dice—so I came to pasta-making late in the game and assumed the lack of truffles meant that they went in at the end. So I just went ahead and made the pasta, assuming that if truffles needed to be added first, they would have been provided. I figured I would add the shaved truffles at the end. Duh! Pasta dough is pretty firm so I should have realized that this wouldn't work.

Grated truffles ready to be put into pasta dough.

The pasta dough came together quite well. The whole process was easier than when I did it two days previously, which seemed like a win to me even though it wasn't the truffle pasta it was supposed to be. Armed with instructions this time, I set about making a second batch with the truffles mixed into the flour at the beginning. I absent-mindedly started to add the eggs to the flour before adding the truffles and then stopped myself. Chef John just scooped some of the flour out of the bowl and told me to mix the truffles into the bit he scooped out and then put it back in the original bowl and continue.

While I was grating truffles on a Microplane with my back turned, someone decided to grab my bowl of flour and use it to dust the table where they were rolling out pasta. That should never have happened as the school insists on using coarser semolina for dusting work surfaces, not finely ground soft wheat flour. Besides, the flour was on my table.

Because the flour needs to be weighed out precisely, there's no way to recover from this, so that batch of pasta went in the trash!

I repeated the process a third time and got it right! I cleaned up my station while the pasta was resting then rolled and cut a sample for Chef John to taste at his request. The instructions I received were to bring a little salted water to a boil, cook the pasta, and give it to him. The only other batch of student-made pasta that was tested was cooked personally by Chef John.

I cooked a few mouthfuls of pasta, tossed it with extra-virgin olive oil and a dash of pepper, and gave it to him. The texture was perfect, but the final product was too salty. It gnawed at me all day because I cook pasta about five times per week and never over salt it. I chalked it up to using a very small quantity of water and not eyeballing the salt correctly. Later, however, I looked at the ingredients of the fresh pasta that I make at home as well as the brand of dry pasta that I use most frequently. My fresh pasta has about one sixth the salt of the school's recipe. The dry pasta has no salt. At home, my salted water compensates for this paucity of salt. Clearly, I will need to use much less salt when making pasta using the school's recipe.

Cutting the pasta was interesting. It was rolled using a manual pasta machine. Chef John wanted it to be rolled on the finest setting, which is almost thin enough to see through. He then wanted it cut on the wider setting of a chitarra. I had heard about chitarra pasta cutters but never had used one.

Chitarra means guitar in Italian. The device is a wooden frame strung with real guitar strings. Most modern chitarra pasta cutters are strung for two different widths depending on which side of the device is used. To use a chitarra, one lays the pasta sheet on top of the strings and rolls the pasta, carefully, with a rolling pin to cut through the pasta sheet. It's really nifty. I think it's a lot more fun than cutting the pasta with a pasta machine.

Chef John also insists that long pasta, such as the tagliatelle I was making, be cut to "regulation" size. Regulation size is twenty-five centimeters, or just about ten inches. After sectioning a sheet of pasta, any piece not regulation size is made into something else like *maltagliati*, which literally means "badly cut" pasta.

Bollito made with pork ribs and served with bread and salsa verde.

The afternoon was crammed full of Chef John demonstrating the preparation of the following dishes, sometimes three at a time! Asterisks (*) mean we also ate the dish!

- Smoked sweet peppers (used for a salsina)*
- Duck bacon (the initial stages)
- Parsley oil*
- Pan-seared orata (a type of sea bass) served on a bed of potato puree with smoked pepper salsina and parsley oil*
- Crispy chicken skin (like chicharrones but made with chicken skin)*
- Panzanella
- Caponata
- Spaghetti aglio e olio*
- Mackerel (sgombro) cooked in vinegar and water with onions
- Roasted eggplant spread*
- Reduced chicken stock (similar to chicken demi-glace)
- Octopus to be cooked sous vide
- Marinated pork fillet
- Bagna cauda (a tangy and pungent anchovy dip)

To tide us over to dinner we had grilled cheese (fontina) sandwiches with porcini mushrooms topped with mayonnaise and some crispy chicken skin.

Focaccia Pugliese with tomatoes, olives, anchovies, and oregano.

We ended the day with a trip to MOPS, a brasserie and birrateca in Catanzaro Lido for apericena. The word apericena is a mash up of the words aperitivo (aperitif) and cena (dinner). During apericena, you buy your drinks, and the restaurant provides small snacks from which one can make a dinner. I had Jack Daniels for €5 a pour. (A pour was way more than a shot! Not a bad price!) Later in the evening I heard from Chef Juan that MOPS also has some very good bourbons. They're on my list for next time. This is clearly a place to return to!

In addition to all the dishes Chef John prepared for us on January 17, here's the rundown of what we and/or Chef John made and ate (*) earlier in the week.

On January 15:

- Northern Italian pasta dough made into:
  - Tagliolini
  - Tagliatelle
  - Farfalle
  - Croxetti
  - Fornarina*
  - Tortellini
  - Agnolotti
  - Cappelletti
- Northern Italian spinach pasta dough
- Northern Italian beet pasta dough
- Chlorophyll extracted from spinach for coloring food
- Meat stuffing for pasta
- Ricotta stuffing for pasta
- Mussels to be put into pasta the next day
- Gnocchi Napoli with tomato sauce, baked and topped with fior di latte, basil, and garlic oil*
- Salsa Napoli

- ★ Individual lasagna made in ramekins:
    - ◆ Seafood
    - ◆ Lamb ragù and wild artichokes
    - ◆ Bolognese

On January 16:

- ★ Garganelli
- ★ Specialty rolls:
    - ◆ Cuttlefish ink*
    - ◆ Walnut and raisin
    - ◆ Sausage and sweet pepper*
- ★ Pasta alla chitarra
- ★ Focaccia
    - ◆ Plain
    - ◆ Peperoncino
    - ◆ Rosemary
    - ◆ Garlic
    - ◆ Pugliese (topped with crushed tomatoes, anchovies, black olives, and oregano)
- ★ Ciabatta
    - ◆ Plain
    - ◆ Whole wheat
- ★ Honey bread
- ★ Biga (a starter for yeast-raised products)
- ★ Pasta allo scoglio (pasta from the reef) made with previously prepared mussels and cuttlefish, with shrimp added, and the cuttlefish ink pasta we made previously*

Gamberi rossi are very delicate shrimp. They are either eaten raw or cooked into a pasta sauce during which they disintegrate.

For lunch we were served polenta with pulled braised pork, Parmesan fonduta, black truffle, and crispy fried carrots and leeks followed by fish poached in fish stock with chlorophyll (to make it green) and topped with a tomato relish. Dessert was amaretto gelato with crushed almonds on top.

For dinner we were served broccoli soup accompanied by the sausage and pepper rolls followed by lasagna with lamb ragù.

Lasagne con Agnello e Carciofi
Lamb and Artichoke Lasagna

If you can't find canned baby artichoke hearts, you can use canned regular artichoke hearts or even frozen artichoke hearts cut into two or three pieces each. The drained weight of the artichoke hearts should be about 480 grams (17 ounces). Although there is no official calibration of pasta machines, something around setting #7 should be correct. Often newer pasta machines can produce exceedingly thin sheets of pasta (up to about #9 or so), which is beyond the capability of "vintage" machines. I find the easiest way to add the besciamella to the lasagna is to put room-temperature, not cold, besciamella in a pastry bag with a wide opening and then pipe it on top. It is not necessary to create a continuous layer of besciamella. Just space the rows of besciamella evenly, using one-third of the besciamella on each layer.

Metric Measure	Ingredient	American Measure
1 liter	Milk	1 quart plus ¼ cup
75 grams	Unsalted butter	5 tablespoons
75 grams	All-purpose flour	½ cup plus 1 tablespoon
To taste	Freshly grated nutmeg	To taste
To taste	Salt, preferably fine sea salt	To taste
To taste	Freshly ground black pepper	To taste
2 (400-gram) cans	Canned baby artichoke hearts	2 (14-ounce) cans
1 recipe	Fresh egg pasta (page 45)	1 recipe
1 recipe	Lamb Ragù (page 46)	1 recipe
125 grams	Freshly grated Parmigiano Reggiano cheese	4½ ounces
To taste	Rosemary Oil (page 262)	To taste

1. Use the milk, butter, flour, and nutmeg to make besciamella following the directions on page 256. Season with salt and pepper. Pour into a metal bowl, cover with plastic wrap that touches the top of the besciamella to prevent the development of a skin, and refrigerate.

2. Drain the artichoke hearts and gently squeeze to rid them of excess liquid.

3. Use a deep, rectangular baking dish that is approximately 23 x 30 centimeters (9 x 12 inches) in size.

4. Roll the egg pasta into long sheets (see headnote) and cut to the length of the baking dish. Use the pasta shortly after rolling so that it does not start to dry and curl. There is no need to precook the pasta.

5. Put a very thin coating of ragù on the bottom of the baking dish. Put a layer of pasta, using ¼ of the pasta sheets, overlapping as necessary. Spread with a thin layer of ragù, then ⅓ of the besciamella, ⅓ of the artichoke hearts, ¼ of the Parmigiano Reggiano cheese.

6. Repeat the layers: pasta, ragù, besciamella, artichoke hearts, and Parmigiano Reggiano cheese.

7. Repeat layers again: pasta, ragù, besciamella, artichoke hearts, and Parmigiano Reggiano cheese.

8. Finish with a layer of pasta. Gently press on the lasagna to level the top. Add a layer of ragù, and then the remaining Parmigiano Reggiano cheese.

9. Drizzle with rosemary oil.

10. Bake at 180°C (350°F) until the lasagna is bubbling and the top is brown, approximately 50 minutes.

11. Allow the lasagna to rest 15 minutes before cutting.

Tip: There will be more ragù than needed for the lasagna. All the other ingredients should be used up in the various layers.

Pasta Fresca all'Uovo
Fresh Egg Pasta

For this pasta, use flour with a fine grind (Italian 00) and low extensibility (W-180). I recommend Paolo Mariani flour for pasta fresca (fresh pasta) or dolci (sweets). Both are 00 grind and have low W values. In a pinch, you could try American pastry flour. Unless you are an expert pasta maker, precisely weighing everything is much easier than a pinch of this and a bit of that. I have converted the metric measures to American measures by weight as volume is too imprecise for this recipe. I recommend, though, that you set your digital scale to metric just this once. When making pasta in the American desert Southwest, I find that I need an extra 10 grams (0.35 ounces) of whole egg to fully incorporate all the flour.

Metric Measure	Ingredient	American Measure
250 grams	Italian 00 flour, W-180	8.82 ounces
2 grams	Salt	0.07 ounces
80 grams	Whole egg, lightly beaten	2.82 ounces
60 grams	Egg yolk, lightly beaten	2.12 ounces

1. Mix the flour and salt in a large bowl.

2. In a separate bowl, combine the whole egg and egg yolk, and gently mix together with a fork.

3. Make a depression in the center of the flour. Add the egg mixture and begin to mix the flour into the egg with a fork. When the dough becomes too stiff for the fork, scrape everything onto a work surface.

4. Change the fork for a bench scraper and your hand. Slide the scraper partway under the flour-egg mixture and then flip it over to bring the flour that was on the bottom to the top. Use your hand and the bench scraper to press the mixture together to fully combine the flour and egg.

5. When the mixture becomes firm enough, you can stop using the bench scraper and use your hands to press and turn the dough until it is homogeneous. Use a pressing motion, not a kneading motion the way you would for bread. That is, press down on the mixture, not out and away from you.

6. Once the dough is homogeneous, form it into a brick shape and wrap very tightly in plastic wrap. The pressure will further help the dough to hydrate.

7. Allow the dough to rest at room temperature for 60 to 90 minutes, until it does not spring back quickly when gently depressed with a finger.

8. Portion, roll, and cut as required for the recipe.

Tip: This dough cannot be rerolled as it will not bond well to itself after rolling. Any scraps can be cut into irregular pieces, called maltagliati in Italian, air-dried if desired, and used in soup or another dish.

 Ragù di Agnello
Lamb Ragù

This is a wonderful sauce for pasta, especially long pasta such as spaghetti. Garnish each serving with freshly grated Parmigiano Reggiano cheese and pass extra cheese at the table. If you don't have fresh rosemary, use 1 teaspoon dried rosemary, crumbled. Imported Italian passata (tomato puree) often comes in jars that weigh 700 grams. Use two of these.

Metric Measure	Ingredient	American Measure
150 grams	Minced carrot	5 ounces
150 grams	Minced onion	5 ounces
2 cloves	Garlic, minced	2 cloves
45 grams	Unsalted butter	3 tablespoons
450 grams	Ground lean lamb	1 pound
2 tablespoons	Extra-virgin olive oil	2 tablespoons
250 milliliters	Dry red wine	1 cup
1,400 grams	Passata (tomato puree)	49 ounces
500 milliliters	Water	2 cups
1 tablespoon	Fresh rosemary, minced	1 tablespoon
To taste	Salt, preferably fine sea salt	To taste
To taste	Freshly ground black pepper	To taste

1. Sauté the carrot, onion, and garlic in the butter until the onion is golden. Do not brown any of the vegetables. Set aside.

2. Brown the lamb in the olive oil until lots of brown bits develop, seasoning with salt along the way. While it is cooking, break up the lamb with a wooden spoon so that it is in tiny crumbles.

3. When the lamb is well-browned, add the sautéed vegetables and sauté approximately 2 minutes longer.

4. Add the wine and boil gently, uncovered, until the wine is almost completely evaporated.

5. Add the passata, water, rosemary, and salt and pepper to taste. Boil gently for 2 hours. If the sauce becomes too thick, add a bit of water and partially cover the pot. At the end, the sauce should be reduced by half.

Tip: If there is oil pooling on top of the sauce, which should not be the case if the lamb was lean, allow the sauce to sit off heat for a few minutes after cooking and then gently spoon off the excess oil.

Linguine allo Scoglio
Linguine "from the Reef"

Given the amount of coastline in Italy, Italians have an amazing number of pasta and seafood dishes. Some versions of this pasta add clams. Others omit the shrimp in favor of clams, mussels, and calamari. Use this as a starting point to design your own recipe.

Metric Measure	Ingredient	American Measure
200 grams	Small, headless, peel-on shrimp (U 51–60)	7 ounces
60	Live mussels	60
2 tablespoons	Extra-virgin olive oil	2 tablespoons
3 cloves	Garlic, bruised with a chef's knife	3 cloves
250 milliliters	Dry white wine	1 cup
150 grams	Cherry tomatoes	5 ounces
1 recipe	Mollusk Ragù (page 50)	1 recipe
500 grams	Dry linguine	~1 pound
125 grams plus more	Salt, preferably fine sea salt, divided	7 tablespoons plus more
To taste	Freshly ground black pepper	To taste
2 tablespoons	Minced parsley or basil chiffonade	2 tablespoons

1. Bring 2 liters (2 quarts) of water seasoned with 50 grams (3 tablespoons) of salt to a boil. Add the shrimp and return to a boil. Cover, remove from the heat, and allow the shrimp to rest for 1 minute.

2. Drain and plunge the shrimp into ice water to stop cooking. Drain when cool. Peel and de-vein the shrimp.

3. Quickly wash the mussels in cold water. Remove any beards.

4. Sauté the garlic in a heavy-bottomed Dutch oven until golden. Add the wine and boil until reduced by half. Remove and discard the garlic.

5. Add the cleaned mussels to the wine, cover the pot, and cook at a medium boil until the mussels are all open, approximately 3 minutes. Immediately strain the mussels through a sieve, reserving the cooking liquid and the mussels separately. Discard any mussels that do not open.

6. When cool enough to handle, remove the mussels from their shells, if desired.

7. In a large sauté pan, sauté the tomatoes over medium-high heat until they just begin to blister, approximately 2 minutes. Gently press on the tomatoes to burst the skin. Reserve.

8. Bring 3 liters (3 quarts) of water seasoned with 75 grams (¼ cup) of salt to a rolling boil.

9. Meanwhile, add the liquid from the mollusk ragù to the sauté pan used for the tomatoes (no need to wash the pan) and heat gently.

10. Add the pasta to the boiling salted water and cook at a rapid boil for approximately 2 minutes less than the minimum cooking time on the package for al dente pasta, stirring frequently to prevent sticking.

11. Drain the pasta, reserving the pasta-cooking water.

12. Add the par-cooked pasta to the liquid in the sauté pan and finish cooking at a moderate boil, adding the reserved mussel-cooking liquid, and then the reserved pasta-cooking water 1 ladle at a time, shaking the pan and stirring the pasta, until the pasta is al dente, leaving the sauce liquid enough to just coat the pasta. Adjust the salt and pepper while finishing the pasta.

13. With the last ladle of liquid, add the calamari from the mollusk ragù, shrimp, mussels, and cherry tomatoes to the pasta. Taste and adjust the salt and pepper.

14. Garnish each serving with a sprinkle of minced parsley or basil chiffonade.

RAGÙ DI MOLLUSCHI
Mollusk Ragù

Calamari either need to be flash cooked (as in fried calamari) or stewed for a long time. Anything in between results in a texture resembling rubber bands. This ragù can be used as a pasta sauce in its own right. Garnish each serving with fresh mint or basil, garlic oil, and coarse breadcrumbs browned in extra-virgin olive oil. You can also use it as part of a more-involved seafood pasta, such as Linguine "From the Reef" (page 48).

Metric Measure	Ingredient	American Measure
150 grams	Calamari or cuttlefish	5 ounces
1 tablespoon	Extra-virgin olive oil	1 tablespoon
1 clove	Garlic, bruised with a chef's knife	1 clove
500 milliliters	Vegetable Broth (page 161)	2 cups
To taste	Salt, preferably fine sea salt	To taste
To taste	Freshly ground black pepper	To taste

1. Cut the calamari into a 1-centimeter (½-inch) dice. Reserve.

2. In a small heavy-bottomed saucepan, sizzle the garlic in olive oil until golden. Remove and discard the garlic.

3. Add the calamari to the garlic-flavored oil. Sauté over medium heat until most of the liquid that comes out of the calamari evaporates.

4. Add the broth, season with salt and pepper, and simmer, partially covered, until tender, approximately 75 to 90 minutes.

5. When done, there should be about 250 milliliters (1 cup) of liquid left. If not, either add water or boil uncovered (as needed) to reach that amount.

Clockwise from top: Spaghetti aglio e olio (spaghetti with garlic and oil) garnished with peperoncino piccante (hot peppers) and breadcrumbs. (See page 89 for a recipe.) Lasagne with lamb ragù. (See page 44 for a recipe for lasagne with lamb ragù and artichokes.) Pasta allo scoglio (Pasta from the reef) made with cuttlefish ink pasta and seafood. (See page 48 for a recipe for pasta allo scoglio. Black pasta is optional but dramatic.)

Pizza Tre Volte

JANUARY 22

Friday, January 18, was market day. The mercatino (little outdoor market) in Soverato, about a fifteen-minute drive from the school, is truly compact, but the quality and variety of the products on offer are amazing. We bought lots of produce and fish for the school. Many of us also bought things for ourselves. Outings to the market are planned for almost every Friday.

I bought ricotta infornata, which is fresh sheep's milk ricotta shaped into little cylinders and baked. The ricotta was made by the vendor using milk from her own sheep. She also baked the cheese herself.

Beautiful vegetables at the weekly outdoor market in Soverato.

After the market we went to a kitchen and restaurant supply store. A number of students needed chef coats so it was a logical stop. I looked at the other items on offer and made mental notes about the prices of items that I need…um…okay, want, not "need"! Some of the items are not available in the States, like a deep sauté pan with a wicked curve, perfect for finishing pasta in a sauce. I see two of these in my future. Other items can be had in the States on the web, like silicone molds and a chitarra for pasta, but being able to see and touch them makes a big difference. I suspect I'll be visiting this store most Fridays when we go to the market.

We got back about 1:30 p.m. and had lunch. The first course was a trifecta of braised mackerel, crisped sous vide octopus with cannellini bean puree, and shrimp crudo (made with gamberi rossi) accompanied by a hazelnut puree. This was followed by panzanella (bread and tomato salad) that was made the previous day.

After lunch we went to the pastry lab to roll out dough for pizza fritta, which is a dish that consists of a deep-fried pizza dough (rolled very thin at the school, though sometimes rolled overly thick in restaurants) topped with an array of toppings that usually includes tomato sauce, fior di latte, and extra-virgin olive oil, among others.

Chef John made a Nutella knock-off that was way better than the real thing. It was just a mixture of about 40 percent melted milk chocolate and 60 percent roasted pureed hazelnuts with a pinch of salt. This was used to make a sweet pizza fritta along with a generous sprinkling of powdered sugar. Tasting everything is a necessity!

We had a few free hours before we had to show up in the pizzeria with the wood-burning oven to try our hands at making pizza. I opted for topping mine with 'nduja, buffalo mozzarella, extra-virgin olive oil, oregano, and a bit of tomato sauce and "pizza cheese" (as it is called here). It was quite the hit, with Chef Juan and two of the other staff reaching for pieces as soon as I cut it.

An antipasto of shrimp crudo (raw shrimp), octopus sous vide, and braised mackerel. (See page 171 for a recipe for octopus sous vide.)

After everyone had made at least one pie each, I suggested that we have a pizza play-off pitting Chef Juan against his wife, Mariana, and Ryan against fellow kitchen assistant Erlyn. The winner of each round was to be pitted against the other. Folks started to go to bed early, and although we completed the first two rounds, we never got to the finals. This was probably a good thing, given that the judging was quite variable.

During pizza making and eating, Ryan was our DJ. He started playing current international songs but then veered into Italian ones. "L'Italiano" is one of my favorites, but I couldn't explain it enough for Ryan to recognize it. I played it for him the next day, and it since has been added to his playlist, which makes me quite happy. For some reason it's brought a smile to my face from the first time I heard it.

ANCHOVIES, FROGS' LEGS, AND QUAIL

Saturday morning, January 19, was very busy with prep: chopping, slicing, dicing, gutting, and cleaning. I think I am now an expert at cleaning anchovies having done many dozen at the ICI. (Twist off the head and pull carefully to remove the guts while they're still attached to the head; use a finger to open the fish along the belly; peel out the spine; sepa-

Tending to my pizza in the wood-fired oven.

rate the filets; remove the dorsal fin from one of the filets; remove any remaining pectoral and ventral fins; rinse in 3.5 percent salt water; line up in a tray; repeat.)

We had to lollipop frogs' legs, which is kind of like making drumettes from chicken wings. We also had to tunnel-bone quail, which entails removing all bones except the furthest bones in the wings and legs without cutting the skin or making any incisions. One goes through the neck and body cavity openings that are already present in the butchered quail. The same technique can be applied to any bird. I think it's a great skill to have, but I can't imagine when I'll tunnel-bone any fowl unless I decide to get into the turducken business!

All this took four and a half hours in the kitchen before our first break.

In the afternoon, we were shown the preparation of and tasted (*) the following dishes:

- ★ Pasta alla vongole made with pasta alla chitarra con scorza d'arancia (pasta with clams made with pasta flavored with orange zest and cut on the chitarra)*
- ★ Rana pescatrice (monkfish) cooked in fumetino—a fragrant stock (we ate this a day later)
- ★ Orecchiette con rape e salsiccia (orecchiette pasta with broccoli rabe and sausage)*
- ★ Ossobuco (we ate this another day)
- ★ Gnocchi sardi con salsa alle erbe (saffron gnocchi with a bacon, tomato, and herb sauce)*

Sometime during the afternoon, Chef John made pistachio gelato for everyone. We have an entire week coming up where we learn to make gelato!

For dinner, five of us made sandwiches and salad for the group. The sandwiches were made on focaccia with cooked ham, salami, buffalo mozzarella, tomato, basil, salt, and olive oil. Dessert was puff pastry stuffed with pastry cream and topped with white chocolate ganache.

Sunday, January 20, was another busy day. We observed Chef John prepare three types of risotto (each of which we ate before 10:30 a.m.!):

- ★ Risotto alla Milanese (saffron risotto)
- ★ Risotto alla Parmigiana con porri e aceto balsamico (Parmesan cheese risotto with sautéed leeks and balsamic vinegar)
- ★ Risotto al nero di seppia con frutti di mare (cuttlefish ink risotto with seafood)

Chef John's technique is a little different from mine, and I will need to try it his way. He does not stir after the wine is added until it completely evaporates. He keeps more liquid in the rice during cooking than I do. At the end, he adds cheese and butter, as I do, but his butter is frozen and he uses a classic French technique to "fluff up" the risotto. I don't fluff my risotto, but I guess I'll learn!

The ossobuco from the previous day was finished and served with the risotto alla Milanese, sprinkled with gremolata (finely minced garlic, parsley, and lemon zest).

Chef John started to marinate the dozens and dozens of anchovies that we had cleaned the previous day. We also tested a portion of baccalà (salted cod) that had been soaking for a few days to see if it was ready to cook, but it was still too salty, so it went back into the water and in the fridge.

Chef John pan-roasted broccoli florets that had been briefly blanched. They were later turned into a simple sauce for mafalde pasta that we had for lunch.

The afternoon saw the preparation of:

- Italian meringue (which is different from both French meringue and Swiss meringue)
- Caramel sauce
- Pâte à bombe (a beaten egg yolk and hot syrup base for many desserts)
- Glassa nera (a glassy candy coating)
- Tiramisù (made both in a large dish and in a martini glass, which was very cool)

Later in the afternoon, we got to be hands-on again, pulling mozzarella this time. The mozzarella is aging under fresh water as I write this and will ultimately be soaked in salt water for a day or so before being used.

Pastry and Pizza

All day Monday, January 21, was spent in the pastry lab watching Chef Juan demonstrate the preparation of a number of fundamental pastry-making components (like a fruit coulis and tempered chocolate) followed by the creation of spumone (which is not like the American spumoni) and a variation on tiramisù.

On Monday evening, we had our third pizza session since Friday! This one involved the use of the electric pizza oven. It pretty much followed the format of the wood-oven pizza session, with each of us making one pizza and sharing, followed by a few additional ones.

I chose to make pizza with 'nduja, a fried egg, fresh peperoncino, and peperoncino oil in addition to a little tomato sauce and pizza cheese. The oven needed to be cleaned, so the raw pizza sat on the table too long and stuck when I tried to get it onto the peel. Rather than pitch it, Chef Chris made it into a large dumpling-shaped calzone. It was a big hit. One of my classmates named it Il Mostro, The Monster. Chef Juan thought it was the perfect breakfast!

I made another one that did not stick to the peel and came out of the oven flat. It was equally good but, interestingly, somewhat different in taste and texture having been baked flat as opposed to closed.

My second "electric pizza" with 'nduja, fried egg, fresh peperoncino, olio santo (peperoncino oil), tomato sauce, and cheese. (See page 62 for a recipe for pizza sauce.)

In my next post, I'll describe what we did in the pastry lab before the pizza session, as well as talk about our trip to Sicily.

Olio all'Aglio
Garlic Oil

I always have a squeeze bottle of garlic oil beside my stove along with several other flavored oils. I often use it to sauté ingredients for which I would have first sautéed garlic to flavor the oil. More often, though, I use it to finish a dish to add a bit of vibrant garlic flavor at the end.

Metric Measure	Ingredient	American Measure
125 grams	Garlic, thinly sliced	4 ounces
500 grams	Extra-virgin olive oil	2 cups

1. Combine the garlic and olive oil in a nonreactive container, such as a large glass jar.
2. Cover loosely and swirl several times per day for 3 days.
3. Strain the oil and discard the solids. Store at room temperature.

Mafalde con i Broccoli
Mafalde Pasta with Broccoli

Mafalde are a long, flat pasta with wavy edges. It is very effective at gripping sauces that have a bit of heft to them.

Metric Measure	Ingredient	American Measure
60 milliliters	Extra-virgin olive oil	¼ cup
4 cloves	Garlic, minced	4 cloves
1 (60-gram) can	Anchovies packed in in olive oil	1 (2-ounce) can
450–500 grams	Broccoli florets	~1 pound
125 milliliters	Dry white wine	½ cup
500 grams	Dry mafalde	~1 pound
To taste	Salt, preferably fine sea salt	To taste
To taste	Freshly ground black pepper	To taste
55 grams	Freshly grated Parmigiano Reggiano cheese	2 ounces

1. In a large sauté pan, combine the olive oil and garlic. Sauté on low heat until the garlic is fragrant. Add the anchovies and their oil. Increase the heat to medium and sauté, stirring frequently, until the anchovies disintegrate, 1 to 2 minutes.

2. As soon as the anchovies have darkened slightly, add the broccoli florets. Sauté until the florets have turned bright green, 2 to 3 minutes. Add the wine, scrape up any bits stuck to the pan, cover the pan, and cook on low until the wine has evaporated.

3. Bring 3 liters (3 quarts) of water seasoned with 75 grams (¼ cup) of salt to a rolling boil.

4. If the broccoli florets are not tender by the time the wine has evaporated, add the boiling salted water 1 ladle at a time and cook, covered, until tender. This is not a dish for crunchy vegetables; broccoli is the sauce, and the texture should be soft but not mushy.

5. Add the pasta to the boiling salted water and cook at a rapid boil for approximately 2 minutes less than the minimum cooking time on the package for al dente pasta, stirring frequently to prevent sticking.

6. Drain the pasta, reserving the pasta-cooking water.

7. Add the par-cooked pasta to the broccoli mixture in the sauté pan and finish cooking at a moderate boil, adding the reserved pasta-cooking water 1 ladle at a time, shaking the pan and stirring the pasta until the pasta is al dente, leaving the sauce liquid enough to just coat the pasta. Adjust the salt and pepper while finishing the pasta.

8. Off the heat, add the cheese and then flip and stir the pasta to emulsify the cheese and sauce. Add a bit more cooking water if the sauce is too thick.

9. Add a generous drizzle of olive oil to each serving.

ORECCHIETTE CON CIME DI RAPA E SALSICCIA
Orecchiette Pasta with Broccoli Rabe and Sausage

If you don't have Garlic Oil (page 57), bruise 3 to 4 cloves of garlic with the side of a chef's knife and sauté gently in 60 milliliters (¼ cup) of extra-virgin olive oil until golden brown to light brown, depending on preference. Discard the garlic and reserve the oil. The stems of broccoli rabe can be stringy, so it is important to peel them as described.

Metric Measure	Ingredient	American Measure
400 grams	Broccoli rabe	13 ounces
300 grams	Italian sausage, sweet or hot, in casing	10 ounces
To taste	Cayenne pepper	To taste
250 milliliters	Chicken Broth (page 15) or Vegetable Broth (page 161)	1 cup
500 grams	Dry orecchiette	~1 pound
60 milliliters	Garlic Oil (page 57)	¼ cup
To taste	Salt, preferably fine sea salt	To taste
To taste	Freshly ground black pepper	To taste
55 grams	Freshly grated Pecorino Romano cheese	2 ounces
To taste	Olio Santo (page 147), optional	To taste

1. Cut the broccoli rabe into pieces. The first cut should be just below the point where the thinner stems from the florets come together to form the thicker stem, keeping the florets together. Reserve the florets separately from the leaves and thicker stems.

Pizza Tre Volte

2. Peel the stems. Using a sharp paring knife, slip the blade just under the outer layer of one of the stems. Press your thumb against the side of the knife to catch the outer layer and then peel down, like a banana, to remove the fibrous outer layer. Repeat the whole way around the stem. Peel all the stems. Cut the stems into pieces about 5-centimeters (2 inches) long.

3. Bring 3 liters (3 quarts) of water seasoned with 75 grams (¼ cup) of salt to a rolling boil.

4. Meanwhile, prick the sausage with a fork in multiple places. In a large sauté pan, sauté the sausage without using oil, if possible. If the sausage does not release enough fat, add a small amount of extra-virgin olive oil. When the sausage is browned, remove it and allow it to cool slightly. Do not clean the sauté pan.

5. Cut the sausage lengthwise into quarters then across into 1-centimeter (½-inch) pieces. The sausage will likely not be fully cooked.

6. Return the sausage to the sauté pan and cook on medium-high heat until well browned. Just as the sausage finishes cooking, add cayenne pepper to taste. Allow it to "bloom" in the oil for 2 to 3 seconds then immediately add the broth to keep the cayenne from burning.

7. Cover the sauté pan and simmer until the liquid has evaporated. Remove the pan from the heat.

8. When the water comes to a boil, add the peeled broccoli rabe stems and leaves and boil until just tender, approximately 2 to 3 minutes. Lift the stems out of the water and plunge into ice water to stop cooking.

9. Add the florets to the boiling water and cook 1 to 2 minutes, until just tender. Add the florets to the ice water with the stems. Drain the cooked and cooled broccoli rabe in a sieve.

10. Add the pasta to the boiling water used to cook the broccoli rabe and cook at a rapid boil for approximately 2 minutes less than the minimum cooking time on the package for al dente pasta, stirring frequently to prevent sticking.

11. Drain the pasta, reserving the pasta-cooking water.

12. Add the par-cooked pasta to the sausage in the sauté pan and finish cooking at a moderate boil, adding the reserved pasta-cooking water 1 ladle at a time, shaking the pan and stirring the pasta, until the pasta is al dente.

13. About 1 minute before the pasta is done, add the cooked, drained broccoli rabe and the garlic oil. Season with salt and pepper.

14. Continue to sauté the mixture, adding pasta-cooking water as needed to create a sauce liquid enough to just coat the pasta. Adjust the salt, pepper, and cayenne.

15. Off the heat, add the cheese and then flip and stir the pasta to emulsify the cheese and sauce. Add a bit more cooking water if the sauce is too thick.

16. Garnish each portion with a drizzle of olio santo, if desired.

PASTA PER PIZZA
Pizza Dough

This is an unusual pizza dough, but it is perennially a big hit at our frequent pizza nights. When making this dough in the dry deserts of the American Southwest, I find that I need to increase the beer from 72 grams to 162 grams because the flour is drier. The use of diastatic malt is optional, but it aids browning. This recipe will make four 35-centimeter (14-inch) pizzas. For individual pizzas, portion the dough into 200-gram (7-ounce) portions. Antimo Caputo Pizzeria Flour has the correct grind and W value, though you can also use Caputo Chef's Flour, which has a slightly higher W value. Note that even the liquid ingredients are weighed for this recipe.

Metric Measure	Ingredient	American Measure
900 grams	Italian 00 flour, W-280	31.75 ounces
4.5 grams	Diastatic malt powder, optional	0.16 ounce
1.8 grams	Active dry yeast	0.05 ounce
72 or 162 grams (see headnote)	Beer	2.54 or 5.71 ounces (see headnote)
360 grams	Water	12.70 ounces
90 grams	Heavy cream	3.17 ounces
7.2 grams	Sugar	0.25 ounce
27 grams	Salt, preferably fine sea salt	0.95 ounce
As needed	Extra-virgin olive oil	As needed

1. Combine the flour, diastatic malt powder, and yeast in the bowl of a stand mixer fitted with a dough hook. Begin to mix on medium-low and then slowly add the beer down the side of the bowl.

Pizza Tre Volte

2. After the beer has been added, slowly add the water and then the cream in the same manner.

3. Sprinkle in the sugar then the salt.

4. Continue mixing until the dough comes together and cleans the side of the bowl. Continue to mix until there is good gluten formation. You can test the gluten formation by stopping the mixer and pinching a bit of dough and pulling it. You want the dough to stretch and form strands. This will take about 5 minutes.

5. Divide the dough into the desired number of portions (see headnote).

6. Lightly oil the bottom of one or more containers with tight-fitting lids (or use a dough box).

7. Completely remove any trace of oil from your hands or the dough will not bond to itself. Shape the portioned dough into balls. Put each portion of dough on a dry work surface. Cup your hands around the sides of the ball and rotate them under the dough gently pulling the dough under. Turn the dough 90 degrees and repeat. After a few turns you should have a ball of dough that is smooth and taut on top.

8. If any seams are open on the bottom, pinch them together to close.

9. Put each ball of dough in the oiled container. After all balls are formed, lightly oil them without turning them over. Cover tightly and refrigerate 48 hours.

10. Remove the dough from the refrigerator and keep at room temperature for 4 to 6 hours before shaping and baking.

SALSA PER PIZZA
Pizza Sauce

Pizza sauce in Italy is the simplest of affairs. It consists of excellent quality canned San Marzano tomatoes passed through a food mill and seasoned with salt. In a pinch you could use excellent quality Italian passata made from San Marzano tomatoes.

Metric Measure	Ingredient	American Measure
As needed	Canned Italian San Marzano tomatoes in puree	As needed
To taste	Salt, preferably fine sea salt	To taste

1. Pass the tomatoes through a food mill to remove the seeds and skin.

2. Season to taste with salt.

3. Refrigerate until ready to use.

Ricotta Infornata
Baked Ricotta

Ricotta infornata drizzled with a bit of extra-virgin olive oil and sprinkled with some freshly ground black pepper or peperoncino powder makes a great antipasto with bread, with or without other dishes such as Caponata (page 216), Bomba Calabrese (page 145), and Roasted Olives (page 76). The more liquid in the ricotta, the more it will slump as it bakes. Homemade ricotta (page 246) will hold its shape better than store-bought ricotta because it will lose more water, but both will taste great. Cheese molds are available online.

1. Fill as many 100-milliliter (3-ounce) cheese molds as desired to the top with ricotta.

2. Place the filled molds on a nonreactive rack placed in a nonreactive sheet pan or large rectangular plastic container. Cover tightly and refrigerate for approximately 48 hours.

3. Line a half-sheet pan with parchment. Remove the ricotta from the molds by inverting them, one at a time, and gently tapping them on the parchment-lined sheet pan. The ricotta should release easily. Leave about 5 centimeters (2 inches) between each cheese.

4. Bake at 230°C (450°F) with convection until darkly brown in some spots.

5. Cool on the parchment-lined pan.

6. If not using immediately, chill in the refrigerator and then wrap tightly and return to the refrigerator.

7. Warm to room temperature before serving.

Risotto al Parmigiano
Parmesan Cheese Risotto

This is the most basic risotto recipe and a very good place to start if you've never made risotto before. If desired, you can use finely minced shallot to replace the onion and garlic. Be sure that the chicken broth is not too concentrated. When in doubt, thin the broth with water. You may need slightly more or less broth. I never add salt to my homemade broth. If the broth is salted, adjust the salt in the recipe as appropriate.

Metric Measure	Ingredient	American Measure
1.5 liters	Chicken Broth (page 15)	1½ quarts
3 tablespoons	Extra-virgin olive oil	3 tablespoons
½ small	Onion, finely diced	½ small
1	Garlic clove, minced	1
300 grams	Arborio or carnaroli rice	1½ cups
150 milliliters	Dry white wine	Scant ¾ cup
1½ teaspoons	Salt, preferably fine sea salt	1½ teaspoons
½ teaspoon	Freshly ground black pepper	½ teaspoon
90 grams	Freshly grated Parmigiano Reggiano cheese	1 cup
30 grams	Unsalted butter at room temperature	2 tablespoons

1. Bring the broth to a simmer in a small saucepan.

2. Meanwhile, put the olive oil, onion, and garlic in a heavy-bottomed saucepan of approximately 3.5-liter (4-quart) capacity. Gently heat the pan and sauté until the onion is soft but not at all brown.

3. Turn the heat to medium and add the rice. Sauté for 2 to 3 minutes, stirring frequently, until all the rice grains show an opaque core surrounded by a translucent exterior. Do not brown the rice.

4. Add the wine and boil gently, stirring frequently, until the wine has completely evaporated.

5. Add approximately 125 milliliters (½ cup) of simmering broth and ⅓ of the salt. Over medium to medium-low heat, gently boil the rice, stirring frequently until the broth has evaporated. It is important that the rice actually boil so that much of the broth evaporates without entering the rice grain. This is what will coax the starch out of the rice to create a creamy risotto. Continue in this manner, adding ⅓ of the salt with each of the next

2 ladles of broth, until the rice is al dente, creamy on the exterior but slightly chewy in the center.

6. Stir frequently to prevent the rice from sticking and browning, especially as the cooking proceeds and the rice starch begins to form the characteristic creamy liquid surrounding the individual grains of rice. As cooking progresses, it will not be possible to allow all the liquid to fully evaporate due to the starch. Wait as long as you can, stirring frequently, without letting the risotto stick and turn brown before adding more broth. The cooking time for the rice, once the first ladle of broth is added, will be approximately 18 minutes.

7. Off the heat, stir in the black pepper, Parmigiano Reggiano cheese, and butter. If the risotto is dry, add more hot broth (or water if you've run out of broth). Risotto should be pourable but not watery. Taste and adjust the seasoning. Serve immediately.

BEYOND SATIETY

JANUARY 25

I haven't had the sensation of hunger in days. That doesn't mean I'm not eating everything that's being put in front of me. Everything must be tasted. Raw ingredients are tasted before being used. Food being prepared is tasted frequently during preparation. The final product must be tasted before being served. Food prepared by one of the chefs is always tasted (or sometimes actually eaten in larger quantities) because it's being prepared to demonstrate a particular dish or food product.

Weight gain is the side effect. If one is eating when one is not hungry, there is no alternative but to gain weight. It's that sacrifice I am making to achieve a goal. In this instance, the goal is to understand and be able to prepare traditional Italian regional cuisine and then to be able to riff on that same cuisine to create new dishes.

One really can't focus on the weight gain. It goes with the territory. Just like medical students, interns and residents can't focus on the excessive caffeine consumption needed to counteract the effects of not getting enough sleep. It goes with the territory, or at least it used to. (Don't get me started about the negative educational consequences of substantially reduced work hours for medical professionals in training! The change was meant to address a perceived problem and created unintended, but wholly predictable, consequences.)

SICILY SOJOURN

On January 22, we went to Sicily for the day. (As part of the school's itinerary, we travel to different parts of Italy to taste different food.) We left Baia dell'Est at 6 a.m. At 6:15, we were at Soverato Dolci for an Italian breakfast: coffee and pastry. Chef John recommended the cornetti (croissants) because they were made in-house, which, he said, was often not the case. He told me I should have "several." I heeded part of his advice but had just one. I chose a cornetto alle noci (croissant with walnuts). I thought it might have ground walnuts on the inside, but instead it had a luscious warm creamy walnut paste that started running down my chin. Someone

Arancini bigger than a fist on the ferry to Messina, Sicily. (See page 71 for a recipe.)

else had a pistachio cornetto and it had the same type of filling. An espresso doppio (double espresso) rounded out my breakfast.

We were on the bus at 6:45 a.m., bound for Reggio Calabria and the ferry to Sicily. After a short ride we pulled onto the beautiful ferry at 9:55. Once we were parked on board, we headed to the vessel's café (of course), and by 10:05 we were chowing down on arancini the size of my fist. One probably provided enough calories for an entire day.

We were back on the bus at 10:20 a.m., and at 10:30 we drove into Messina. We headed for Taormina, reaching there at 11:15 a.m. (There is also a train to Taormina. It travels from Calabria right onto a special ferry with train tracks and continues on after reaching Sicily! The passengers never get off the train.)

After a couple of group pictures in Taormina, we were on our own until 12:50 p.m., at which time we were to meet for lunch. Seven of us headed for the town's famous amphitheater built by the Greeks in the third century BCE and subsequently expanded by the Romans.

We headed back to our meeting place a little late, but before we got there we saw another part of our group sitting outside a bar with a round of Aperol spritzes at 1 p.m. Mariana, Chef Juan's wife, was with the group. Already late for lunch, Mariana managed to massage lunch plans and we all got a round of the spritzes before making it to the restaurant (some of us with Aperol spritzes in Styrofoam cups) at 1:30. Here we were in one of the most heavily touristed (and, therefore, expensive) towns in Italy, a town that has been a tourist destination since Roman times, and an Aperol spritz cost only €6.50! Bowls of nibbles came to the table free of charge.

The amphitheater in Taormina was built by the Greeks and expanded by the Romans.

Lunch started with individual antipasto plates of three cured meats, three cheeses, caponata, fried eggplant, and olives. The first course was pasta alla Norma. The second course consisted of veal rolls stuffed with prosciutto and cheese, rolled in breadcrumbs, and gently sautéed. These were served with mashed potatoes. Desert was tiramisù and gelato. An amaro and coffee followed.

We rolled out of the restaurant at 3:30 and had another hour to explore the town before boarding the bus for the return trip. Siesta, which typically lasts from 1 p.m. to 4 or 5 p.m. (hey, this is Southern Italy, after all!), wasn't quite over, so many of the shops were still closed.

Taormina is known for its ceramics, and I wanted to purchase something. The one shop that I was able to get into had many items that were unpriced, making it difficult to shop. As I was about to ask prices, I spied a platter that was priced at €1500. Based on this, I decided there was no need to ask for pricing of items that, at best, would have been totally unnecessary impulse purchases. Besides, I suspect I'll head back to Sicily in the near future at a time when I won't be bringing a steamer trunk full of kitchen equipment home with me!

Antipasto in Taormina.

We were back on the bus at 4:30 p.m., heading for the port in Messina. Before reaching the ferry dock, though, the bus made a stop. Chef Juan disappeared and then reappeared with bags full of cannoli! It was the first food I refused since the program began. Once on the ferry, nobody got off the bus except one smoker who needed his fix.

Back at the school, not one of us wanted dinner. We all headed to our rooms. Exams were scheduled to start the next day and one-third of the class had to take a practical exam, the contents of which were not divulged. I was scheduled in the second group, with my exam a day later.

As you may recall, in my previous post I promised to describe what we did in the pastry lab on January 21, the day before we went to Sicily. Here's the rundown of what Chef Juan demonstrated the preparation of:

- ★ Strawberry coulis
- ★ Pan di Spagna (subsequently cut into savoiardi)
- ★ Masa chablon (chocolate coating)
- ★ Mascarpone cream (for tiramisù) starting with the preparation of pâte à bombe

- ★ Salsa al caffè (coffee sauce)
- ★ Tempered chocolate
- ★ White chocolate lace
- ★ Tiramisù
- ★ Strawberry spumone

Chef Juan's modern interpretation of tiramisù. (See page 76 for a traditional tiramisù recipe.)

Chef John kept feeding us during the day we spent in the pastry lab with Chef Juan. At 10:30 a.m. small plates of bagna cauda and a bread roll flavored with cuttlefish ink appeared. At 11:50 he sent in seared swordfish with caponata, capers, and a roasted black olive crumble. At 1:30 p.m. we got bollito di maiale with polenta and little cubes of aspic made from a chicken demi. There was to be one more dish arriving that somehow didn't. There were no complaints when it didn't arrive.

We finished in the pastry lab at 4 p.m. I managed to get in a good walk before pizza making (and the next round of eating) started at 6.

Thursday was the first of two exam days. It was, mercifully, a free day until 4:30 p.m. for those of us who were not scheduled for exams. At that time, we had a lecture by Dr. Bill Schindler, an anthropologist and fascinating speaker. He spoke about human dietary history. He plans on being here for two more days. It will be very interesting to see what he presents us.

Chef John's bollito with polenta.

Spritz
Aperol Spritz

A spritz can be made with a number of lightly bitter spirits such as Aperol, Select, Campari, and Cynar. It has been a popular drink in Italy for over 100 years. Select is very similar to Aperol, whereas Campari and Cynar are slightly more bitter.

Metric Measure	Ingredient	American Measure
90 milliliters	Prosecco	3 ounces
60 milliliters	Aperol or Select	2 ounces
Splash	Soda water or seltzer	Splash
1 slice	Orange	1 slice

1. Put ice in a wine glass.
2. Add the prosecco, Aperol, and seltzer to the wine glass. Stir gently.
3. Garnish with an orange slice.

Arancini di Riso
Arancini

Arancini are typically the size of a small fist. They can be round or pointed, whichever you prefer. The usual filling is a meat ragù and peas. For the meat filling, I prefer to make a batch of Ragù Bolognese (page 260) and then strain out as much meat as I need for the Arancini. Yes, there will be slightly less meat in the ragù that is left, but it will still be a magnificent sauce for pasta and you've got a whole extra meal for the same amount of work as one! In Italy, saffron comes already powdered in little packets of approximately 0.1 to 0.125 grams. If using saffron threads, crush them thoroughly.

For the Rice

Metric Measure	Ingredient	American Measure
1.2 liters	Water	5 cups
2½ teaspoons	Salt, preferably fine sea salt	2½ teaspoons
500 grams	Arborio or carnaroli rice	1.1 pound (2½ cups)
0.1–0.125 grams	Saffron, powdered or crushed	1 large pinch
45 grams	Unsalted butter	3 tablespoons
75 grams	Freshly grated Parmigiano Reggiano cheese	2½ ounces

1. Bring the water and salt to a boil in a heavy-bottomed saucepan. Add the rice and saffron. Stir, cover tightly, and cook over very low heat without stirring until the liquid is absorbed, approximately 15 minutes.

2. Stir in the butter and Parmigiano Reggiano cheese. Spread the rice in a half-sheet pan and cover. Inverting another half-sheet pan on top works well. Allow to cool to room temperature.

FINAL ASSEMBLY

Italians sometimes use a flour and water paste instead of eggs when breading food for frying as is typical in this recipe.

Metric Measure	Ingredient	American Measure
240 grams	Italian 00 flour, W-180	1¾ cups
1 teaspoon	Salt, preferably fine sea salt	1 teaspoon
400 milliliters	Water	1¾ cups
120 grams	Meat from Ragù Bolognese (page 260), strained (see headnote)	¼ pound
80 grams	Thawed frozen baby peas	⅓ cup
25 grams	Freshly grated Pecorino Romano cheese	1 ounce
To taste	Freshly ground black pepper	To taste
As needed	Fine dry breadcrumbs	As needed
As needed	Neutral oil, such as corn or sunflower	As needed

1. Combine the flour and salt. Slowly add the water, mixing with a fork, to avoid lumps. After all the water is added, mix thoroughly. Cover and refrigerate 1 hour to allow the flour to fully hydrate.

2. Combine the meat, peas, and Pecorino Romano cheese. Season with salt and pepper, if needed.

3. Divide the cooled cooked rice into 10 portions. Holding one portion in your hand, flatten it and then cup your hand to create the beginning of a ball shape with a depression in the middle. Add approximately 1 tablespoon of the filling and then close the ball and smooth the rice. If desired, shape into a cone rather than a ball at this point. Repeat with the remaining cooked rice.

4. Remove the flour-and-water mixture from the refrigerator. Thin with water if necessary so that it just coats the back of a spoon. Roll each rice ball in the flour-and-water mixture then in the breadcrumbs.

5. Refrigerate 1 hour, uncovered, to allow the coating to adhere.

6. Bring 10 centimeters (4 inches) of oil to 170°C (340°F) in a heavy-bottomed saucepan or deep fryer.

7. Fry the arancini, a few at a time, until deep brown. Drain on paper towels. Serve immediately.

 Cannoli Siciliani
Cannoli

This recipe has been in my family for four generations. It has always been made with American all-purpose flour, so that is what I am recommending. The ingredients and quantities, however, are very similar to Maestro Paolo Caridi's recipe for cannoli.

Metric Measure	Ingredient	American Measure
330 grams	All-purpose flour	2½ cups
1 tablespoon	Granulated sugar	1 tablespoon
1 tablespoon	Cocoa powder	1 tablespoon
50 grams	Lard, melted and cooled slightly	3½ tablespoons
3	Large eggs	3
45 milliliters	Wine, white or red	3 tablespoons
As needed	Neutral oil, such as corn or sunflower	As needed

1. Combine the flour, sugar, and cocoa powder in the bowl of a stand mixer outfitted with a paddle. Mix on low to combine.

2. With the mixer running, pour in the melted lard.

3. Add the eggs one at a time. When combined, add the wine and mix until a smooth dough is formed. You may need to finish the dough by hand.

4. Form the dough into a compact shape and wrap tightly in plastic wrap. Allow the dough to rest at room temperature for 1 hour.

5. Form the dough into approximately walnut-sized balls. With a rolling pin, roll into an oval, the long dimension of which is slightly shorter than your cannoli form and the short dimension is large enough to wrap around the form with some overlap. (Note: The exact size of the balls depends on the size of your cannoli forms and how thin you roll the dough.) The ideal thickness is 2 millimeters or $1/12$ inch (which is less than $1/8$ inch and more than $1/16$ inch). You can also roll sheets of dough through a pasta machine and cut the sheets into squares instead of ovals. There should be approximately 3 dozen shells.

6. Heat 7 centimeters (3 inches) of oil to 175°C (350°F) in a heavy-bottomed saucepan or deep fryer.

7. While the oil heats, wrap each cannoli mold with a piece of dough, overlapping slightly to form a tube. The dough should stick to itself, but if it doesn't, use a dab of water.

8. Fry the shells in hot oil until brown. Remove them from the molds before they harden or they may break. Drain the shells on a rack to maintain crispness.

9. Continue frying until all the shells are made.

Filling and Assembly

It is best to fill the shells shortly before serving or they will become soft. The filling, however, can be made several hours in advance and refrigerated, tightly covered. Pour off any liquid that might collect around the filling.

Metric Measure	Ingredient	American Measure
1 kilogram	Ricotta	2¼ pounds
250 grams	Granulated sugar	1¼ cups
1 tablespoon	Vanilla extract	1 tablespoon
1 teaspoon	Powdered cinnamon	1 teaspoon
As needed	Chopped pistachios, for garnish	As needed
As needed	Chopped dark chocolate, for garnish	As needed

1. Line a sieve with cheesecloth. Put the ricotta in the cheesecloth-lined sieve. Place the sieve in a bowl and cover everything with plastic wrap. Refrigerate at least 24 (up to 48) hours to allow excess liquid to drain off.

2. Combine the drained ricotta, sugar, vanilla extract, and cinnamon in the bowl of a stand mixer outfitted with a whisk. Beat until slightly fluffy, about 2 to 3 minutes.

3. Fill a piping bag with the filling and pipe it into the cannoli shells, putting a bit in from each end, being sure to reach the center.

4. Garnish one end with chopped pistachios and the other with chopped chocolate.

Pasta alla Norma
Pasta alla Norma

The most traditional way to serve Pasta alla Norma is to deep fry slices of eggplant and put them on top of the pasta. I prefer this method as it is lighter but still very flavorful. If you choose to use the traditional method, don't dice and sauté the eggplant. Slice it approximately ½ centimeter (¼ inch) thick, salt it liberally, allow it to drain for 1 hour, rinse, and pat dry. Deep fry in neutral oil, such as corn or sunflower, until brown, approximately 2 minutes. Drain on paper and top each portion of pasta with some of the eggplant. Garnish as below.

Metric Measure	Ingredient	American Measure
2 tablespoons plus more to garnish	Extra-virgin olive oil	2 tablespoons plus more to garnish
300 grams	Eggplant, large dice	10 ounces
½ recipe	Basic Tomato Sauce (page 131)	½ recipe
500 grams	Dry short pasta, such as penne	~1 pound
To taste	Salt, preferably fine sea salt	To taste
To taste	Freshly ground black pepper	To taste
1 tablespoon	Basil chiffonade	1 tablespoon
50–60 grams	Ricotta salata, shredded	⅔ cup

1. Bring 3 liters (3 quarts) of water seasoned with 75 grams (¼ cup) of salt to a rolling boil.

2. Meanwhile, heat 2 tablespoons of olive oil in a large sauté pan. Sauté the eggplant on medium heat until beginning to soften. Add the tomato sauce and boil gently until reduced by approximately 20 percent.

3. Add the pasta to the boiling salted water and cook for approximately 2 minutes less than the minimum cooking time on the package for al dente pasta, stirring frequently to prevent sticking.

4. Drain the pasta, reserving the pasta-cooking liquid. Add the par-cooked pasta to the sauce in the sauté pan and finish cooking at a moderate boil, adding the reserved pasta-cooking water 1 ladle at a time, shaking the pan and stirring the pasta, until the pasta is al dente.

5. Adjust the salt and pepper.

6. Portion the pasta onto warm plates. Top each with a drizzle of extra-virgin olive oil, some basil chiffonade, and a generous sprinkle of ricotta salata.

OLIVE ARROSTITE
Roasted Olives

Roasted olives are good to nibble on their own or as part of an antipasto platter. Some recipes call for roasted olives as their flavor is more concentrated that regular cured olives. Be sure to use olives with pits. You can make these in any quantity desired; just be sure not to crowd them on the sheet pan. In Italy these would be made with fresh raw olives for cooking, not curing. Olives of this type are not readily available in the United States. Brine-cured olives work well.

Metric Measure	Ingredient	American Measure
200 grams	Brine cured black olives	7 ounces
1 tablespoon	Extra-virgin olive oil	1 tablespoon

1. Rinse and dry the olives. Toss with the olive oil.
2. Spread the olives on a parchment-lined half-sheet pan.
3. Roast at 200°C (400°F) until aromatic and slightly shriveled, approximately 20 minutes.

TIRAMISÙ
Tiramisù

While the original recipe for tiramisù may not have contained rum, many current versions do. If you don't want to use alcohol, just use more espresso, but you may need to adjust the amount of sugar. Italian savoiardi are not really ladyfingers as is sometimes thought. They are dry biscuits and not soft cakes. The dryness is important to allow the expresso to be absorbed.

Metric Measure	Ingredient	American Measure
1.1 liters	Espresso, cooled (see Tip)	37 fluid ounces
360 milliliters	Dark rum	1½ cups
200 grams	Sugar (divided)	1 cup
6	Eggs, separated	6
650 grams	Mascarpone	23 ounces
⅛ teaspoon	Cream of tartar	⅛ teaspoon
500 grams	Imported Italian savoiardi	17½ ounces
350–450 grams	Dark chocolate (60–70% cacao) grated, shaved or finely ground in food processor	12–16 ounces
As needed	Cocoa powder	As needed

1. Mix the espresso, rum, and 100 grams (½ cup) of the sugar until the sugar is dissolved. Set aside.

2. Using a stand mixer with a paddle attachment, beat the egg yolks and the remaining 100 grams (½ cup) sugar until the sugar is dissolved. Beat in the mascarpone until fluffy.

3. In a clean bowl and using the whisk attachment, beat the egg whites and cream of tartar until stiff. Fold a large spoonful of the stiff egg whites into the mascarpone mixture to lighten it. Gently fold in the remaining egg whites.

4. Put a thin layer of the mascarpone mixture in a flat, deep dish large enough to hold half the savoiardi in a single layer.

5. Dip the savoiardi in the espresso-rum mixture, being sure to hold them under the liquid for a few seconds and then allowing the excess liquid to drip out. Put half the savoiardi in a layer on top of the mascarpone mixture in the dish.

6. Spread half of the remaining mascarpone mixture on top of the savoiardi. Add a layer of thinly shaved chocolate and dust generously with the cocoa powder.

7. Repeat the layers one more time, using enough cocoa powder to completely cover the top of the tiramisù.

8. Cover tightly and refrigerate overnight.

Tip: You can make enough espresso shots to get the needed quantity or you can cheat by putting 100 grams (1½ cups less 3 tablespoons) of ground espresso in a drip coffee pot and brew it using 1.25 liters (42 fluid ounces) water.

Tip: Before assembling the tiramisù, plan how to place the savoiardi in a baking dish to achieve two layers. Each layer should use half the savoiardi.

Horses Galloping through Fields of Clover

JANUARY 27

The last few days have been pretty low-key. Well, except for the exam, that is!

Exam days were Wednesday and Thursday, January 23 and 24. We were randomly assigned to one of three groups and scheduled for our exam on either Wednesday afternoon, Thursday morning, or Thursday afternoon. Wednesday morning was free for all of us.

Exam Day

My exam was scheduled for Thursday morning, so I had Wednesday free until a lecture by Dr. Bill Schindler at four-thirty. "Dr. Bill" took the salumi (meat curing) course about three years ago and has since done some collaboration with Chef John. Dr. Bill,[1] an anthropologist, focuses on understanding human foodways from prehistory to modern times. He is an enthusiastic and engaging teacher. I hope to spend some time with him at the Eastern Shore Food Lab.[2]

With my exam scheduled for 8 a.m. on Thursday, I went to bed early on Wednesday. I woke up at 3 a.m. and could not get back to sleep. Other than not wanting to embarrass myself, I had nothing substantive riding on this exam. I guess not being embarrassed is motivation enough. I knew the exam would not really be about recipes. It would be about technique and process. That's not something that can be learned in ten days. So really, I'd

Dinner rolls, with beet powder, made by the students in my testing group. (See page XX for a recipe.)

---

[1] You can find out more about Dr. Bill at www.ancestralinsight.com; https://www.facebook.com/drbillschindler; and https://twitter.com/drbillschindler?lang=en.
[2] You can find out more about the Eastern Shore Food Lab at https://eatlikeahuman.com/eastern-shore-food-lab/.

been preparing for this exam since I started cooking at the age of seventeen. I either had it or I didn't. Nonetheless, I have to admit I had performance anxiety.

I had to make risotto alla Parmigiana (Parmesan cheese risotto), scaloppine di maiale con salsa di marsala (pork cutlets with marsala sauce), spaghetti aglio e olio (spaghetti with garlic and oil), and dinner rolls with beet powder (that turned them fuchsia). In general, it was designed to be a low-pressure exam (right!) though there were a few things done to trip us up. We all had to share pasta-cooking water, which was bubbling away on the stove when we got to the kitchen. The water, however, was not salted. (Lesson: Taste *everything!*)

I was the second one to start dinner rolls after finishing the other three dishes. When I got to the pastry lab, I was told: "The ingredients are all over there [pointing]." I started to weigh out flour, not noticing that another student had removed a second container of flour and put it on a different table (until that student brought it to my attention). The two flours had different "W" values (a measure of the strength of the flour). The recipe called for a particular W value, which could only be achieved by mixing the two flours in a precisely calculated ratio. Although we had learned that flours could be combined to achieve the desired W value, all breads that we made until exam time used one specific flour of the desired W value so I wasn't even thinking about the need to mix. (Lesson: Read *everything!*)

(**Note:** Flour sold in Italy is often labeled with a W value. This is not true in the United States. After getting home I will need to source flour with known W values. I'm not sure how that's going to go.[3])

Having successfully salted the pasta water and calculated the correct ratio of flours for the specialty rolls, I felt like I had done a pretty good job on my first exam. I had the afternoon off until the didactic session with Dr. Bill that evening.

Dr. Bill's second session involved knapping stone to make sharp stone knives then using them to butcher a rabbit. There were also lessons on starting fire using sticks and making rope from plant fiber. Making a stone tool was essential since we had to have at least one to butcher our rabbit. Starting a fire and making rope were not essential to the evening's activities. I briefly assisted one other student with the (failed) fire thing before doing the rabbit thing.

---

[3] Update: It has gone moderately well but not completely satisfactorily. Specification sheets for flours from Antimo Caputo, a well-respected flour mill in Naples, are online. The spec sheets contain W values, though the bags of flour themselves do not. That's manageable. The problem is that Caputo does not produce flours with low W values that I am able to find commercially available. My pasta flour, one that I have really come to like, is from Paolo Mariani. The only way I could find the W value was to write the company. I tried to inquire about the W values of other flours, but I have either not received responses or have received responses to a completely different question (one that I didn't ask).

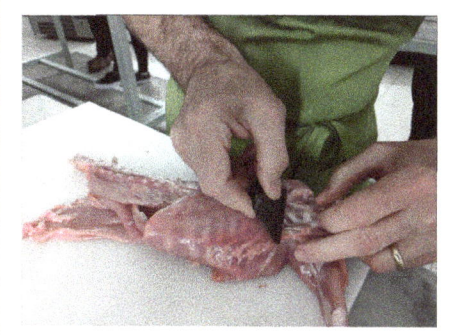
Butchering a rabbit with my stone knife.

Stone tools are incredibly sharp! Sharper than my expensive Japanese ceramic knives. They get dull quickly, though, and can only be sharpened by re-making the tool, which I see as distinct disadvantages. To be sure, if an incredibly sharp instrument is needed, a well-made stone tool will be sharper than any modern man-made knife. Rarely, however, is that degree of sharpness needed for a cook. In addition, stone tools often have several sharp sides, so it's quite easy to slice through fingers and hands while trying to cut something else.

Butchering the rabbit was a worthwhile experience and the knowledge gained is directly transferrable to doing so with a metal knife. It is also a good prelude to butchering a pig, which we will do in the coming days as part of our week of salumi, otherwise known as "Dead Animal Week" or more specifically, "Pig Week." Chef John turned the rabbits into a fabulous cacciatore for Saturday's lunch. The jus from the cacciatore was then used as the main component of a quick sauce for incredibly delicious house-made pappardelle (made with 30 percent whole wheat flour) served as the first course before the rabbit.

Friday was market day and we all went to the mercatino at 9 a.m. A side trip to the kitchen and restaurant supply store scored me two large sauté pans perfect for finishing pasta in sauce and several plastic grates for drying pasta, draining cheese, curing meats, and glazing pastry. I searched and searched Amazon and the Webstaurant store and could not find plastic grates (nor could I find the specific type of sauté pans I bought, which are made in Italy).

I have now officially started my hoard of items to be brought back to the States.

A quick trip to the liquor store after the mercatino was unsuccessful in securing a bottle of bourbon. They only had one, Rebel Yell, and it was €50! I'll stick with my Jim Beam at €13 until I find something better. After the liquor store, and a quick side trip for Dr. Bill to buy a present for his wife, we went to a wine tasting.

An array of olives at the weekly market in Soverato.

The Joy of Calabrian Vino

Fabio, one of the owners of the Panino Lab (which I wrote about in the first dispatch), is also a sommelier. He has a room in the back of the Panino Lab set up for wine tasting. We tasted four different—and excellent—Calabrian wines. Fabio walked us through the tasting process and criteria with the first wine. We then each had to evaluate the remaining three wines and discuss our thoughts. (This exercise rekindled my longstanding desire to take the one-month sommelier training course at the Culinary Institute of America in California. For now, I'll settle for the wine tasting and pairing lessons that are part of this course.)

The first course of Saturday's lunch was pappardelle made with 30 percent whole wheat flour with a simple sauce of rabbit jus and topped with shaved truffles. (See page 86 for a recipe, truffles are optional.)

Occasionally I can identify some of the different flavors in wine, things like ripe berries, leather, grapefruit, and vanilla, for example. Whenever I do this, which isn't often and is always when I am with a sommelier or wine aficionado who is doing the same thing, Frank (my husband…I can't forget my husband) gets a very serious look on his face, tastes and swishes the wine, and then says something like "horses galloping through fields of clover" or "ducks waddling down the hill in a rainstorm." So far he hasn't quite hit the flavor profile of any wine, but sooner or later…who knows?

After the wine tasting we reconvened in the kitchen with our chef togs for a lacto-fermentation lesson. Dr. Bill decided to demonstrate rather than make it a hands-on session as planned. He put up four different kinds of vegetables to ferment, including sauerkraut.

In the short break before dinner, I was finally able to put my feet up and enjoy a glass of bourbon. The next day, Saturday, was our first completely free day since starting the course thirteen days earlier!

Brodo Concentrato di Pollo
Concentrated Chicken Stock

In general, traditional Italian cuisine does not make use of super-concentrated stock. There are some traditional dishes, however, that benefit from the extra punch of flavor that can be delivered by a concentrated stock. The Rabbit Ragù (page 86), which can also be made with chicken, is one such recipe. Chicken thigh bones and wing tips work well for this recipe. Just as the Rabbit Ragù can be made with chicken, this chicken stock can be made with rabbit.

Metric Measure	Ingredient	American Measure
950 grams	Chicken bones with some meat	2 pounds
To taste	Salt, preferably fine sea salt	To taste
To taste	Freshly ground black pepper	To taste
As needed	All-purpose flour	As needed
80 milliliters	Extra-virgin olive oil	⅓ cup
30 grams	Tomato paste, double concentrate	2 tablespoons
700 milliliters	Dry red wine	3 cups
150 grams	Finely diced carrot	5 ounces
150 grams	Finely diced onion	5 ounces
50 grams	Finely diced celery	1¾ ounces
3 liters	Water	3 quarts plus ⅔ cup

1. Generously salt and pepper the chicken. Toss the chicken in flour and shake off the excess.

2. Put the olive oil in a heavy-bottomed Dutch oven. Add the chicken to the cold oil. Put the pot on medium-high heat and cook, stirring frequently, to create lots of brown bits. Be vigilant not to burn the flour.

3. Add the tomato paste and cook, stirring constantly, until slightly darker, about 30 to 60 seconds, being careful not to burn the tomato paste.

4. Add the wine and boil until the liquid is almost completely evaporated. Because of the flour, it will not be possible to cook off all the liquid, which will become quite thick.

5. Add the diced carrot, onion, and celery along with the water.

6. Boil gently, uncovered, until the liquid is reduced to approximately 750 milliliters (25 ounces or just over 3 cups), stirring occasionally at the beginning

but increasingly frequently as the broth reduces. Plan on about 3 hours to cook the stock.

7. Cool slightly then strain the stock. Refrigerate until cold and then portion and freeze, if desired.

PANINETTI

Little Bread Rolls

Pane is the Italian word for bread. *Pani* is plural. *Paninetti* is a diminutive form that can mean small bread rolls or sandwiches depending on the context. Paninetti are a great accompaniment to antipasto. They freeze exceptionally well and can go directly from the freezer to a 180°C (350°F) oven to heat up. If thawed, they take less than 90 seconds. Frozen paninetti will take a bit longer.

BIGA

Metric Measure	Ingredient	American Measure
240 grams	Italian 00 flour W-300 to W-320	1¾ cups
0.72 grams	Active dry yeast	¼ teaspoon
120 grams	Ice water	½ cup

1. Twenty to 24 hours in advance of making the dough, use the ingredients listed to make the biga following the instructions on page 213.

ROLLS

Paninetti can be made with extra-virgin olive oil, butter, lard, and even cocoa butter. Feel free to experiment with these and other fats based on the final flavor profile desired. Olive oil makes more tender rolls compared to solid fats. The fact that each roll is only two or three bites accommodates flavors that might not be appropriate for more sustained eating. Some possible variations are provided.

Metric Measure	Ingredient	American Measure
500 grams	Italian 00 flour W-220	3¾ cups
4 grams	Active dry yeast	1⅛ teaspoons
300 grams	Water	1¼ cups
10 grams	Sugar	¾ tablespoon
1 recipe	Biga (immediately preceding)	1 recipe
10 grams	Salt	1¾ teaspoons
100 grams	Oil or fat (see headnote)	7 tablespoons
As desired	Flavorings and/or inclusions	As desired

1. Combine the flour and yeast in the bowl of a stand mixer fitted with a dough hook. Begin to mix on low. Stream in the water and then add the sugar. After a basic dough forms, add the biga, cutting it into four pieces and adding them one at a time.
2. After the mixture is well combined, sprinkle in the salt and mix on medium-low until a strong gluten network forms.
3. Slowly add the oil or fat, reducing the speed of the mixer if necessary. After all the oil is incorporated, increase the speed and mix until the dough is smooth and elastic.
4. Shape the dough into a taut ball (see directions for shaping pizza dough on page 62). Put the dough in a bowl rubbed with olive oil. Rub the top of the dough with olive oil and cover the bowl tightly with plastic.
5. Allow the dough to rest for 30 minutes.
6. Divide the dough into portions of 15 grams (½ ounce) for use on an antipasto plate or 20 grams (⅔ ounce) for dinner rolls. Form taut balls.
7. Arrange the dough balls on half-sheet pans lined with silicone mats or parchment. Allow the dough to rise in a 37°C (99°F) oven until it does not spring back when pressed lightly with a finger, approximately 1 to 2 hours. (Note: Add humidity to the oven by placing a container of just-boiled water in the bottom of the oven along with the dough balls.)
8. Bake the rolls at 180°C (350°F) for 12 to 15 minutes, until just light golden brown on the bottom.
9. Cool the rolls on the sheet pans, covered with a cloth to retain moisture.

VARIATIONS

Squid Ink: Combine 8 grams of squid ink with enough water to make 300 grams (1¼ cups) and make the rolls as described. (Squid ink from Italy comes in 4-gram packets.)

Walnut Raisin: Use butter for the fat. Add 62 grams (2¼ ounces) of chopped walnuts and 62 grams (2¼ ounces) of raisins to the dough just before step 3.

Rosemary-Garlic: Use 50 grams (3¾ tablespoons) of extra-virgin olive oil, 40 grams (3 tablespoons) of Rosemary Oil (page 262), and 10 grams (¾ tablespoon) of Garlic Oil (page 57).

Oregano: Add 1.2 grams (1¼ teaspoons) of crushed dried oregano. Use olive oil for the fat.

Pasta Integrale con Ragù di Coniglio
Whole Wheat Pasta with Rabbit Ragù

If you don't want to use rabbit, you can substitute bone-in skinless chicken thighs. After braising the rabbit, it is shredded and combined with the sauce ingredients. One batch of ragù is sufficient for two batches of homemade whole wheat pasta. Extra rabbit can be frozen.

Braised Rabbit

Metric Measure	Ingredient	American Measure
60 milliliters	Extra-virgin olive oil	¼ cup
4 cloves	Garlic, bruised with the side of a chef's knife	4 cloves
1.1 kilograms	Rabbit, dressed	2½ pounds
To taste	Salt, preferably fine sea salt	To taste
1 medium	Carrot, chopped	1 medium
1	Celery stick, chopped	1
1 small	Onion, chopped	1 small
250 milliliters	Dry white wine	1 cup
2	Bay leaves, preferably fresh	2
5	Fresh sage leaves	5
1 sprig	Fresh rosemary	1 sprig
4	Whole juniper berries	4
12	Whole black peppercorns	12

1. In a heavy-bottomed shallow pot, sauté the garlic in olive oil until fragrant.

2. Add the rabbit, meaty side down. Season the rabbit well with salt, and sear on one side only. If the garlic starts to brown too much, put it on top of the rabbit.

3. Without moving the rabbit, add the carrot, celery, and onion. Add the wine and then the bay leaves, sage leaves, rosemary, juniper berries, and black peppercorns.

4. After the wine has boiled for a brief period, loosen the rabbit pieces. Cover the pot and simmer until the rabbit shreds easily, approximately 2 hours, adding a bit of water if needed.

5. Allow the rabbit to cool in the braising liquid and then bone the rabbit and shred it, being sure to eliminate any gristle or chewy bits of meat. There should be about 340 grams (11 ounces) of shredded meat.

6. Strain the braising liquid. Discard the solids and reserve the liquid. There should be about 200 milliliters (¾ cup) of cooking liquid.

7. Divide the rabbit into two equal portions. Add half the cooking liquid to each portion. Freeze if not using immediately.

PASTA AND ASSEMBLY

If you don't want to use homemade pasta, you can substitute 400 grams (14 ounces) of dry whole wheat pasta.

Metric Measure	Ingredient	American Measure
1 recipe	Whole Wheat Pasta (page 90)	1 recipe
275–300 milliliters	Concentrated Chicken Stock (page 83)	1 cup plus 3 tablespoons
½ recipe	Braised Rabbit, shredded (page 86)	½ recipe
To taste	Rosemary Oil (page 262)	To taste
45 grams	Freshly grated Parmigiano Reggiano cheese	1⅓ ounces
To taste	Salt, preferably fine sea salt	To taste
To taste	Freshly ground black pepper	To taste

1. Roll out the pasta to approximately #6 on the pasta machine. Cut into tagliatelle or pappardelle. Toss with a bit of semolina, form into loose mounds, and allow to dry a few hours before using, tossing occasionally to keep it from sticking together.

2. Bring 3 liters (3 quarts) of water seasoned with 75 grams (¼ cup) of salt to a rolling boil.

3. Gently warm the concentrated chicken stock in a large sauté pan.

4. When the chicken stock is bubbling, add ½ recipe of shredded, braised rabbit with ½ of the braising liquid. Season with salt and pepper.

5. Add the pasta to the boiling salted water and cook at a rapid boil until almost cooked, stirring frequently to prevent sticking. If using dry pasta, boil for approximately 2 minutes less than the minimum cooking time on the package for al dente pasta.

6. Drain the pasta, reserving the pasta-cooking water.

7. Add the par-cooked pasta to the rabbit in the sauté pan and finish cooking at a moderate boil, adding the reserved pasta-cooking water 1 ladle at a

time, shaking the pan and stirring the pasta, until the pasta is al dente, leaving the sauce liquid enough to just coat the pasta. Adjust the salt and pepper while finishing the pasta.

8. Mix in a few squirts of rosemary oil.

9. Off the heat, add the cheese and then flip and stir the pasta to emulsify the cheese and sauce. Add a bit more cooking water if the sauce is too thick.

Scaloppine di Maiale al Marsala
Pork Cutlets with Marsala

This dish cooks in just a few minutes, and it is best to serve it as soon as it is ready or the sauce will separate. You can break it into three steps, however. Flour and refrigerate the pork in advance. Do the initial sauté of the pork and spread it out on a half-sheet pan to cool quickly. Make the pan sauce and rewarm the pork at the last minute. You may need more butter than is called for; however, do not use an excessive amount or it will not fully emulsify and will float to the top of the sauce.

Metric Measure	Ingredient	American Measure
500 grams	Lean, boneless pork loin	~1 pound
As needed	All-purpose flour	As needed
90 grams	Unsalted butter	6 tablespoons
100 milliliters	Dry Marsala wine	6½ tablespoons
1½ tablespoons	Sweet Marsala wine	1½ tablespoons
To taste	Salt, preferably fine sea salt	To taste
To taste	Freshly ground black pepper	To taste

1. Cut the pork into scaloppine approximately 6 millimeters (¼ inch) thick. (*Note:* This will be much easier if you use a very sharp knife and put the pork in the freezer until it firms up but does not freeze solid, approximately 30 to 45 minutes, depending on the diameter of the loin.)

2. Thoroughly dust the scaloppine with flour, shaking off any excess. If you have time, put the pork on a rack and refrigerate for 30 to 60 minutes to allow the flour to adhere better.

3. In a large sauté pan, melt 60 grams (4 tablespoons) of butter over medium heat. When the foam subsides, add as many pieces of pork as will fit comfortably. Sauté, turning once until each side is just golden. Cool on a half-sheet pan, seasoning the pieces with salt and pepper.

4. Cook the rest of the pork, using more butter if necessary. Do not clean the pan.

5. To finish the dish, add the remaining 30 grams (2 tablespoons) of butter to the pan used to sauté the pork. Once it melts, add the dry and sweet Marsala wine. Bring to a gentle boil, swirling the pan to emulsify the butter and wine. There will be some bits of flour left from cooking the pork that will aid in emulsifying the sauce.

6. Add the pork and simmer briefly just to heat through. Season the sauce with salt and pepper and serve immediately.

Spaghetti Aglio e Olio
Spaghetti with Garlic and Oil

For such a simple dish, there is a dizzying array of variations. Should the garlic be minced, sliced, or bruised? Should it be cooked until soft, golden, or brown? There was even a time when I sautéed the garlic in three batches to different degrees of "doneness" to get (in theory) a greater depth of flavor. In the end, I think this classic recipe is best. What is key to all the variations, though, is cooking the garlic enough to tame its bite, creating a mellow garlicy sweetness. The addition of peperoncino (chile), fresh or ground, is optional.

Metric Measure	Ingredient	American Measure
140 milliliters	Extra-virgin olive oil	9½ tablespoons
6–8 cloves	Garlic, thinly sliced	6–8 cloves
1–2 teaspoons	Cayenne pepper or 2 to 4 fresh hot red peppers, sliced, optional	1–2 teaspoons
500 grams	Dry spaghetti	~1 pound
55 grams	Freshly grated Parmigiano Reggiano cheese	2 ounces
To taste	Salt, preferably fine sea salt	To taste
To taste	Freshly ground black pepper	To taste

1. Bring 3 liters (3 quarts) of water seasoned with 75 grams (¼ cup) of salt to a rolling boil.

2. Meanwhile, in a large sauté pan, gently sauté the garlic in the olive oil until lightly golden. If using fresh hot peppers, add them with the garlic. If using ground red pepper, add it just a few seconds before adding the pasta so that it does not burn. If the garlic is ready before the pasta, remove it from the heat and add a bit of the pasta-cooking water to stop the cooking process.

3. Add the pasta to the boiling salted water and cook at a rapid boil for approximately 2 minutes less than the minimum cooking time on the package for al dente pasta, stirring frequently to prevent sticking.

4. Drain the pasta, reserving the pasta-cooking water.

5. Add the par-cooked pasta to the liquid in the sauté pan and finish cooking at a moderate boil, adding the reserved pasta-cooking water 1 ladle at a time, shaking the pan and stirring the pasta, until the pasta is al dente, leaving the sauce liquid enough to just coat the pasta. Adjust the salt and pepper while finishing the pasta.

6. Off the heat, add the cheese and then flip and stir the pasta to emulsify the cheese and sauce. Add a bit more cooking water if the sauce is too thick.

Pasta Integrale
Whole Wheat Pasta

When testing this recipe in the United States, I used Bob's Red Mill stone-ground whole wheat flour and Paolo Mariani 00 flour for pasta fresca. In Italy I typically use Divella flour. Atmospheric conditions can influence the flour-egg ratio. You may need to add a sprinkling more flour in a humid environment or a few grams more egg in a dry environment.

Metric Measure	Ingredient	American Measure
100 grams	Stone-ground whole wheat flour	3½ ounces
200 grams	Italian 00 flour for fresh pasta	7 ounces
3 grams	Salt	½ teaspoon
160 grams	Lightly beaten whole egg	5⅓ ounces

1. Combine the flours and salt. Mix well with a fork.

2. Mound the flour on a work surface (such as a kitchen counter or pasta board). Spread the flour out, making a large well in the center with high flour "walls" around the well.

3. Pour the egg into the well, being careful not to allow it to run over. If this is a concern, add the egg in two or three additions.

4. Using the fork, work in a circular motion around the egg, bringing in a bit of flour at a time and mixing it with the egg.

5. Once enough flour has been added that the egg is no longer runny, change the fork for a bench scraper and your hand. Slide the scraper part way under the flour-egg mixture and then flip it over bringing the flour that was on the bottom to the top. Use your hand and the bench scraper to press the mixture together to fully combine the flour and egg.

6. Ultimately, when the mixture becomes firm enough, you can stop using the bench scraper and use your hands to press and turn the dough until it is homogeneous. Use a pressing motion, not a kneading motion the way you would for bread. That is, press down on the mixture, not out and away from you.

7. Once the dough is homogeneous, form it into a brick shape and wrap very tightly in plastic wrap. The pressure will further help the dough to hydrate.

8. Allow the dough to rest at room temperature for 1 hour. Portion, roll, and cut as required for the recipe.

Pig Week

FEBRUARY 3

The pig (well, actually it was a pig and a half) arrived, unceremoniously, in the back of a van on Sunday, January 27.

The pigs were raised by a local family that also has a restaurant. They (the pigs, not the family) were fed restaurant scraps (really good food) and finished with hazelnuts and chestnuts for the last three weeks or so. Hazelnuts and chestnuts are plentiful here.

Each half-pig weighed about 165 pounds. Getting to the school from the nearest access point for a vehicle involves at least one staircase. Getting a 165-pound side of pig down a staircase is a group effort requiring strength and coordination.

The pigs went into our walk-in cooler to await class on Monday.

In addition to the thirteen of us who are on this three-month odyssey of Italian regional cuisine, we were joined by five additional students for Pig Week. We refer to them as the Pig People. Apparently, we will also be joined by Gelato People, Conserve People, Pastry People, and Cheese People for a week each during the remaining ten weeks. That leaves about six weeks where it'll just be the thirteen of us. I don't think we'll be joined by any Alcohol People for our week of mixology and distilling.

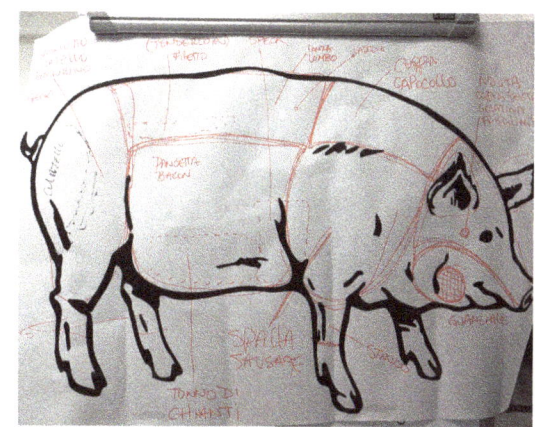

A sketch of the basic butchering cuts of the pig.

On Monday, January 28, Chef John demonstrated how to butcher a pig into the primal cuts for processing into traditional Italian salumi (and discussed a few variations on the cuts based on the objectives of the person doing the butchering). Afterward, the other two half-pigs were brought into the kitchen for us to butcher. I have three pages of (sometimes cryptic) notes on how Chef John butchered the pig.

A guilty pleasure: poaching eggs in frischilimiti (little bits of porky goodness)

But first, of course, we had to taste. We tasted at least seven different cured meats, all but one of them made at the school.

After the pig was butchered into primal cuts, several large cuts were salted as part of the initial cure. These included:

- Pancetta rotolo (rolled pancetta)
- Pancetta tesa (flat pancetta)
- (American) bacon
- Capocollo

After the butchering, Chef John wanted to completely disinfect the kitchen, so we didn't prepare dinner in the kitchen that evening. Instead we went to La Tavernetta, the restaurant in the hotel on the same property as the school. It was a special event, with one table full of local chefs and us at another table. The meal was intended to highlight three versions of a local stewed tripe dish, morzello di Catanzaro, each flavored with a different hot pepper. The first course was an 'nduja-stuffed potato puree on top of caciocavallo fonduta. Then came three courses of stewed tripe served inside of bread. After the second, Mariana asked that we just get the stew, minus the bread, for the third round as the bread was not getting eaten (much of the tripe was not getting eaten either, but that's a different matter). The meal finished with pistachio gelato on crème anglaise topped with melted chocolate.

On Tuesday, we continued with making:

- "Franken-fileto" (see below)
- Guanciale (cured pork jowl)
- Porchetta (see below)
- Pickled pork (like corned beef but made with pork)
- Lardo (a yummy slab of cured pork fat—similar to salt pork but better—not to be confused with rendered "lard," which is called strutto in Italian)
- Prosciuttino (similar to prosciutto but smaller as the weather in Calabria is not conducive to curing an entire ham)
- Speck
- Tonno del Chianti

Butchering a pig for Italian artisan salumi (*salumi* is the Italian word that is equivalent to the French word *charcuterie*) creates a whole new perspective. In the

States, cuts like the loin and tenderloin are among the most expensive. When purchasing a whole pig, every part of the animal costs as much as every other. The most valuable cuts for curing are not the loin and tenderloin because they are too lean. Much of those cuts ended up being made into sausage!

One of the tenderloins was turned into a Frankenstein version of a cured meat ("franken-fileto"). The loin was carefully butterflied and topped with a layer of fatback that was pounded thin. The combination, about 80 percent tenderloin and 20 percent fat, was salted for curing, tightly rolled in plastic wrap for shape, and hung in the refrigerator for 48 hours before being unwrapped, tied, and hung in the hanging room.

A mid-morning snack of frischilimiti and eggs with cotechino and a little bread roll. (See page 16 for a recipe for cotechino with lentils and page 84 for a recipe for little bread rolls.)

'Chetta Extravaganza

Traditional porchetta is made from a whole suckling pig with the bones removed. Porchetta-style roasts abound in Italy. The one we made consisted of a slab of pork belly (the cut from which bacon and pancetta are made) rolled around the loin, tied, and roasted for hours. Traditional seasonings include garlic, rosemary, and fennel. Before rolling it, Chef John opted to slather the meat with a massive quantity of pureed truffles. (We have consumed an obscene quantity of fresh truffles since starting this course.) The porchetta then went into the fridge to be pulled out for dinner on Wednesday.

Chef John got creative and demonstrated the production of rabbit porchetta using twenty rabbit bellies and rabbit fat. (Remember the rabbits we butchered with stone knives?) The "rabbitchetta" was cooked sous vide and then chilled, smoked, and brushed with maple syrup. (Okay, so not really Italian, but it was good!) He also made a "lambchetta" from four lamb bellies that ended up being served as a snack of lamb and eggs a few days later.

Dinner was at a local pizzeria as the kitchen, once again, needed to be sanitized.

Wednesday, January 30, started with a lecture on the science of meat curing by Chef Juan. Other than herbs and spices for flavoring, the only product used at the school to cure meat is salt. Absolutely no nitrates or nitrites are added.[1]

---

[1] Update, since my original stint at ICI, I have been back many times. Chef Juan has taken a deep dive into Italian salumi. He is now convinced that using nitrate and/or nitrite salts is an essential practice from a food safety perspective.

A few days prior when we were butchering the pigs, anything not destined for a specific purpose was put into one of two piles labelled "Bollito #1" and "Bollito #2." *Bollito* simply means boiled. Bollito #1 contained bones (like ribs) with some meat attached. Bollito #2 contained all the other bits and pieces (specks of meat, gristle, silver skin, fat that wasn't good for sausage making, or other products). These were all soaked for a day in cold water in the fridge and then boiled…and boiled…and boiled. The head and ears were also boiled.

Bones with meat attached (like ribs) from Bollito #1 were served with some broth, salsa verde, and bread as a snack! The fat skimmed off the top of all the bollito pots was turned into strutto (lard). Bits of meat from the head were turned into 'nduja or coppa di testa (head cheese). Any remaining bits became friscilimiti, a Southern Italian specialty with cracklings (pork fat with layers of meat and skin still attached) and eggs. The broth was concentrated to make gelatin.

The friscilimiti (all those tiny bits of cooked pork) were crisped in a sauté pan with lard (of course, being Pig Week), eggs were nestled on top, and when the eggs were appropriately cooked, they were served as a morning snack with cotechino and bread.

The rest of Wednesday was devoted to seasoning batches of meat for our cured salami and fresh sausage. The cured salami included:

- Salsiccia (sausage in much of Italy is partially cured and not used fresh as in the United States)
- Soppressata
- Salame Napoli
- Salame Brianza
- Salame gentile
- Ciauscolo
- Salame Milano
- Salame di Fabriano
- Salame felino
- Strolghino
- Lucanica
- Salame di Mugnano
- Tartufo
- Cotechino

After those were made, the eighteen of us were set free to each make a fresh sausage of our choosing. I made mine with 75 percent lean pork and 25 percent fat, and seasoned it with hot red Calabrian pepper, sweet red Calabrian pepper, coarsely ground black pepper, fennel seed, garlic, and red wine.

Making salami is serious business. There is no approximating the proportion of fat and lean. When butchering we separated completely the meat and fat. These were then recombined in specific proportions based on the requirements of each recipe.

Amaretto Bacon and Other Delights

Thursday started off with Chef John continuing the bacon that had been salted three days earlier. The salt and sweet mixture (different for each) was washed off with some sort of alcohol. The one cured with salt and brown sugar was washed in Jack Daniel's, smoked over chestnut wood, then glazed with maple syrup. The salt and white sugar one was rinsed with Amaretto, smoked over pistachio shells, and glazed with a concentrated coffee syrup. The salt-and-honey–cured one was rinsed in brandy, smoked over chestnut wood, and glazed with honey. Each was put in the fridge where they would stay, uncovered, for about a week to allow the glaze to crystallize. At that point they could be used or vacuum-packed and kept in the fridge for up to six months.

The speck was rinsed in grappa, coated with finely ground black pepper, smoked, and then put in netting to be hung and aged before use.

On the spur of the moment midmorning, Chef John took some of the concentrated liquid from Bollito #2 and mixed it with orange-zest-infused 97.5 percent alcohol and some sugar to make "jello" shots. These went in the fridge and appeared at dinner on Saturday.

Chef John then made tonno del Chianti (tuna from Chianti). It is a well-known and beloved pork product that resembles oil-packed tuna. When butchering the pigs, we carefully removed the flap meat. This meat was boiled in a mixture of half vinegar, half water that was abundantly flavored with onions and bay leaves until fork-tender and then cooled in the cooking liquid. It was packed into jars with seasonings and covered with either extra-virgin olive oil or

Ciauscolo tied and ready to age: my first attempt at basket-tying.

the cooking liquid and processed in a boiling water bath. We tasted some tonno del Chianti from the previous production. I am most definitely making this stuff![2]

The rest of the day was spent stuffing all the salami and our personal sausages. The ground pork that was left after each of us took our portion for sausage the previous day had been seasoned for soppressata—nearly twenty pounds of it! A few of us assisted Maria, one of the dishwashers, stuff it into large intestine, as is traditional. (*Note:* "Dishwasher" is a completely inadequate term for all the things that Maria does at the school.)

Although Maria's job is to wash everything and keep the kitchen tidy, she is an expert at curing meat. A warm, caring, and wonderful person, she feels like a grandmother though she's a decade younger than I am. Apparently, she and her sister kill, butcher, and cure four pigs every year—all within about a week! I cannot imagine how they do this. It took four days for eighteen of us, not counting staff, to do a pig and a half.

Tonno del Chianti, boiled pork packed in olive oil with aromatics. (See page 106 for a recipe.)

We went to the hanging room to hang the meats that were ready. Some need to be kept under refrigeration or cured at a warmer temperature before hanging. Cured meats are given a light smoking two or three times a day for the first four days or so after hanging. They do not taste smoky; the smoke acts as another preservative.

Friday morning we went to the mercatino. Friday afternoon saw the production of coppa di testa (head cheese) and 'nduja. We tasted several different versions of head cheese made a few weeks earlier. All were very good and quite different from anything I've had in the States. The best thing made with all the "bits" was 'nduja. 'Nduja is a spicy, spreadable salame. Chef John's version is approximately one third cooked meat (mostly from the head), one third raw fatback, and one-third Calabrian red chile (both as a "paste" that resembles tomato paste in consistency and color as well as dried in powdered form). Everything is stuffed into a casing and hung to age.

Chef Juan made blood sausage and bratwurst. Neither is particularly Italian, though Italians do make blood sausages. Both were great. The blood sausage was revelatory! With the main part of class over for the day, several of us stuck

---

[2] Tonno del Chianti was among the first foods I prepared after returning from Italy. It was part of Easter dinner for twenty people that happened six days after I got home.

around to complete the "maintenance" of the salumi that had been started earlier in the week.

That evening's dinner consisted of all the fresh sausages we had made expertly grilled by Chef Juan and an array of accompaniments.

With Pig Week over, menu planning and execution, our next adventure, was scheduled to start the next day, Saturday, February 2, at 11 a.m.

PANCETTA TESA
Flat Pancetta

I find pancetta tesa one of the easiest cured meats to make. Pork belly is rubbed with a seasoning mix, allowed to cure in the fridge for a short time, rinsed with water and vinegar, and put back in the fridge until it loses about 20 percent of its weight. There's no rolling, no tying, no chopping, no grinding. In the end, you'll have an amazing cured-pork product to add to many recipes. Pieces of pancetta make great gifts, too! Feel free to experiment with herbs and spices, but do not modify the salt or Prague powder as these are essential for safe curing. Prague powder #2 can be purchased online. Do not use Prague powder #1. All ingredients are calculated as a proportion of the weight of the pork belly. You'll have a little bit of arithmetic to do, but it is not complicated. Feel free to use metric or American measures. Weighing the pork belly in grams or ounces will result in answers that are easier to understand than using kilograms or pounds.

Ingredient	Proportion
Pork belly without skin	
Juniper berries	0.00160
Whole black peppercorns	0.00450
Nutmeg, grated fresh	0.00320
Allspice, whole	0.00320
Cinnamon stick, preferably Ceylon or Saigon	0.00320
Cloves, whole	0.00064
Garlic, minced	0.01340
Salt, preferably fine sea salt or canning and pickling salt	0.03000
Prague powder #2	0.00220
Dry white wine or apple cider vinegar, for rinsing	As needed
Crushed black peppercorns, for coating	As needed

1. Select a pork belly of uniform thickness for even curing. I usually get one around 4.5 kilograms (10 pounds). It's really no more work to cure a big one than a small one, and it keeps well in the freezer cut into portions and vacuum-sealed.

2. Calculate the quantity of each ingredient.
   a. Weigh the pork belly. Using grams or ounces will be easier than using kilograms or pounds.
   b. Multiply the weight of the pork belly by the proportion of each ingredient listed to get the amount of the ingredient needed in either grams or ounces. For example:
      i. If the pork belly weighs 4500 grams, the amount of black peppercorns to use is: 4500 grams x 0.00450 = 20.25 grams.
      ii. If the pork belly weighs 160 ounces (10 pounds), the amount of salt to use is: 160 ounces x 0.03000 = 4.8 ounces.

3. Put the juniper berries, black peppercorns, nutmeg, allspice, cinnamon stick, and cloves in a very small blender jar or a blade-type coffee grinder. Grind to a powder.

4. Mix the spices with the minced garlic, salt, and Prague powder.

5. Put the pork belly in a large, rectangular, nonreactive, food-safe tub. I use a plastic or acrylic dough box. Even though stainless steel is theoretically nonreactive, I don't recommend leaving it in contact with the salt mixture for the length of time needed to cure the pork.

6. Rub the pork belly all over with the curing mixture, making sure to cover all surfaces, including the sides. Use all of the curing mixture.

7. Put the tub with the pork belly in the refrigerator. Turn the pork every 2 to 3 days for 7 to 10 days until it is uniformly firm. I suggest pressing the pork belly with your index finger before putting it in the refrigerator to get a feeling for how soft it is. Test it every 3 days to keep track of how the texture changes. When in doubt, cure it for the full 10 days (1 or 2 days longer won't hurt, either).

8. Remove the pork belly from the refrigerator and rinse it with cool water to remove the salt and spices.

9. After the water rinse, douse it with a generous amount of vinegar and then wipe it dry.

10. Rub the pork belly with coarsely ground black peppercorns. Weigh the pork and note the weight.

11. Place the pork belly, fat side up, on a nonreactive, preferably plastic, ventilated rack inside a nonreactive tub. Refrigerate the pork, uncovered, until it has lost 20 to 25 percent of its weight, roughly 6 weeks, plus or minus.

12. Wrap the pork tightly in plastic wrap and refrigerate for 3 to 4 days to allow some of the dryer edges to rehydrate.

13. Portion and freeze what you will not use within about 2 weeks. It will keep in the freezer for a year or more, if it is vacuum-sealed.

Tip: White wine vinegar is traditionally used in Italy to cleanse meats while curing. Wine vinegar is inexpensive in Italy; not so in the United States. Feel free to substitute apple cider vinegar. You will never notice the difference.

Porchetta
Slow-Roasted Pork

Traditionally, Porchetta is made from a whole pig, but similarly spiced home versions exist throughout Italy. Growing up, my mother made a version of this roast without the fennel seeds. The roast was much smaller as it was intended to serve a family of four. When cooking for a crowd, I reach for this recipe. Italians are masters of low-and-slow cooking. You could shorten the cooking time by a couple of hours, but please, don't try the French/American high-heat-short-cooking-time method. It will be another dish entirely!

Initial Seasoning

Metric Measure	Ingredient	American Measure
8½ grams	Whole fennel seeds	3½ teaspoons
9 grams	Whole black peppercorns	1½ tablespoons
32 grams	Salt, preferably fine sea salt	2 tablespoons
5½ grams	Minced fresh rosemary	3½ teaspoons
40 grams	Chopped garlic	1⅓ ounces
4–6 grams	Crushed red pepper	½ teaspoon
As needed	Olive oil	As needed
3 kilograms	Boneless pork shoulder (approximate weight)	7 pounds

1. In a small blender jar, grind the whole fennel seeds, whole black peppercorns, and salt to a powder.

2. Add the rosemary and grind again.

3. Add the garlic, red pepper, and a few tablespoons of olive oil. Grind again. Add enough olive oil to make a paste that is not runny, processing as needed.

4. Unroll the pork shoulder on a work surface cut-side up. Slice partway through any thick pieces of meat to create flaps without separating the meat. It won't look pretty at this point but don't fear.

5. Rub the paste over all the cut surfaces of the pork shoulder, not the edges. Roll up the roast, more or less putting the flaps back where they were. Tie the roast with butcher's twine to create a tight, thick cylinder. A second pair of hands is useful for this part but not essential.

6. Put the tied roast, fat side up and seam down, into a nonreactive, oven-safe pan with a tight-fitting lid, just large enough to hold the roast. I like using an oval enameled cast iron Dutch oven.

7. If the roasting pan does not have a cover that seals tightly, snuggle a piece of plastic wrap all around the roast before covering the pan.

8. Cover the roasting pan and refrigerate for 2 days.

Final Seasoning and Cooking

Metric Measure	Ingredient	American Measure
2½ grams	Whole fennel seeds	¾ teaspoon
3 grams	Whole black peppercorns	1½ teaspoons
3 grams	Salt, preferably fine sea salt	½ teaspoon
1½ grams	Minced fresh rosemary	1½ teaspoons
10 grams	Chopped garlic	⅓ ounce
180 milliliters	Dry white wine	¾ cup

1. Remove the pork shoulder from the refrigerator 60 to 90 minutes before roasting.

2. In a small blender jar, grind the whole fennel seeds, whole black peppercorns, and salt to a powder.

3. Add the rosemary and grind again.

4. Add the garlic and grind again.

5. Rub the spice mixture over the top of the roast. Pour the white wine into the bottom of the pan.

6. Cover the pan and roast at 120°C (250°F) for 10 hours, occasionally basting with pan juices after the first 5 hours.

7. Uncover the pan for the last hour of roasting. If necessary (but usually not), add a bit of water to the pan if the pan juices evaporate.

8. Put the roast on a serving platter.

9. Skim the fat from the pan drippings. Shred the meat with two forks. Drizzle some of the defatted drippings over the meat. Serve the remaining drippings at the table.

SALSICCIA CALABRESE
Calabrian Sausage

For this, and most sausage, a ratio of 25 percent fat to 75 percent lean meat is good. As a general rule, a pork shoulder is close to these proportions. On the other hand, pork belly is about 50 percent fat. You could use a fifty-fifty mixture of pork belly and lean pork to achieve the correct proportion of fat to lean. As with all my salumi recipes, I calculate the ingredients as a proportion of the amount of meat. There is no guessing involved and the seasoning is consistent from batch to batch. I usually start with about 2½ kilograms (5 pounds, or so) of pork.

Ingredient	Proportion
Boneless pork shoulder	
Salt, preferably fine sea salt	0.0260
Whole fennel seed	0.0053
Crushed red pepper	0.0055
Sweet ground red pepper, such as unsmoked paprika	0.0066
Freshly ground black pepper	0.0009
Chopped garlic	0.0190
Ice water	0.0700
Dry red wine or more ice water	0.0350

1. Cut the pork into strips approximately 2½ x 2½ x 15 centimeters (1 x 1 x 6 inches) in size. Lay the strips, without touching, on silicone-lined half-sheet pans and put in the freezer until firm but not frozen solid, approximately 30 minutes.

2. When the pork is firm, grind it using a coarse (approximately 9-millimeter or ⅜-inch) grinder disk. If you are making a large quantity of sausage, catch the meat in a bowl set in a larger bowl of ice water to keep it cold.

3. Weigh the ground pork and then calculate the amount of each ingredient needed by multiplying the weight of the meat, in grams or ounces, by the proportion of the ingredient. (See the recipe for Pancetta Tesa, page 99, for examples.)

4. Add the salt, fennel seed, crushed red pepper, sweet ground pepper, and black pepper to the ground meat. Using a stand mixer fitted with a paddle, beat the mixture until the spices are homogeneously distributed, approximately 1 minute.

5. In a blender jar, puree the garlic and ice water. Add the mixture to the meat. Rinse the blender jar out with the red wine and add to the meat.

6. Beat the meat mixture for another minute, or until it becomes sticky. This stickiness is essential so that the sausage holds together and does not crumble when cooked.

7. Stuff the mixture into 32- to 35-millimeter hog casings (see page xviii for information on hog casings). Use a large pin or a sausage pricker to release any air pockets that form. (Note: I generally make this sausage in a continuous run, but you can twist the casing every so often to make links if you desire.)

Salsiccia Toscana
Tuscan Sausage

My original versions of this sausage used a spice blend that I purchased from a butcher in Bagni di Lucca, Tuscany. When the spice blend ran out, I had to recreate it. For the Lucchese spice blend, use 1 part whole cloves, 2 parts cinnamon stick, 2 parts whole allspice berries, and 2 parts broken-up whole nutmeg by weight. Grind the spices to a fine powder in a small blender jar or coffee grinder.

Ingredient	Proportion
Boneless pork shoulder	
Salt, preferably fine sea salt	0.026
Freshly ground black pepper	0.004
Lucchese spice blend (see headnote)	0.004
Garlic, chopped	0.015
Dry white wine	0.100

1. Cut the pork into strips approximately 2½ x 2½ x 15 centimeters (1 x 1 x 6 inches) in size. Lay the strips, without touching, on silicone-lined half-sheet pans and put in the freezer until firm but not frozen solid, approximately 30 minutes.

2. When the pork is firm, grind it using a coarse (approximately 9-millimeter or ⅜-inch) grinder disk. If you are making a large quantity of sausage, catch the meat in a bowl set in a larger bowl of ice water to keep it cold.

3. Weigh the ground pork then calculate the amount of each ingredient needed by multiplying the weight of the meat, in grams or ounces, but the proportion of the ingredient. (See the recipe for Pancetta Tesa, page 99, for examples.)

4. Add the salt, black pepper, and Lucchese spice blend to the ground meat. Using a stand mixer fitted with a paddle, beat the mixture until the spices are homogeneously distributed, approximately 1 minute.

5. In a blender jar, puree the garlic and some of the white wine. Add the mixture to the meat. Rinse the blender jar out with the remainder of the white wine and add to the meat.

6. Beat the meat mixture for another minute, or until it becomes sticky. This stickiness is essential so that the sausage holds together and does not crumble when cooked.

7. Stuff the mixture into 32- to 35-millimeter hog casings (see page xviii for information on hog casings). Use a large pin or a sausage pricker to release any air pockets that form.

8. Tie each end of the casing after stuffing a moderately long length. Using butcher's twine, tie the large sausage into links of approximately 100 grams (¼ pound) each. To do this, weigh the sausage and calculate how many links to make by dividing the weight in grams by 100 (or dividing the weight in ounces by 4). Ignore any numbers after the decimal place and tie the sausage into the required number of even-sized links.

Tonno del Chianti
Tuna of Chianti (Pork Confit)

Chianti is a completely land locked region of Tuscany. Tonno del Chianti (tuna of Chianti) is a reference to the method of preserving pork in olive oil that is reminiscent of tuna preserved in olive oil. Tonno del Chianti makes an excellent addition to an antipasto plate. I like using pork shoulder (pork butt) because the collagen helps to moisten the meat as it cooks. Canning and pickling salt is pure salt. It contains no additives of any sort.

To Cook the Pork

Metric Measure	Ingredient	American Measure
1.2 liters	White wine vinegar	5 cups
1.2 liters	Water	5 cups
2 medium	Onions, thinly sliced	2 medium
2 teaspoons	Whole black peppercorns	2 teaspoons
4	Bay leaves, preferably fresh	4
36 grams	Canning and pickling salt or fine sea salt	1.27 ounces (6½ teaspoons)
1.5–1.8 kilograms	Bone-in pork shoulder (pork butt)	3–4 pounds

1. In a nonreactive pot, bring all the ingredients except the pork to a boil. Simmer 2 minutes.
2. Add the pork, cover the pot, and simmer until the pork is very tender, 1½ to 2 hours.
3. Remove the pork from the liquid. Strain the liquid and discard the solids.
4. Pour the strained liquid over the pork and refrigerate, covered tightly, overnight.

To Can the Pork

Metric Measure	Ingredient	American Measure
1 recipe	Cooked, cooled pork (immediately preceding)	1 recipe
As needed	Canning and pickling salt or fine sea salt	As needed
As needed	Cooking liquid (immediately preceding)	As needed
As needed	Garlic cloves	As needed
As needed	Bay leaves, preferably fresh	As needed
As needed	Fresh chile peppers	As needed
As needed	Extra-virgin olive oil	As needed

1. Break the pork into bite-sized pieces, discarding bones and gristle.

2. Gently, without pressing, pack the pork into 250-milliliter (½-pint) Mason jars.

3. To each jar add ¼ teaspoon of salt, 1 tablespoon of cooking liquid, 1 garlic clove cut in half, and 1 bay leaf. Add 1 chile pepper sliced lengthwise, if desired.

4. Fill each jar with extra-virgin olive oil, using a thin knife to free any air bubbles.

5. Add a plastic spacer to the top of each jar to keep the solids below the level of the olive oil.

6. Seal with new lids.

7. Put the jars into a pot of room-temperature water that reaches at least 5 centimeters (2 inches) over the top of the jars. Bring the water to a boil and process for 40 minutes.

8. Remove the jars from the water and allow them to cool. Store at a cool room temperature. Do not refrigerate until opened.

Chef Juan ready to carve porchetta filled with truffles. (See page 101 for a more traditional recipe for porchetta.)

Pig Week 107

DISPATCH #9

THE BARBER MAKES HOUSE CALLS

FEBRUARY 11

"You look like a priest."

I heard those exact words three times during my first week at the Italian Culinary Institute. The first time was from Chef John. The second time was from Chef Juan. The third time was from another student.

Although the design of my chef's coat is the standard shape, the collar of this particular coat has a slightly more relaxed and lower cut. That means my undershirt shows through the notch in the collar. The dark gray coat, coupled with a white undershirt, looks very much like the Roman collar worn by priests—a particularly resonant similarity in a Catholic country.

Being the psychiatrist in the room, especially a psychiatrist who reminds people of priests, has its moments. Mostly, I focus on cooking and don't deal with the reality of my prior career. It's actually quite fascinating to be a student again and turn my day-to-day experiences over to a crew of people who are consummate experts in their field. The content of what I did before is really not relevant. In this context, I am a student. My goal is to soak in as much information as I can.

A riff on spaghetti alla carbonara made with duck bacon cured and smoked at the Italian Culinary Institute.

The major task of this past week was to develop and execute a menu as part of a team. Our class of thirteen was divided into two groups. My group of seven was assigned lunch and the group of six was assigned dinner. Because the lunch group had slightly less time than the dinner group (at least theoretically), the extra person in our group made sense.

Menu planning started on Saturday, February 2. After being randomly assigned to our respective groups, we went off to develop a menu concept.

The parameters were basic. The menu had to include a trio of antipasti, an antipasto tris. This was to be followed by a first course, or primo piatto, in Italian. In an Italian meal, a primo is either pasta, rice, or a soup. The next course was another primo, which is not part of the typical sequence of an Italian meal, though it could happen for a special occasion.

After our second primo we were to make a secondo. A secondo in an Italian meal is the "protein," such as meat, fish, or poultry. To complicate it further, once again it was to be a secondo tris with three different dishes on the plate, accompanied by a contorno (a side dish). The meal was to end with a dolce tris (you got it, three different desserts on the same plate). We had to present four different breads, one with the antipasto, one with the secondo, and two on the table. Luckily the wine pairings were handled (this time) by the chefs at the Institute.

Our team was instructed to cook Northern Italian food. The other team got Southern Italian. We spent Saturday afternoon working out a proposed menu. Our initial menu was this:

Antipasto Tris
Bruschetta con Zucchine sott'aceto
Fiori di Zucca Fritti
Rotolino di Zucchine con Ricotta

Primo Piatto #1
Risotto alla Parmigiana con Frico e Aceto Balsamico

Primo Piatto #2
Farfalle ai Funghi e Mentuccia Romana (aka Niepita to my Tuscan father-in-law)

Secondo Piatto Tris e Contorno
Tartare di Manzo
Bistecca alla Griglia
Fettine di Manzo in Umido con Olive Nere
Cannellini alla Toscana
Paninetti con Rosmarino

Dolce Tris
Pera Affogata nel Vino Rosso con Crumble di Castagne
Torta di Mele e Castagne
Pannacotta di Castagne

Sul Tavolo
Grissini
Ciabatta

A torta di frutta made by Chef Juan for one of our lunches.

After devising our menu on Saturday, we were free. Sunday was a non-school day. I had work to do so I stayed at the school while everybody else went on day trips. That meant I had the washing machine to myself! We all share a washing machine, so this was a big advantage. The other interesting twist was that Chef John insisted that they would make lunch for me even though I repeatedly said I'd be happy to cook for myself. I am in an apartment with a kitchen, after all.

Cooking for myself was a nonstarter with Chef John, so I enjoyed a relaxing day of work and laundry punctuated by lunch. I was told we would all have lunch in the kitchen. The crew, including Chef John, Chef Juan, Chef Chris, Ryan and Erlyn (the kitchen assistants), Mariana (Chef Juan's wife and the overall coordinator of the program), and at least one of the dishwashers, if not others, works every day. That means they cook every day. It didn't seem strange that I would join them in the kitchen for a meal.

At 1 p.m. I walked from my apartment to the school. Upon entering the front room, which is set up as a bar (both for espresso and alcohol) with a counter as well as two bistro tables, I noticed that one of the bistro tables was set for two. I was not eating in the kitchen. The chefs had prepared a meal for me and I was dining with Mariana.

The antipasto made by my menu execution group featured zucchini flowers done three ways.

As each course came out, Chef John appeared to describe it. The first course was fusilloni (large fusilli) with a sauce of 'nduja and tomato. The 'nduja was made that morning, specifically for lunch. Chef said he knew I like 'nduja.

The next course was a bright salad with orange.

Following that was braised pickled pork made in the style of corned beef. This was something that had been started during the just-ended Pig Week. Small bread rolls rounded out the meal.

The rest of Sunday passed in bliss. Monday morning was my scheduled appointment at the questura to register my residence in Italy. It was also the morning when my team was scheduled to present our proposed menu to Chef John.

The appointment went well. The fingerprinting part was actually fun. The two guys doing the fingerprinting were surprised I was a student (I assume due to my age), but once they heard what I was studying and where the school was located, the whole event became quite jocular. One of the guys had gotten married at the hotel on the property shared with the school. That became the focus of conversation.

I got back to the school half an hour into the scheduled meeting with Chef John to discuss our proposed menu. Much of the menu was nixed by Chef, though a few dishes remained. The rest of the day was spent in meetings with Chef, interspersed with team meetings during which we tried to integrate Chef's recommendations to refine our menu.

The menu we ended up with was:

Antipasto Tris
Fiore di Zucca Crudo con Insalata di Zucchine
Fiore di Zucca Fritto con Caviale
Fiore di Zucca al Forno con Ricotta, Bottarga e Zafferano
Paninetti con Olive

Primo Piatto #1
Risotto ai Funghi Porcini con Aceto Balsamico

Primo Piatto #2
Pappardelle con Ragù di Coniglio

Secondo Piatto Tris e Contorno Tris (Crudo, Cotto, Stracotto)
Tartare di Manzo con Broccoli Crudi
Bistecca alla Griglia
Rotolo di Manzo con Prosciutto, Lardo di Colonnata, e Funghi Selvatici
Broccoli Saltati
Broccoli Brasati
Paninetti con Rosmarino

Dolce Tris
Pera Affogata nel Vino Rosso con Panna e Nocciole
Tiramisù alle Nocciole
Gianduia Caldo

Sul Tavolo
Focaccia al Parmigiano
Ciabatta

We started prepping for our meal on Tuesday morning. We also had to prepare lunch for everyone that day. The other group of students prepped on Tuesday afternoon and prepared dinner for everyone.

A Night to Remember... or Not

Pasta alla Norma with the more traditional topping of fried eggplant.

Thursday was the big day. We had to prepare and serve our meal to ten people: the other six students and four faculty. When I've prepared meals for people, rarely have I had the experience of being able to just cook. Usually I'm cooking and trying to spend time with the dinner guests. This was different. As stressful as I thought it would be, because we had to get each course out on time and many of them had to be prepared at the last minute, it wasn't. Just being able to concentrate on preparing the food perfectly and on time (without trying to spend time with guests) was actually a Zen-like experience.

That evening, after the other group finished dinner service, limoncello shots came out. Things went downhill from there. I went to bed at a respectable hour, but apparently the evening involved beer pong, conga dancing, and passing out. The whole party got shut down when Mariana discovered that four people dancing in the conga line were not students at the school.

Friday was very subdued and consisted of our usual market visit followed by a tour of the fourth-largest coffee roaster in Italy (Guglielmo) and then a free afternoon before dinner. After weeks of attempts, the barber finally made it to campus. Three of us got haircuts. Things are different in Italy. The little white paper "collar" barbers put around a customer's neck is made of a crepe paper–like substance rather than the thin tissue paper collars used in the States. It also has an adhesive and therefore sticks to itself. The stretchy quality of the paper coupled with the adhesive means it produces a pretty good seal around one's neck. After the cape was put on, the crepe-paper collar was turned down over it, creating a neat edge.

An American-style buffet was served for dinner the day after our big menu executions.

The Barber Makes House Calls

Truffle pappardelle set out to dry. (See page 45 for a recipe for pasta dough that can be cut into any desired shape.)

My cut used a combination of an electric clipper on the sides and scissors on the top. A straight razor, with a disposable blade, was used to trim the periphery: sideburns, neck, temples. It also removed some little fuzzy hairs on my forehead. I've never had that done before. I think he did a great job and the whole thing, including the house call, cost just €15!

After the haircuts, a few of us worked with Chef Juan on dinner of grilled burgers (pork, not beef—this is southern Italy, after all, and Pig Week had just ended!) and various side dishes. Everyone went to bed early. The next phase of our education was scheduled to begin the following morning: Dead Vegetable Week.

FETTINE DI MANZO IN UMIDO CON OLIVE NERE
Thinly Sliced Beef Braised in Tomato Sauce with Black Olives

Italians often cook with unpitted olives. I've been served whole unpitted olives on pizza numerous times. You can use brine-cured or oil-cured olives in this dish, as desired. Leave the pits in for the most authentic experience but be sure to warn your dinner guests!

Metric Measure	Ingredient	American Measure
1 kilogram	Thinly sliced beef, such as sirloin	2¼ pounds
As needed	Flour, for dredging	As needed
80 milliliters	Extra-virgin olive oil	⅓ cup
4–5 cloves	Garlic, bruised with a chef's knife	4–5 cloves
60 milliliters	Tomato paste	¼ cup
2 teaspoons	Minced fresh rosemary	2 teaspoons
3–4 sprigs	Fresh parsley, minced	3–4 sprigs
3–4	Fresh sage leaves, minced	3–4
2	Bay leaves, preferably fresh	2
½ teaspoon	Dried oregano	½ teaspoon
160 milliliters	Dry wine, red or white	⅔ cup
375 milliliters	Chicken Broth (page 15) or Vegetable Broth (page 161), or water	1½ cups
2 tablespoons	Salted capers, rinsed	2 tablespoons
15–20	Black olives, preferably Italian	15–20

| To taste | Salt, preferably fine sea salt | To taste |
| To taste | Freshly ground black pepper | To taste |

1. Lightly pound the beef with a mallet. Season the beef with salt and pepper and then dredge in flour, shaking off the excess.

2. Heat the olive oil in a heavy sauté pan. Add the garlic and sauté until the garlic is light brown. Discard the garlic.

3. Sauté the beef in the garlic-flavored oil on high heat until it is well browned on both sides. Do this in batches. Remove and reserve the beef.

4. Sauté the tomato paste in the oil remaining in the sauté pan until the color darkens slightly and it smells sweet, 1 to 2 minutes. Add the herbs and stir to combine. Add the wine and simmer to evaporate it.

5. Add the broth and season with salt and pepper. Add the beef and any accumulated juices. Simmer, partially covered until very tender, approximately 2 hours, turning the beef every 30 minutes. Add the capers and olives after the first hour.

6. As the beef cooks, adjust the seasoning.

 Fiori di Zucca Fritti
Fried Zucchini Blossoms

Fried zucchini blossoms are one of the joys of summer. They are very good stuffed, but I prefer them plain. They become irresistibly crunchy. When we have these in our house, everyone is in the kitchen because the blossoms get eaten within moments of coming out of the oil. You can obviously make as many blossoms as you want, but I suggest 24 because that's not too many for 4 people. I usually use water to make the batter, but seltzer makes a crispier coating. Beer adds another layer of flavor that I think is better if the blossoms are stuffed, but you decide.

Metric Measure	Ingredient	American Measure
135 grams	All-purpose flour	1 cup
5 grams	Salt, preferably fine sea salt	1 teaspoon
240 milliliters	Water, seltzer, or beer	1 cup
24	Zucchini blossoms	24
As needed	Neutral oil, such as corn or sunflower	As needed

1. Combine the flour and salt with a fork. Add the liquid a little at a time, mixing with a fork to avoid lumps. Add enough liquid to make a batter that

lightly but thoroughly coats the back of a spoon. It may take more or less liquid than noted.

2. Cover the batter and refrigerate it for 1 hour to allow the flour to fully hydrate.

3. Meanwhile, break off the base of the zucchini blossoms at the point where the little green tendrils are attached. Remove the tendrils and stamen, which should pretty much stay attached to the stem end of the blossom.

4. After being refrigerated, the batter will have thickened. Slowly add more liquid to return the batter to the consistency noted in step 1.

5. Heat 7 to 8 centimeters (3 inches) of oil to 175°C (350°F).

6. Dip each blossom into the batter, gently scraping off any excess on the edge of the bowl.

7. Fry the blossoms a few at a time until the coating is crispy and just beginning to brown. The delicate flavor of the blossoms will be completely overshadowed by the taste of the coating if it gets too brown.

8. Drain the fried blossoms on a metal rack to maintain their crunch. Salt the blossoms and serve immediately.

Fusilloni con Sugo di 'Nduja e Pomodoro
Fusilloni Pasta with 'Nduja and Tomato Sauce

'Nduja is a spicy, spreadable salame from Calabria. It is produced in a range of heat levels, though commercially available products are rarely incendiary. If you are lucky enough to snare some homemade 'nduja (like mine), it can set your hair on fire. If the quantity of 'nduja called for in this recipe will make it too spicy for you, swap some of it out for very finely minced soppressata or other similar salame, which will give the "cured" meat flavor with much less heat.

Sugo di 'Nduja

Metric Measure	Ingredient	American Measure
100 grams	Chopped onion	3½ ounces
100 grams	Chopped carrot	3½ ounces
50 grams	Chopped celery	1¾ ounces
3 cloves	Garlic, chopped	3 cloves
3 tablespoons	Extra-virgin olive oil	3 tablespoons
150 grams	'Nduja	5½ ounces

100 milliliters	Dry red wine	6½ tablespoons
700 grams	Passata (tomato puree)	24½ ounces
To taste	Salt, preferably fine sea salt	To taste
To taste	Freshly grated black pepper	To taste

1. Finely mince the onion, carrot, celery, and garlic by pulsing in a food processor. Pulse the carrot and garlic first until medium-fine. Add the celery and pulse briefly. Add the onion and pulse until everything is finely minced. Do not create a puree.

2. If substituting salame for some of the 'nduja, chop it and then mince it in the food processor after removing the vegetables.

3. In a heavy-bottomed saucepan, sauté the onion, carrot, celery, and garlic in the olive oil until soft.

4. Add the 'nduja and salame, if using, and sauté until the 'nduja fully renders its fat and everything sizzles together for a few minutes.

5. Add the wine and boil until completely evaporated.

6. Add the passata. Fill the passata jar halfway with water and swish it around to loosen the last bits. Add the water to the saucepan. Season with salt and pepper. Simmer, partially covered, approximately 45 minutes, stirring occasionally.

7. Taste and adjust the seasoning.

PASTA AND ASSEMBLY

Fusilli are corkscrew-shaped pasta. Fusilloni are large fusilli. I like them for this dish because they hold the textured sauce particularly well. Substitute another rustic-style pasta if you cannot find fusilloni. Extra sugo freezes well

Metric Measure	Ingredient	American Measure
½ recipe	Sugo di 'Nduja (immediately preceding)	½ recipe
500 grams	Dry fusilloni	~1 pound
To taste	Salt, preferably fine sea salt	To taste
To taste	Freshly ground black pepper	To taste
50 grams	Freshly grated Pecorino Romano cheese	1¾ ounces
2 tablespoons	Minced parsley	2 tablespoons

1. Bring 3 liters (3 quarts) of water seasoned with 75 grams (¼ cup) of salt to a rolling boil.

2. Meanwhile, gently heat the Sugo di 'Nduja in a large sauté pan.

3. Add the pasta to the boiling salted water and cook at a rapid boil for approximately 2 minutes less than the minimum cooking time on the package for al dente pasta, stirring frequently to prevent sticking.

4. Drain the pasta, reserving the pasta-cooking water.

5. Add the par-cooked pasta to the sauce in the sauté pan and finish cooking at a moderate boil, adding the reserved pasta-cooking water 1 ladle at a time, shaking the pan and stirring the pasta, until the pasta is al dente, leaving the sauce liquid enough to just coat the pasta. Adjust the salt and pepper while finishing the pasta.

6. Off the heat, add the cheese and parsley and then flip and stir the pasta to emulsify the cheese and sauce. Add a bit more cooking water if the sauce is too thick.

7. Serve immediately.

Brodo di Funghi
Mushroom Broth

Except in rare instances, I do not include the stems from cremini or button mushrooms when preparing recipes. I clean the stems and store them in the freezer. When I have enough, I make mushroom broth and then freeze it in small portions. It is a great way to add flavor to dishes that include mushrooms. I also add it to soups, stews, and savory meat dishes. The process couldn't be simpler. Adjust the amount of water for whatever quantity of mushroom stems you have.

Metric Measure	Ingredient	American Measure
500 milliliters	Chopped mushroom stems	2 cups
2 liters	Water	2 quarts

1. Combine the mushroom stems and water in a pressure cooker.[1] Cook for 65 minutes under pressure. Allow the pressure to release naturally.

2. Alternatively, on the stovetop, simmer the mixture, covered, for approximately 4 hours. Add water to return the volume to approximately the starting amount.

3. Strain and cool the broth.

---

[1] An electric pressure cooker, such as an Instant Pot, makes the process hands-off

Pere Affogate nel Vino Rosso
Red-Wine Poached Pears

Use pears that are still firm but just beginning to have a bit of a "give" when pressed. This recipe can be easily doubled. Although the pears are wonderful served on their own with just a bit of the syrup, consider topping them with some lightly sweetened whipped cream and chopped hazelnuts.

Metric Measure	Ingredient	American Measure
500 milliliters	Dry red wine	2 cups
500 milliliters	Water	2 cups
265 grams	Granulated sugar	1 1/3 cups
7–8 centimeters	Cinnamon stick	3 inches
1 teaspoon	Whole cloves	1 teaspoon
1/3	Whole nutmeg, cracked into several pieces	1/3
3	Cardamon pods, cracked open	3
4 large	Pears	4 large

1. Put all the ingredients except the pears in a heavy-bottomed, nonreactive saucepan. Bring to a boil.

2. Meanwhile, peel and quarter the pears and carefully remove the cores.

3. When the liquid comes to a boil, add the pears. Return the liquid to a low boil (more than a simmer).

4. Cook until the pears can be easily pierced with a sharp knife but are not mushy or falling apart. (Note: To hold the pears under the poaching liquid, put a saucer that just fits inside the pot on top of the pears.)

5. When the pears are cooked, remove them to a heatproof bowl.

6. Boil the poaching liquid quickly until it is reduced to approximately 375 milliliters (1½ cups).

7. Strain the syrup over the pears. Refrigerate overnight.

Risotto ai Funghi
Mushroom Risotto

This is a wonderful first course to serve in the fall and winter. I have written this recipe for the easiest mushrooms to find: white button mushrooms. The technique, however, works for most any mushroom. If you need something to do with all the mushroom stems, see the recipe for Mushroom Broth (page 118). You can substitute mushroom broth for about one-quarter of the chicken broth if you want.

Metric Measure	Ingredient	American Measure
675 grams	Button mushrooms, caps only	1½ pounds
2 tablespoons	Extra-virgin olive oil	2 tablespoons
To taste	Salt, preferably fine sea salt	To taste
2 cloves	Garlic, minced	2 cloves
½ teaspoon	Dried marjoram or oregano	½ teaspoon

1. Rinse the mushroom caps and wipe with a cloth to remove dirt.
2. Slice the mushroom caps approximately 3 millimeters (⅛ inch) thick.
3. In a large sauté pan, heat the olive oil over medium-high heat until it shimmers. Add the mushrooms and toss to coat.
4. As soon as the mushrooms have absorbed all the oil, turn the heat to low and generously salt the mushrooms. Stir frequently.
5. After the mushrooms have begun to release liquid, turn the heat to high and cook until all the liquid evaporates. Continue to sauté until some of the mushrooms turn golden and others get a few brown flecks.
6. Remove the mushrooms from the heat and immediately add the minced garlic and marjoram. Stir for about 1 minute to allow the garlic to cook in the residual heat.
7. Reserve the mushrooms.

FOR THE RICE

Metric Measure	Ingredient	American Measure
5 grams	Dried porcini mushrooms	⅙ ounce
1.5 liters	Chicken Broth (page 15)	1½ quarts
3 tablespoons	Extra-virgin olive oil	3 tablespoons
½ small	Onion, finely diced	½ small
1	Garlic clove, minced	1
300 grams	Arborio or carnaroli rice	1½ cups
150 milliliters	Dry white wine	Scant ¾ cup
1½ teaspoons	Salt, preferably fine sea salt	1½ teaspoons
½ teaspoon	Freshly ground black pepper	½ teaspoon
90 grams	Freshly grated Parmigiano Reggiano cheese	3¼ ounces
30 grams	Unsalted butter at room temperature	2 tablespoons

1. Cover the porcini mushrooms with 100 milliliters (⅖ cup) of water. Soak until the mushrooms are soft, approximately 15 minutes. Remove the mushrooms from the liquid and squeeze out the extra liquid. Reserve the soaking liquid.

2. Finely mince the mushrooms.

3. Bring the broth to a simmer in a small saucepan.

4. Meanwhile, put the olive oil, onion, garlic, and minced porcini mushrooms in a heavy-bottomed saucepan of approximately 3.5-liter (4-quart) capacity. Gently heat the pan and sauté until the onion is soft but not brown.

5. Turn the heat to medium and add the rice. Sauté for 2 to 3 minutes, stirring frequently, until all the rice shows an opaque core surrounded by a translucent exterior. Do not brown the rice.

6. Add the mushroom soaking liquid, leaving any grit behind and boil gently, stirring frequently, until the liquid has completely evaporated.

7. Add the wine and boil gently, stirring frequently, until the wine has completely evaporated.

8. Add approximately 125 milliliters (½ cup) simmering broth and ⅓ of the salt. Over medium to medium-low heat, gently boil the rice, stirring frequently until the broth has evaporated. (Note: It is important that the rice actually boil so that much of the broth evaporates without entering the rice grain. This is what will coax the starch out of the rice to create a creamy risotto.)

Continue in this manner, adding ⅓ of the salt with each of the next 2 ladles of broth, until the rice is al dente, creamy on the exterior but slightly chewy in the center.

9. Stir frequently to prevent the rice from sticking and browning, especially as the cooking proceeds and the rice starch begins to form the characteristic creamy liquid surrounding the individual grains of rice. As cooking progresses, it will not be possible to allow all the liquid to evaporate due to the starch. Wait as long as you can, stirring frequently, without letting the risotto stick and turn brown before adding more broth. The cooking time for the rice, once the first ladle of broth is added, will be approximately 18 minutes.

10. When you estimate that you have about 2 more ladles of broth to add, scrape in the cooked button mushroom caps. Stir well and continue cooking the rice as described above.

11. Off the heat, stir in the black pepper, Parmigiano Reggiano cheese, and butter. If the risotto is dry, add more hot broth (or water if you've run out of broth). Risotto should be pourable but not loose. Taste and adjust the seasoning. Serve immediately.

Semifreddo sandwiched between two thin layers of sponge cake, glazed in chocolate, and sprinkled with chopped hazelnuts and white chocolate.

Dead Vegetable Week

Beautiful broccoli rabe appears during conserves destined for a pasta dish. (See page 135 for a recipe for orecchiette pasta with broccoli rabe and sausage.)

FEBRUARY 15

Conserve Week, or "Dead Vegetable Week," began on Saturday, February 9. It was a jam-packed (no pun intended, well, maybe) week of brewing beer, fermenting apple cider, distilling spirits, mixing drinks, and preserving fruits and vegetables by drying, salting, smoking, pickling, packing in oil (sott'olio), and packing in vinegar (sott'aceto). But first it began with a brief critique by the chefs of our menu execution from earlier that week. Comments to the whole class were general. Comments to the teams were more specific. Individual comments were provided if requested.

I requested, and a day or two later Chef John and I retired to a corner of the adjacent restaurant during a non-service time. He looked at me with this "why are we here" look. I reminded him that I was coming to see if he had any feedback about my performance. He looked at me and said, "You, no!" We then went on to chat about other food-related topics, like what I wanted to do in the culinary world.

Eggplant diced for Bomba Calabrese. (See page 145 for a recipe.)

I owe a debt of gratitude to David Locke and Bill Forte, chefs I work with at the annual Palm Desert Food and Wine Festival, who convinced me that I would hold my own against others with professional culinary training and that I shouldn't spend time in a course that taught the basics. Their advice was to dive into a specialized course that focused on what I wanted to learn, hence my time at the Italian Culinary Institute.

Chef John makes salmon bacon.

FERMENTATION FUN

The first day of Dead Vegetable Week was pretty low-key. It consisted of an introduction to fermentation and distillation that served the purpose of showing us that making beer and wine and distilling alcohol are actually quite easy but can contribute immeasurably to the uniqueness of one's cuisine.

We started to ferment two types of beer: ale and pils. We also started to ferment apple cider. The process is similar to fermenting grapes to make wine. Since this was not the season to make wine, apple cider was the stand-in. We also put up a wild ferment of fruit peelings and cores and other bits without the addition of packaged yeast.

We used a small copper still to distill a grain-based ferment (beer) and a fruit-based ferment (wine). Honestly, beer was a pain. With only 4.2 percent alcohol and a very small still, it was not realistic to distill enough to do anything substantive. Distilling wine, with an alcohol content three times that of beer, was definitely more satisfactory.

To make the product useful, even as the base for extracting essential oils from citrus peels and other fruits, the alcohol would have needed to have been distilled at least twice more. Nonetheless, the experience of actually distilling something showed how manageable and effective the process could be. Updates on our ferments will continue for weeks until we're ready to bottle them. As for the distillate, I'm not sure what ever became of it.

After our introduction to fermentation and distillation, Conserve Week got into full swing on Sunday the tenth. Before work started on vegetables, however, Chef John felt the need to demonstrate several dishes. We had three plates of pasta before 2 p.m. Each of the dishes had copious (and I mean copious) amounts of rendered pork fat from either guanciale or speck.

The pasta dishes included pasta alla gricia, pasta all'Amatriciana, and linguine with caramelized onions and speck (a nontraditional, but very yummy, dish created by Chef John).

In between the pasta dishes, Chef John demonstrated how to make vegetable demi. In French cooking, a demi-glace is a highly concentrated stock made in a very prescribed way. Chef doesn't use the term demi-glace, just demi, as he doesn't make "real" French demi-glace. His highly concentrated stocks, however, add a tremendous amount of flavor to dishes. In addition to the concentrated stock itself, Chef John refines the fat from the each demi and uses it to enhance dishes in place of butter or extra-virgin olive oil.

We got lessons on cleaning artichokes and making meatballs, starting giardiniera, butchering salmon (okay, so there are a few non-vegetables included in Dead Vegetable Week), curing salmon, curing and smoking salmon bellies to make salmon bacon, making salmon jerky, stuffing and conserving hot peppers, pickling apples, roasting tomatoes, making and conserving apple marmalade and mostarda, as well as cooking and conserving pleurotus mushrooms (a luscious mushroom variety that takes hours to cook but ends up meaty and tender).

Lunch was Chef John's "very bastardized" risotto alla fiorentina. It contained all the ingredients in a traditional risotto alla fiorentina (gizzards, chicken livers, and tomato sauce) but with a great deal more finesse and technique.

BOMBA CALABRESE

On the eleventh we started bomba Calabrese, a spicy conserve of finely diced eggplant, onions, sweet peppers, and hot peppers preserved in oil. The eggplant is peeled, thinly sliced, heavily salted, and allowed to drain for a day. It is then cut in a small dice, rinsed in boiling white wine vinegar, then pressed through a vegetable press to remove as much liquid as possible.

When squeezing the second batch, Gerard turned the crank one half-turn too far and eggplant cubes went shooting out of the top of the press and stuck to the ceiling! There was no way Chef John could say that we did not adequately squeeze the eggplant.

We also learned the calculations for sugar syrups as well as Chef John's method for cooking dried beans (similar to mine) and then finishing them for a dish (removing them from the cooking liquid, cooking them until they dry out to create fond on the bottom of a pot, and then returning the cooking liquid and simmering briefly to release the fond and flavor the broth…not like mine!). There was also the making of a smoked pepper puree, candied peperoncini (hot peppers), balsamic vinegar–cured onions, and spicy eggplant in oil to be served as an antipasto.

Chef John demonstrated other conserves that were not traditional, like zucchini bacon (if you've been reading these posts, you've probably noticed that Chef John has a "thing" for baconizing anything that can be baconized), sun-dried tomato conserve, scallion sauce, and pickled potatoes. There were also pickled zucchini, pickled arugula (which seemed a lot like leftover salad), salmon jerky, and "veggie 'nduja" (basically another variant on eggplant, sweet peppers, hot peppers, and extra-virgin olive oil).

We wrapped up the day with our first session on mixology. Our mixology instructor is Evangelos Triantafyllopoulos (Agelos) from Athens. He is truly a gifted mixologist and an owner of the White Monkey Bar in Athens. He is a fun-loving, jocular person who has the perfect persona to be a bartender, but he is also a very serious, driven, and hard-working person below that persona.

We learned his method (and several recipes) for making flavored syrups—and very creative ones at that—using sous vide. (Yet another reason I am happy I bought a sous vide set-up last year!) He then demonstrated (and we tasted) a whole series of classic cocktails plus twists on them.

The morning of the twelfth we went to a nearby agriturismo (a farm designed for receiving guests). It's owned by the same folks who own the Panino Lab where we've had lunch and also a wine tasting. We picked oranges, lemons, and mandarins—hundreds upon hundreds of them. Really, probably thousands of them!

After a brief stop at the supermarket, we were back at the Italian Culinary Institute processing citrus. I was initially on washing duty with a couple of other students. This took about two hours. After that, I joined everyone else who was zesting, peeling, and supreme-cutting the citrus. After a quick lunch of cavatelli with scallion sauce (sautéed scallion tops simmered with simple tomato sauce), we were back to processing citrus for a short while.

Chef John demonstrated how to candy orange peel (well, really, just the first day of a three-day process) and made a batch of orange marmalade. Chef John also whipped up a batch of orecchiette with pancetta and rapini to feed us again, just a few hours after lunch.

Cocktail Time

We were then turned over to Agelos for more lessons in mixology. This included making foams, infusing spirits with the flavors of fat (like bacon and pancetta), and making cold infusions of spirits and fruits and other aromatics. He also showed us a neat trick of almost instantaneously infusing spirits with citrus zest using a carbon dioxide cartridge and beverage carbonator.

The second of four food and cocktail pairings prepared by the chefs and Agelos on February 14.

Agelos then made (and we drank) another whole series of classic cocktails plus twists on those cocktails. Bourbon featured prominently in these cocktails, and Agelos knew of my love of bourbon, so I frequently got a whole drink for myself rather than one to share among others in the class. I have to say that pancetta-infused bourbon, a little simple syrup, coffee bitters, and a lemon zest garnish makes a mighty tasty "twist" on an Old Fashioned! I'm looking forward to repeating this with bacon-infused bourbon when I get back to the States.

The third of four food and cocktail pairings prepared by the chefs and Agelos on February 14.

MORE CITRUS

After mixology class, a handful of us went back to the kitchen for an hour and a half before dinner to help process more citrus. As it turned out, staff worked on citrus all day, every day, for the rest of the week!

Because we had been making sugar syrups of different concentrations for both conserves and mixology, Chef Juan ended the day with a brief lecture on the formula for creating a solution with any desired sugar content, regardless of the sugar content of the starting solution. For example, you would add less sugar to fruit juice than to coffee to get a solution with the same amount of sugar (because the fruit juice contains some sugar). While this is important for conserves and mixology, it is critical for gelato (which has its own week in the near future). The formula is:

$$X = (P_F \times SO) - ZO / 1 - P_F$$

Where:

- P_F = Desired brix
- SO = Quantity of original solution (in grams)
- ZO = Sugar content of SO (in grams) = Quantity of SO (in grams) x percentage of sugar in SO
- X = Amount of sugar to be added (in grams)

(*Note:* Brix is a measure of the sugar in a solution on a percentage basis, that is weight of sugar in grams divided by total weight of solution in grams.)

An Excursion to Tutto Calabria

February 14 started out with an excursion. On the way to the bus, we were met by Chef Juan handing out heart-shaped chocolate candy to celebrate Valentine's Day. Once on the bus, we headed to Tutto Calabria, a local artisanal producer of peperoncino (pepper) products. Calabria is known for its peperoncino, both hot and sweet.

Tutto Calabria has been around since 1970, having been started by the father of the three siblings who now run the company. Although Tutto Calabria products are exported to the States, only a limited number of items from their line are available. I bought a few jars of peperoncino piccante (hot pepper) products that I have never seen in the States.

We came back and had lunch (cacio e pepe followed by meatballs in tomato sauce). After a short break we were back to our mixology lessons with Agelos. He made some sours (including one that started with hazelnut gelato) and a blazer (a cocktail set on fire as it is poured back and forth between the two parts of the shaker). He ended the lesson with a variety of martinis.

His dirty martini is made with a little oil floating on top rather than olive juice. He made two: one with rosemary-infused olive oil and one with oil from bomba Calabrese (a hot pepper conserve we made in house) and a garlic and bay leaf–infused extra-virgin olive oil. He called this the Steak Dirty Martini since it would pair perfectly with a steak. His Breakfast Martini was similar to a Cosmo but included orange marmalade instead of pomegranate juice.

The view from my terrace was just glorious this week.

Agelos's Breakfast Tequila Martini was the best Margarita I've ever had. In addition to marmalade in the mix and a bit of salt on the rim, he put freshly ground black pepper on top. We ended the session with an Espresso Martini garnished with coffee beans and topped with a few drops of coffee bitters.

After another brief break, we were back for a food and cocktail pairing from 5:30 p.m. to 6:30 p.m. Four different foods were paired with four different cocktails. All of the combinations were very good but, honestly, afterward I was at my limit of caloric intake for the day. The school made arrangements to take everyone out to dinner at 8:30 p.m. in honor of Valentine's Day. Unable to eat or drink anything else, I decided not to go. It was the first school-sponsored activity that I missed since

I arrived. (Admittedly, I cut out early on some of the evenings that involved beer pong and blackouts, but I was there for the beginning of all of them!)

Today wrapped up our attention to cocktails and the majority of conserves, though we will make a few from time to time as other products come into season. We'll either see, do, or hear about the final steps on a number of the products that were started this week. We'll do a round of baking with new products we haven't made before. This evening ended with a pizza party, but not just any pizza party; it's a contest of sorts. You'll hear all about it in the next dispatch.

SALSA DI POMODORO
Basic Tomato Sauce

This is a tomato sauce that can be used on its own exactly as prepared, adjusted with other aromatics and herbs as desired, or used as a component in more complicated tomato sauces. If you keep Rosemary Oil (page 262) and Garlic Oil (page 57) next to the stove and have a few spices and butter at the ready, you can create endless variations on this sauce when finishing pasta in the sauté pan. Each will be different without any indication that they are actually the same tomato sauce. This makes enough sauce for approximately 1 kilogram (2¼ pounds) of pasta.

Metric Measure	Ingredient	American Measure
100 grams	Very finely diced onion	3½ ounces
100 grams	Very finely diced carrot	3½ ounces
50 grams	Very finely diced celery	1¾ ounces
3 tablespoons	Extra-virgin olive oil	3 tablespoons
1 (1-kilogram) can	Peeled tomatoes in tomato puree	1 (35-ounce) can
To taste	Salt, preferably fine sea salt	To taste
To taste	Freshly ground black pepper	To taste

1. In a heavy-bottomed saucepan, sweat the onion, carrot, and celery in the olive oil until soft and the onion is golden, approximately 15 minutes. Do not brown the vegetables.

2. Meanwhile, pass the tomatoes through a food mill to remove the seeds and any bits of skin and core.

3. Add the tomatoes to the vegetables. Season with salt and pepper. Simmer, partially covered approximately 15 minutes.

4. Allow the sauce to cool slightly then either pass it through the food mill or use an immersion blender to puree it completely.

CACIO E PEPE
Cacio e Pepe

Cacio e Pepe, a traditional Roman pasta, has very few ingredients. The sauce is nothing more than Pecorino Romano cheese (called cacio in the Roman dialect) emulsified with the pasta cooking water and seasoned with black pepper. I find using a blender to combine the cheese and some of the cooking water reduces the likelihood of creating a lumpy or non-emulsified sauce. Toasted cracked peppercorns and freshly ground peppercorns add textural notes and subtly different flavors.

Metric Measure	Ingredient	American Measure
2 tablespoons	Whole black peppercorns	2 tablespoons
500 grams	Dry spaghetti	~1 pound
200 grams	Freshly grated Pecorino Romano cheese	7 ounces
To taste	Salt, preferably fine sea salt	To taste
To taste	Freshly ground black pepper	To taste

1. Toast the whole peppercorns in a dry skillet over medium-low heat until fragrant. Immediately remove the peppercorns from the skillet to prevent overcooking from residual heat. Coarsely crush the toasted peppercorns with a mortar and pestle.

2. Bring 3 liters (3 quarts) of water seasoned with 75 grams (¼ cup) of salt to a rolling boil.

3. Add the pasta to the boiling salted water and cook at a rapid boil for approximately 2 minutes less than the minimum cooking time on the package for al dente pasta, stirring frequently to prevent sticking. At this point the spaghetti should be bendable. If it is too undercooked, it is likely to break in the sauté pan.

4. Meanwhile, put the Pecorino Romano cheese in a blender jar.

5. Drain the pasta, reserving the pasta-cooking water.

6. Put the par-cooked pasta and 2 ladles (approximately 250 milliliters or 1 cup) of pasta-cooking water into a large sauté pan. Add the toasted cracked black peppercorns. Cook the pasta at a moderate boil, adding the reserved pasta-cooking water 1 ladle at a time, shaking the pan and stirring the pasta, until the pasta is al dente. Because you will be adding more water along with the cheese, there should be very little liquid in the pan when the pasta is al dente.

7. Just as the pasta finishes cooking, add 1 ladle of pasta-cooking water to the cheese in the blender and puree. Add more water if needed to make a pourable slurry. Pour the cheese puree into the pasta.

8. Immediately remove the pasta from the heat to prevent the cheese from clumping.

9. Add a bit more pasta-cooking water in the blender jar to capture the remaining cheese and add it to the pasta.

10. Off the heat, flip and stir the pasta to emulsify the cheese and make a creamy sauce. Add a bit more cooking water if the sauce is too thick.

11. Add more freshly ground black pepper to taste.

12. Serve immediately.

ARANCIA CANDITA
Candied Orange Peel

For the modest amount of work involved in preparing home-candied orange peel, the flavor is truly infinitely better than anything you can buy. Use the freshest oranges you can find. The same process also works for lemons.

Metric Measure	Ingredient	American Measure
As desired	Fresh oranges	As desired
As calculated plus more for coating	Granulated sugar	As calculated plus more for coating
As calculated	Water	As calculated

1. Wash and dry fresh, unblemished oranges. Using a sharp knife, score through the peel to the flesh below, quartering the peel. Remove the peel without breaking. If there is a large amount of white pith on the underside of the peel, use a dull knife or a spoon to scrape out some of it to create an even layer.

2. Cut the peel into strips approximately ½-centimeter (¼-inch) wide.

3. Weigh the prepared peel.

4. Juice the oranges once the peel is removed.

5. Make a syrup as follows:

    a. Multiply the weight of the peel (in grams or ounces) by 3. Multiply the result by 0.66. That is the amount of sugar to use (in grams or ounces).

    b. Multiply the weight of the peel (in grams or ounces) by 3. Multiply the result by 0.34. That is the amount of liquid to use (in grams or ounces).

    c. For the liquid, strain the juice and add enough water to reach the desired weight.

    d. Combine the sugar and liquid. Bring to a boil, stirring occasionally.

6. Add the prepared peel to the boiling syrup. Return to a boil and boil for 90 seconds. Remove from the heat. Cover the pot and allow the peel to cool for about 30 minutes.

7. Remove the peel from the syrup and lay the pieces out on a rack without them touching. Allow it to dry overnight, uncovered, at room temperature. Cover the syrup and allow it to remain at room temperature.

8. Repeat the process of bringing the syrup to a boil, boiling the peel for 90 seconds, allowing the peel to cool partially in the syrup, and laying it out on a rack overnight on the second day and again on the third day.

9. On the fourth day, after the peel has dried overnight from the third boil, roll the peel in granulated sugar.

10. Store the candied peel in a loosely covered container until all tackiness is gone, approximately 3 days. Cover tightly and refrigerate.

Pasta all'Amatriciana
Pasta all'Amatriciana

The usual cured pork product for this dish is guanciale, not pancetta. Guanciale can be difficult to source in the United States, so feel free to substitute pancetta. Guanciale has more fat than pancetta. If you use it, you may need to remove a bit of the rendered fat before adding the chile pepper. Using basic tomato sauce creates a smoother texture. If you want a more rustic dish, use canned tomatoes. Crush the contents of a 793-gram (28-ounce) can of whole peeled tomatoes using your hands so that it still has some texture but no big pieces. Weigh out 580 grams (20 ounces) and save the rest for another use. Use the crushed tomatoes in place of the Basic Tomato Sauce.

Metric Measure	Ingredient	American Measure
250 grams	Guanciale or pancetta cut in matchsticks	9 ounces
1 small	Whole dried red chile pepper, optional	1 small
80 milliliters	Dry white wine	⅓ cup
550 grams	Basic Tomato Sauce (page 131)	19 ounces
500 grams	Dry spaghetti or bucatini	~1 pound
100 grams plus more to garnish	Freshly grated Pecorino Romano cheese	3½ ounces plus more to garnish
To taste	Salt, preferably fine sea salt	To taste
To taste	Freshly ground black pepper	To taste
To garnish	Basil chiffonade	To garnish

1. In a large sauté pan, sauté the guanciale until the it is golden brown. Add the chile pepper, if using. Continue to sauté the guanciale, with or without the chile, until crispy.

2. Remove and reserve the guanciale but keep the rendered fat in the sauté pan.

3. Add the white wine to the sauté pan and boil until it completely evaporates, scraping up any brown bits from the pan.

4. Add the tomato sauce (or hand-crushed canned tomatoes) and salt and pepper to taste. Simmer approximately 10 minutes.

5. Bring 3 liters (3 quarts) of water seasoned with 75 grams (¼ cup) of salt to a rolling boil.

6. Add the pasta to the boiling salted water and cook at a rapid boil for approximately 2 minutes less than the minimum cooking time on the package for al dente pasta, stirring frequently to prevent sticking. At this point the pasta should be bendable. If it is too undercooked, it is likely to break in the sauté pan.

7. Drain the pasta, reserving the pasta-cooking water. Add the par-cooked pasta to the sauce in the sauté pan and finish cooking at a moderate boil, adding the reserved pasta-cooking water 1 ladle at a time, shaking the pan and stirring the pasta, until the pasta is al dente leaving the sauce liquid enough to just coat the pasta.

8. Add the cooked guanciale with the last ladle of pasta-cooking water.

9. Off the heat, add the cheese and then flip and stir the pasta to emulsify the cheese and sauce. Add a bit more cooking water if the sauce is too thick. Taste and adjust the salt and pepper.

10. Garnish each portion with extra freshly grated Pecorino Romano cheese and a sprinkling of basil chiffonade.

Pasta alla Gricia
Pasta alla Gricia

Pasta alla Gricia predates the arrival of tomatoes to Europe. You will notice that Pasta all'Amatriciana (immediately preceding) is basically Pasta alla Gricia with tomatoes. Some recipes for gricia include onions or garlic. If you choose to add one or the other, sauté it in the rendered fat after the guanciale is removed. Common pasta shapes to use include rigatoni, bucatini, and spaghetti.

Metric Measure	Ingredient	American Measure
250 grams	Guanciale or pancetta cut in matchsticks	9 ounces
500 grams	Dry rigatoni, bucatini, or spaghetti	~1 pound
20 grams plus more to garnish	Fresh parsley, minced	1/3 cup plus more to garnish
100 grams plus more to garnish	Freshly grated Pecorino Romano cheese	3½ ounces plus more to garnish
To taste	Salt, preferably fine sea salt	To taste
To taste	Freshly ground black pepper	To taste

1. Bring 3 liters (3 quarts) of water seasoned with 75 grams (¼ cup) of salt to a rolling boil.

2. Meanwhile, in a large sauté pan, sauté the guanciale until it is crispy.

3. Remove and reserve the guanciale but keep the rendered fat in the sauté pan.

4. Add the pasta to the boiling salted water and cook at a rapid boil for approximately 2 minutes less than the minimum cooking time on the package for al dente pasta, stirring frequently to prevent sticking. At this point the pasta should be bendable. If it is too undercooked, it is likely to break in the sauté pan.

5. Meanwhile, add 2 ladles, approximately 250 milliliters (1 cup), of pasta-cooking water to the sauté pan and bring it to a boil, scraping up any brown bits from the pan.

6. Drain the pasta, reserving the pasta-cooking water.

7. Add the par-cooked pasta to the liquid in the sauté pan and finish cooking at a moderate boil, adding the reserved pasta-cooking water 1 ladle at a time, shaking the pan and stirring the pasta, until the pasta is al dente, leaving the sauce liquid enough to just coat the pasta.

8. Add the cooked guanciale and minced parsley with the last ladle of pasta-cooking water.

9. Off the heat, add the cheese and then flip and stir the pasta to emulsify the cheese and sauce. Add a bit more cooking water if the sauce is too thick. Adjust the salt and pepper.

10. Garnish each portion with extra Pecorino Romano cheese and a sprinkling of minced parsley.

If It Doesn't Taste Yummy, It's Worthless

FEBRUARY 20

I am sitting in the servants' quarters as I write this—the servants' quarters of a palazzo in Matera. The Palazzo Gattini, in Piazza Duomo, is now a luxury hotel. Around the corner and down some stairs are the former servants' quarters, now turned into short-term rentals. Ours is in Dimora Santa Barbara hosted by a wonderful father-son duo, Angelo and Ivan.

I couldn't be happier. The suite is massive; definitely bigger than my first house. It has a separate fully-equipped kitchen, a large salon set up as both a living and dining room, a bedroom that is up a flight of stairs and overlooks the living room, and a bathroom.

The floors are marble and granite, the furnishings are antique, and the lighting is soft. It is also blissfully quiet. I could spend weeks, perhaps months, here, but unfortunately, my stay will only last two days.

Let me fill you in on what has happened since last time.

The week of conserves and mixology ended on February 15 with what was billed as a "Pizza Party." Ha! It was not a party; it was a contest. At the end, everyone was

A view of Matera.

hungry because every two students made one small pizza, half of which was eaten by the judges.

A street scene in Matera.

We were randomly assigned to teams of two. Tommy Palmer and I were a team. The premise was that each team had to create a pizza using a maximum of five ingredients, not including the crust, from a basket of ingredients that would change from team to team, and pair it with a creative cocktail using a maximum of five ingredients, not including garnishes, from a well-stocked bar. The clincher was that we would have ten minutes to make and bake the pizza and create the cocktail after we were given our basket of ingredients!

Once the ground rules were laid out, and several hours before the contest was to begin, each team was given time to discuss cocktails with our mixologist, Agelos. The conversation happened at the bar inside the school. When our turn came, Tommy and I each took a seat at a bar stool and Agelos stood behind the bar. He offered us each a shot. We accepted. He poured one for himself too. We talked about strategy for pairing cocktails with pizza and how to have a plan that could be finalized and executed within the allotted ten minutes.

Tommy and I then went off to discuss how we were going to tackle the task, knowing what ingredients we had to work with for the cocktail, but not knowing what would be available to use for the pizza. We also decided that Tommy would make the cocktail and I would make the pizza.

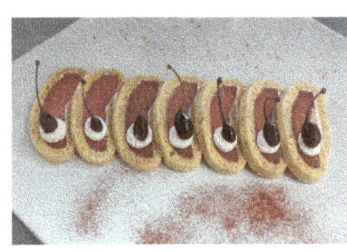
Cured salmon wrapped in a flexible bread spread with cream cheese and topped with caper berries, part of a snack at the Italian Culinary Institute prepared with salmon that was cured during conserves week.

We had a couple of free hours before we had to assemble at 5 p.m. to start the contest. About 4:45 p.m., my husband, Frank, arrived with Zia Fidalma and cousins Massimo and Francesca from Tuscany. They had all met up at the airport in Lamezia Terme and driven to the school together. Chef John saw that they were well-fed with house-cured meats, small sandwiches, and pizza while we had our contest.

Tommy and I had decided that our theme would be Southern Italian. That meant we would do a spicy pizza based on whatever spicy ingredients were available (it was unthinkable that there wouldn't be at least one spicy ingredient), and that our cocktail would have citrus, for which Southern Italy is well known.

We were introduced to our basket of ingredients by Chef John. We had bomba Calabrese, pickled peperoncini, thinly sliced scallions, pizza cheese, Pecorino Romano cheese, anchovies, and sgombro (mackerel) that had been delicately braised. We also learned that the two minutes Chef John took to explain our ingredients were deducted from our ten-minute allotment. We now had eight minutes to make a pizza and a cocktail.

After plates of pasta, Frank and I shared this "salad" as our second course for our lunch at La Cabana restaurant.

I was hoping for arugula and peperoncino oil so that I could top the pizza with something fresh that would also scream Southern Italy, but it wasn't to be.

Tommy went off to make the cocktail: one part lemon syrup, one part Aperol, and two parts gin stirred with ice, poured into a large ice-filled wineglass, topped with prosecco, sprayed with lemon and orange oil from freshly cut peels, and garnished with basil.

For the pizza, I stirred bomba Calabrese into the tomato puree to evenly disperse the heat. I stretched out the crust, topped it with the sauce, pizza cheese (pasta filata), and a small amount of Pecorino. Thinly sliced onions were the closest I was going to come to a vegetable, so I also added those. When the pizza came out of the oven, I topped it with small bits of sgombro for my best attempt at a delicate freshness. I avoided the anchovies as being too strong and the pickled peperoncini as being too acidic.

Although Tommy and I didn't win, Chef John held up a slice of our creation, describing it as a perfectly baked pizza (smile). Many of the students came up to Tommy and told him that they could have drunk our cocktail "all night."

When the contest was over, a few of the students baked pies that were shared, but these still didn't satisfy everyone's hunger. So, while Agelos set about making a dirty vodka martini for Frank, with the dirty part being a few drops of bomba Calabrese oil and a few drops of rosemary-infused extra-virgin olive oil floating on top, Chef Juan and Ryan set about making a kilo of spaghetti aglio e olio. It went so fast that a second kilo followed immediately behind!

When the evening was over, a few of us ended up in Agelos' suite, drinking and talking until 3 a.m. At that point, Agelos was still raring to continue the party, but the rest of us were anxious to get some sleep.

The next morning, I had breakfast with the relatives while Frank slept. Not only was he time shifted by eight hours, but he hadn't slept for forty hours before our 3 a.m. curfew!

If It Doesn't Taste Yummy, It's Worthless

Midmorning the next day, we headed to Soverato Dolci for coffee and pastries before driving to Serra San Bruno in the mountains. The museum was closed so we headed back down the mountain to il mare (the sea), where it was warmer. We had a very nice lunch at La Cabana restaurant on the beach (literally) in Pietragrande, the beach town below the school.

After a few hours of downtime, we went to Al Fondaco for dinner. Al Fondaco serves superbly prepared Calabrian food. We only ordered wine and antipasto to start since the server said that the antipasto was abbondante (abundant). It sure was. Over the course of an hour we got plate after bowl after platter of food. We did manage to order a few plates of pasta after the antipasto (and a second liter of wine), but anything more was unthinkable except, of course, espresso and an amaro.

Rolled and stuffed eggplant at Al Fondaco. (See page 146 for a recipe.)

We went to bed happy and full. We also woke up happy and full!

After a leisurely breakfast on Sunday the seventeenth, we drove to Soverato and walked the lungomare (walkway along the sea) for what Italians would call la passeggiata (an after-meal stroll). Because it was Sunday, lots of folks were doing the same. We had lunch at a small restaurant in Soverato followed by pastry and coffee at Soverato Dolci.

We drove to Lamezia Terme and had an unremarkable drive through the old part of town before heading to the airport and saying goodbye to Zia Fidalma, Massimo, and Francesca.

There were a few of us at the school for dinner. Chef John had prepared an amazing meal of ricotta gnocchi with spicy sausage in tomato sauce followed by a shredded cabbage salad that was followed by beautifully sautéed pork medallions with a rich sauce (I'm ashamed to say I don't remember what the vegetable was!). For dessert we had a caramelized ricotta cheesecake with rum-soaked raisins.

After breakfast the next morning, Frank and I set off for our adventure in Matera, an adventure that started in the servants' quarters of a palazzo in Piazza Duomo. Before that, however, we had some really good sandwiches at an AutoGrill on the Autostrada. The quality of the food in Italy is amazing. Here we were, essentially at a place to grab a quick bite at a highway rest stop, and the sandwiches were memorable! The gas station attendant also ran a small shop selling Calabrian food products. Seasonal and regional are big concepts in Italian food.

Along the lungomare in Soverato (left to right) myself, cousin Massimo, Great Aunt Fidalma, cousin Francesca, and my husband, Frank.

Matera is a UNESCO World Heritage Site. It has a long (and at times disturbing) history. I won't try to recap Matera's history here since that is better covered by travel books and websites, but I will say that it is worth every minute of a long visit. I'm sorry that we're only here for two days.

While in Matera, we tried to eat local food. The area is famous for peppers that are fried until crispy and dark in spots. Interestingly, they are not at all spicy, but they are very flavorful. As Chef John says, "If it doesn't taste yummy, it's worthless."

In my next post, I'll describe what we did in the pastry lab before the pizza session, as well as talk about our trip to Sicily.

FAGIOLI E VERDURE
Beans and Greens

I usually have containers of cooked beans in the freezer that I use for a variety of dishes including pasta e fagioli and beans and greens. The instructions provided here will make more beans than you need for this recipe. I encourage you to freeze the extra. You can use borlotti, cranberry, Roman, or red kidney beans for this recipe.

BEANS

Metric Measure	Ingredient	American Measure
450 grams	Dry beans (see headnote)	1 pound
3 cloves	Garlic, bruised with a chef's knife	3 cloves
3 tablespoons	Extra-virgin olive oil	3 tablespoons
½ teaspoon	Whole black peppercorns	½ teaspoon
1	Bay leaf, preferably fresh	1
1 tablespoon	Salt, preferably fine sea salt	1 tablespoon

1. Wash and drain the beans. Cover generously with water and refrigerate overnight.

2. The next day, drain and rinse the beans. Combine all ingredients, except the salt, in an oven-safe pot with a lid. Add enough water to cover the beans by 5 centimeters (2 inches). Cover the pot and bring the beans to a gentle boil on the stovetop and then cook in the oven at 120°C (250°F) for 1 hour.

3. Add the salt, stir well, and continue cooking until the beans are tender but not mushy. This could be 45 minutes to 1 hour, or longer, depending on the type of beans, their age, and your elevation. Remember, the beans will continue to cook from residual heat for a while after they are removed from the oven.

GREENS AND ASSEMBLY

Greens other than spinach are very much at home in this dish, including endive, escarole, and even broccoli rabe. The cooking time will be longer for other greens.

Metric Measure	Ingredient	American Measure
300 grams	Spinach or other greens (see headnote)	10 ounces
60 milliliters	Extra-virgin olive oil	¼ cup
2 cloves	Garlic, sliced	2 cloves
To taste	Crushed red pepper	To taste
500 milliliters	Cooked beans with cooking liquid to cover	2 cups
To taste	Salt, preferably fine sea salt	To taste
To taste	Freshly grated black pepper	To taste

1. Bring a large pot of heavily salted water to a boil over high heat. Add the spinach. As soon as the water boils, remove the spinach and shock it in a large bowl of ice water. As soon as the spinach has cooled, drain it.

2. Combine the olive oil, garlic, and red pepper in a small sauté pan. Cook over low heat until the garlic is golden. Reserve.

3. In a shallow pan, combine the cooked beans and their cooking liquid with the drained spinach. Simmer approximately 5 minutes, adjusting the salt and pepper.

4. Scrape in the flavored olive oil along with the garlic slices and the red pepper. Simmer 1 minute longer. Serve with lots of crusty bread.

BOMBA CALABRESE
Calabrian Preserved Spicy Eggplant

If you cannot get Calabrian hot chile peppers (peperoncini piccante), use fresh cayenne or serrano peppers. The amounts given here can be increased or decreased. The bell pepper and onion should each be equal to half the weight of the eggplant. If using quantities different from what is listed in the recipe, calculate the salt as noted in the directions.

Metric Measure	Ingredient	American Measure
350 grams	Peeled and sliced eggplant (see below)	12 ounces
See below	Canning and pickling salt	See below
175 grams	Finely diced red bell pepper	6 ounces
175 grams	Finely diced onion	6 ounces
30 grams or to taste	Minced fresh hot red chile pepper	1 ounce or to taste
500 milliliters	White wine vinegar	2¼ cups
As needed	Extra-virgin olive oil	As needed

1. Using a mandoline, slice the eggplant 4.5 millimeters (1/6 inch) thick. Salt the slices liberally on both sides with canning and pickling salt, which contains no additives. Put the slices on a nonreactive rack, such as a plastic grate, set at an angle.

2. Combine the bell pepper, onion, and chile pepper. Weigh the mixture. Add 2.6 percent salt by weight (that is, multiply the weight by 0.026 to get the amount of salt in grams or ounces). For the amounts listed, that would be 9.88 grams (0.34 ounces). Mix well and weigh the vegetables down to keep them under the brine, which will develop quickly.

3. After 12 hours, cut the eggplant into a tiny dice and put the pieces into a heat proof bowl.

4. Pour the bell pepper mixture into a sieve and allow it to drain well.

5. Bring the vinegar to a boil. Pour the boiling vinegar over the diced eggplant. Swish well for approximately 60 seconds to dissolve all the salt. Pour the vinegar-eggplant mixture into the sieve with the bell pepper mixture, allowing it to drain well.

6. Put the drained vegetables into a double thickness of cheesecloth. Put the packet into a vegetable press or a potato ricer and squeeze to remove as much liquid as possible.

7. Weigh the mixture after squeezing out the liquid and add 2.6 percent salt by weight. That is, multiply the weight of the eggplant-pepper-onion mixture by 0.026. Add enough extra-virgin olive oil to create a slurry.

8. Fill clean jars with the slurry. Top up with extra-virgin olive oil, sliding a knife blade into each jar several times to allow air to escape. Seal and allow to mature at room temperature for several weeks before using.

Melanzane Imbottite

Stuffed Eggplant Rolls

To make the breadcrumbs, cut the crust from a few slices of one- or two-day-old Italian bread and whiz it in the food processor. In a pinch, you can use plain panko breadcrumbs. Scamorza, provolone, and mozzarella cheeses will all work, but the flavor will be somewhat different. Heck, you could use a bit of each if you have them in your fridge!

Metric Measure	Ingredient	American Measure
1	Purple eggplant, approximately 450 grams (1 pound) and 25 centimeters (9½ inches) long	1
As needed	Extra-virgin olive oil to brush eggplant	As needed
30 grams	Coarse breadcrumbs	1 ounce
40 grams	Scamorza, Provolone, or Mozzarella cheese, grated	1⅓ ounces
25 grams	Soppressata or other spicy salame, minced	Scant 1 ounce
1–2 cloves	Garlic, minced	1–2 cloves
1½ tablespoons	Minced parsley	1½ tablespoons
7 grams	Grated Pecorino Romano cheese	¼ ounce
3 tablespoons	Extra-virgin olive oil	3 tablespoons

To taste	Salt, preferably fine sea salt	To taste
To taste	Freshly ground black pepper	To taste
~250 milliliters	Basic Tomato Sauce (page 131)	~1 cup
To taste	Dried oregano	To taste

1. Peel the eggplant, if desired. Slice lengthwise into slabs 6 millimeters (¼ inch) thick using a mandoline.

2. Brush one side of each eggplant slice with olive oil. Heat a dry nonstick sauté pan over medium heat. Put as many eggplant slices as will comfortably fit in the pan, oiled-side down. Brush the top of each eggplant slice with olive oil. Cook the eggplant, flipping two or three times, until softened and browned in places but not mushy, approximately 4 to 5 minutes total. Cook the remaining eggplant slices in the same way.

3. Combine the breadcrumbs, scamorza, soppressata, garlic, parsley, Pecorino Romano cheese, and olive oil. Season with salt and pepper.

4. Divide the filling among the eggplant slices, mounding it near the wider end of each slice. Roll the eggplant to encase the filling.

5. Spread a little tomato sauce in the bottom of a baking dish just large enough to hold the eggplant rolls without crowding.

6. Put the eggplant rolls on top of the sauce, seam-side down.

7. Spread a little tomato sauce on the top of each eggplant roll. Sprinkle with oregano.

8. Bake at 180°C (350°C) until heated through, approximately 20 minutes.

OLIO SANTO
Hot Chile Oil

Olio santo (holy oil, as it is playfully called in Calabria) is a common condiment on many tables. It can be made from both dried red chiles and fresh red chiles. Dried chiles are easier to source, so I use them in this recipe. The heat level and flavor profile will vary from chile to chile, but feel free to use whatever dried red chiles you can get. Just be sure they are piccante (spicy)! There is always a squeeze bottle of olio santo by my stove and often one on the table.

Metric Measure	Ingredient	American Measure
25 grams	Dried red chile, stems removed	1 ounce
250 grams	Extra-virgin olive oil	1⅓ cups

If It Doesn't Taste Yummy, It's Worthless

1. Lightly crush the dried chile.
2. Combine the chile and olive oil in a small, nonreactive pot.
3. Heat to 120°C (250°F), stirring often. Immediately remove from the heat and allow to cool to room temperature, uncovered.
4. Repeat the heating and cooling process two more times.
5. After the mixture has cooled for the third time. Pour it into a glass jar. Cover loosely and keep out of direct sunlight.
6. Swirl one or two times each day for 7 to 10 days then strain the mixture. Discard the chile.

CROSTATA DI RICOTTA
Ricotta Tart

Made with ricotta, this is much lighter than an American cheesecake. I always keep jars of lemon oil and orange oil in my refrigerator. They add much more flavor than extract. If you don't have orange oil, you can substitute the finely grated zest of 1 orange.

Metric Measure	Ingredient	American Measure
1 recipe	Pasta Frolla (page 149)	1 recipe
500 grams	Whole milk ricotta, preferably homemade (page 246)	17½ ounces
2 large	Eggs	2 large
175 grams	Granulated sugar	⅞ cup
¼ teaspoon	Salt, preferably fine sea salt	¼ teaspoon
1 teaspoon	Orange oil	1 teaspoon
1 teaspoon	Vanilla extract	1 teaspoon
1 tablespoon	Orange liqueur, such as Cointreau	1 tablespoon
65 grams	Miniature chocolate chips, if desired	2⅓ ounces

1. Roll out the pasta frolla between sheets of parchment or waxed paper until it is large enough to line the bottom and sides of a 27 x 2.5–centimeter (9½ x 1 inch) tart pan with a removable bottom.
2. Cut the pasta frolla level with the top of the pan. Using a fork, prick the bottom of the crust in numerous locations. Refrigerate the crust while making the filling.
3. Using a hand whisk, whisk together the ricotta, eggs, sugar, salt, orange oil, vanilla, and orange liqueur until smooth. Stir in the chocolate chips, if using.
4. Pour the filling into the crust-lined pan.

5. Bake at 180°C (350°F) until set and the crust is brown, approximately 35 to 40 minutes.

6. Cool completely and then remove the sides of the pan.

PASTA FROLLA
Shortcrust Pastry

Pasta frolla is the standard Italian shortcrust pastry for most anything requiring a crust. It is much less fussy than American pie crust. It resembles Scottish shortbread but is slightly less crumbly. Paolo Mariani flour for *dolci* (sweets) is an example of a flour with the correct W-value. Most "vanilla" used in domestic baking in Italy is powdered artificial vanilla. I use powdered real vanilla instead. You could use 1 packet of Italian (artificial) vanilla powder if you want. In place of the lemon oil, you could use the finely grated zest of ½ lemon.

Metric Measure	Ingredient	American Measure
300 grams	Italian 00 flour W-180	2¼ cups
100 grams	Granulated sugar	½ cup
½ teaspoon	Baking powder	½ teaspoon
¾ teaspoon	Powdered vanilla	¾ teaspoon
Pinch	Salt, preferably fine sea salt	Pinch
85 grams	Unsalted butter, chilled	6 tablespoons
¼ teaspoon	Lemon oil	¼ teaspoon
2 large	Eggs	2 large

1. Blend the flour, sugar, baking powder, powdered vanilla, and salt in a food processor.

2. Add the butter, cut into pieces, and lemon oil. Blend until crumbly.

3. Add the eggs and blend until the mixture almost forms a ball.

4. Remove the pastry from the food processor and work by hand until a cohesive mass is formed.

5. Flaten the pasta frolla into a circle, wrap in parchment or waxed paper, and refrigerate for about 30 minutes before using.

6. When rolling out, place the pastry between sheets of parchment or waxed paper.

7. If the dough begins to get too soft as it is being rolled, slide it onto an inverted half-sheet pan and place it in the refrigerator for a few minutes.

How Far Over the Top Can We Go?

FEBRUARY 27

I feel like I'm living in a Fellini movie. Consumption of food and alcohol has reached amazing proportions. Take Monday, for example.

Monday, February 25, was day five of our sommelier training. Sommelier days started in the kitchen with food preparation and consumption and ended with about three to four hours of wine tasting (followed by dinner…and more wine!).

The previous night, Sunday, we went out for pizza, drinks, and karaoke, so Monday started at the unusually late hour of 10 a.m. (except for those of us who had signed up for baking duty).

In the kitchen at 10, Chef John immediately prepared a plate of tortino di semolino (similar to semolina gnocchi but cut into larger pieces) accompanied by a fried egg, steamed spinach, tomato sauce, and feta cheese. Next, we had a bowl of tripe stewed in tomato sauce, topped with battered and fried onion rings and seared foie gras, and accompanied by crostata. Following that was bavette (similar to linguine) with a sauce of baby octopus and tomato sauce and plated with octopus carpaccio.

At this point it was now noon. Only two hours had passed and we had consumed a day's worth of food.

Shortly after noon we were served maltagliati pasta with braised oxtail, fava beans, rosemary oil, and Parmesan cheese. This was followed by a "milkshake" made of house-made fiordilatte gelato, heavy cream, and bourbon vanilla paste! Now it was shortly after 12:30.

Octopus carpaccio. (See page 172 for a recipe.)

We were then turned over to Chef Juan for a lecture on calculating food costs during the height of our postprandial somnolence. At 2:15 p.m. we went into our fifth day of wine tasting with Chef Mark.

We tasted only four wines, a very short list compared to the other days, as Chef Mark McDonald, who is also a sommelier, was making a five-course wine-pairing dinner for us that evening. The afternoon wines were paired with a dish of boned quail stuffed with truffle-and-cream-laced bread stuffing, seared in a mixture of olive oil and lardo di Colonnata, served with a potato and celery root puree, matchstick beets, seared cauliflower, pomegranate syrup, and pomegranate. The idea was to evaluate how each of the wines paired with this very complex dish. (Generally not well, is the answer.)

Cooked and pressed octopus ready to be thinly sliced into carpaccio. (See page 172 for a recipe for octopus carpaccio.)

Blessedly, we had a few hours off so that Chef Mark could cook. Around 4:30 p.m. I headed to my suite. At 5 p.m. I decided to take a quick nap, thinking I really wouldn't sleep. When my alarm went off at 7, I couldn't figure out why the alarm was sounding before the sun had risen. It took me a few moments to realize that it was evening and that I had to be at dinner at 7:30.

Dinner was a five-course meal that was not Italian but was designed to explore wine pairings. The first course was an Indonesian-inspired shrimp curry in coconut milk. Next was a vegetarian plate of broccoli and cauliflower, each prepared three ways including pureed, pickled, and cooked. Next was a Mexican-inspired albondigas soup in a very flavorful broth made from house-cured pancetta and multiple types of dried chile. The main course was chicken thighs braised in beer. The braising liquid was used as the base for a peanut mole. The dish was served with a cornbread that was very much like a corn pudding. Dessert was a tris of Gorgonzola: Gorgonzola cheesecake sprinkled with chopped pistachios, shortbread with a Gorgonzola cream sauce and a sweetened pistachio puree, and a ball of Gorgonzola with orange-blossom honey. Each dish was accompanied by a different wine except for the chicken, which was accompanied by the same beer in which it was cooked.

Doesn't this experience sound like something from a Fellini movie?

This is pretty much how the previous four days had gone as well. The first day of this week-long session was Thursday the twenty-first. It was the first day after our five-day break. In the morning, we went to the market in Catanzaro Lido. Frank, my husband, who was still visiting, came with. While looking at the stall of a vendor selling ceramic and terracotta wares, I was quoted a price of €10 for a ceramic spoon rest. I thought it was expensive compared to other similar items that actually had price tags. I was about to leave when an Italian woman came up and began a very animated conversation with us. I told her, in my limited Italian, that I was a student at the Italian Culinary Institute. The conversation continued for a while with me struggling to understand and respond. Then she pointed out a two-part terracotta contraption meant to hold a candle to heat 'nduja in a small terracotta bowl. The warm 'nduja was to be spread on bruschetta. I confirmed that I loved 'nduja. She told the vendor to give us a good price so I took the plunge and said I'd take the spoon rest and 'nduja warmer, expecting to be quoted something like €25. Instead, the price for both was €13!

When Frank and I wrapped up shopping, we sat at a nearby bar having espresso. (A "bar" in Italy has typically meant a coffee bar; though with the younger generation, and as the language progresses, it could mean either that or a venue selling alcohol or both.) Teresa, our new friend from the market, came by and said she was buying us another round of coffee. She did so and briefly sat with us. She is a commanding presence.

Despite being very lively, she spoke Italian (to us) clearly and slowly so that I understood almost everything, learning about her children who are living in Russia, for example.

Following the market, we went to Scolacium Archaeological Park. The area of the park was originally inhabited by the Greeks, followed by the Romans, followed by… you get it, the usual story of Italy! It was discovered when the owner was working on his olive grove.

Back at school, lunch was a multicourse affair that included rabbit, which Frank loved. (Don't tell his mother! He's convinced her that he doesn't like rabbit, which, of course, isn't true. He's also convinced her that he doesn't like fish and soup, which also isn't true.)

That afternoon was our first session with Chef Mark. We were instructed in a method to analyze wine and tasted five different wines. I'm sad to say that I didn't make any notes about dinner, nor did I take any pictures, so it's lost. Though I know for sure that I didn't have any wine!

Zuppa di Pesce, Frogs' Legs, and Beyond

The next morning, we started with a hands-on lesson in the kitchen. Afterward, Chef John used many of the ingredients we had prepped to make dishes for us to eat. I took the lead on making spinach pici. Pici are thin, rolled pasta similar in length to spaghetti but a little thicker and hand-rolled. As I write this, the pici have not shown up on any plate served to us. Sometimes the chefs eat the food, sometimes (but rarely) it is disposed of, and sometimes it appears weeks later!

First to be prepared and served was broccoli rabe and (huge balls of) burrata dressed with extra-virgin olive oil (we go through gallons per week), lemon juice, anchovies, and garlic all blitzed in a food processor. Following that we had a riff on a Sicilian

Broccoli rabe and burrata with lemon-anchovy dressing. (See page XX for a recipe.)

dish: pasta alla sarde (pasta with sardines), but made with anchovies, which Chef John prefers to sardines. We tasted house-cured bottarga and then moved on to an exceedingly complex zuppa di pesce (fish soup).

Pasta alla sarde but made with anchovies instead of sardines.

To make the fish soup, Chef John first made a light fish stock from bones and heads with some veggies and tomato puree. He cooked mussels and added the cooking liquid to the broth, which was ultimately frappéd and strained before using. He baked whole langostino after coating the tails in seasoned breadcrumbs. He sautéed shrimp in shrimp butter, which was made by combining equal parts butter and fresh whole shrimp and cooking and mashing them together until the shrimp started to crackle and brown, at which time the butter was strained and the shrimp discarded. He cooked branzino (sea bass) filets in butter. Then and only then was the soup assembled. Into the bowls went mussels, branzino, shrimp, and fish broth. On top went the langostino. A piece of focaccia was artistically inserted along the side.

The soup was followed by lollipopped frogs' legs (which we had previously prepped and which had been frozen for a couple of weeks) cooked in brown butter and then doused with prosecco. After the frogs' legs he made sarde in saor, a Venetian dish of floured and deep-fried sardines layered with an onion mixture. The onion mixture is made by cooking lots of thinly sliced onion in lots and lots of olive oil. When soft, vinegar, sugar, and raisins are added. Mercifully, this dish needed to marinate, so it didn't get served until dinner.

Chef John also demonstrated how to make conserved tuna and his version of eggplant Parmigiana. The Parmigiana also appeared at dinner. The tuna is in jars waiting for another day!

At this point, Chef Mark got us for an afternoon of wine tasting. We tasted seven wines before I took a predinner nap!

One-Hour Delay

The next day, February 23, started with making two breads: honey bread and butter bread. Both would end up on plates over the next two days. Most notably, the butter bread was used to make soft-shell crab sandwiches!

Chef John then made, and we ate, fish tartare with crispy fish skin. Following this was a beautiful octopus carpaccio (the extra of which would be served on the twenty-fifth along with pasta and a sauce of baby octopus). Chef John then made two different olio cotura dishes: one salmon and one spatula. Spatula is a long fish with nasty sharp teeth that looks like a barracuda. Olio cotura basically involves poaching something in oil. We ate both of these later in the day served with a caper foam that Chef Juan whipped up.

The day in the kitchen ended with vitello tonnato, traditionally thinly sliced cold poached veal served with tuna fish mayonnaise and capers. Rather than poach the veal, Chef John cooked it sous vide. The small amount of liquid from the sous vide was incorporated into the mayonnaise along with house-cured tuna. After the vitello tonnato we had tomato soup made from house-canned tomato puree followed by cotoletta alla Milanese, thinly sliced veal or beef, breaded and fried in clarified butter! We went to the dining room for lunch (yes, lunch) of pasta with a sauce of pureed house-cured and smoked salmon and cream.

Chef Mark then started an afternoon of wine tasting. I think we had six wines based on my notes.

On the twenty-fourth, Chef John demonstrated the cooking of the oxtail that was served on the twenty-fifth with pasta and fava beans. He also started the baby octopus sauce for the next day. With those demos out of the way, he cooked something that was served to us: chickpeas with infused olive oil, the kind of simple peasant food I love!

We then had tuna croquettes served with the shrimp demi followed by sausages made of baccalà (salted cod) for which Chef Juan stood in the back of the kitchen for over an hour stuffing tiny, tiny casings using a funnel and his fingers, served with polenta and salsa livornese! We made two kinds of arancini, but after I deep-fried the first batch, the remainder were put away for another day (sometimes restraint shows through, but not often).

Chef John started the tripe that was served the next day as well as his take on Buffalo wings that involved turkey wings, peperoncino picante, and twenty hours of sous vide before the cooking liquid got turned into a sauce using 'nduja and butter! These didn't make it to the table until the afternoon of the twenty-sixth, when they were served with a beer tasting headed up by Chef Mark.

Chef John then demonstrated the preparation of the quail that would end up on a tasting plate the next day (along with truffle stuffing seared in olive oil, lardo di Colonnata, and other tasty bites). The day in the kitchen ended with battered and fried soft-shell crabs served on butter bread with tomato sauce and cheese.

Chef Mark's wine tasting involved five wines. We had a few hours to recover before going out for pizza, karaoke, and alcohol. The school paid for the first round of drinks for everyone. A few of us then ordered another drink, not knowing that Chef Mark would buy bottles of liquor for the table! I was among those with the smallest alcohol consumption that evening (three Jack Daniel's, two Obans, two rums, and about three or four gins, one of which involved a bottle being poured into my mouth—well, mostly onto my face—while on the dance floor).

You now understand why the next day started at 10 a.m. instead of 9.

Baccala (salted cod) sausage with polenta and salsa Livornese.

ANTIPASTO DI BURRATA E CIME DI RAPA
Burrata and Broccoli Rabe Antipasto

Often I just serve an antipasto and pasta for dinner. Some of my favorite pasta dishes are low-protein affairs so I look for an antipasto that can fill the gap. Burrata and broccoli rabe adds protein to the meal with an amazing textural contrast. In Italy, you can find burrata almost the size of tennis balls. Feel free to use several smaller ones if large ones are not available. Serve this at room temperature so that the burrata is creamier. The quantities below are for one person; scale up as necessary.

Metric Measure	Ingredient	American Measure
2–3 stalks	Broccoli rabe	2–3 stalks
2 teaspoons	Anchovy-Garlic Paste (page 29)	2 teaspoons
1 tablespoon	Extra-virgin olive oil	1 tablespoon
2 teaspoons	Freshly squeezed lemon juice	2 teaspoons
1 large	Ball of burrata	1 large
To taste	Salt, preferably flaky sea salt	To taste
To taste	Freshly ground black pepper	To taste

1. Cut the broccoli rabe into pieces. The first cut should be just below the point where the thinner stems from the florets come together to form the larger stem, keeping the florets together. Reserve the florets separately from the leaves and thicker stems.

2. Peel the stems. Using a sharp paring knife, slip the blade just under the outer layer of one of the stems. Press your thumb against the side of the knife to catch the outer layer and then peel down, like a banana, to remove the fibrous outer layer. Repeat the whole way around the stem. Peel all the stems. Cut the stems into pieces about 5 centimeters (2 inches) long.

3. Bring 3 liters (3 quarts) of water seasoned with 75 grams (¼ cup) of salt to a rolling boil.

4. When the water comes to a boil, add the peeled broccoli rabe stems and leaves and boil until just tender, approximately 2 to 3 minutes. Lift the stems out of the water and plunge into ice water to stop cooking.

5. Add the florets to the boiling water and cook 1 to 2 minutes or until just tender. Add the florets to the ice water with the stems. Drain the cooked broccoli rabe in a sieve.

How Far Over the Top Can We Go?

6. Thin the anchovy-garlic paste with the olive oil until it is just pourable. Add the lemon juice. Taste and adjust the olive oil and lemon juice to suit your preferences.

7. Put the broccoli rabe stems and leaves on the bottom of a plate. Put the burrata on top. Put some of the florets on top of the broccoli rabe and sprinkle the rest around the plate.

8. Drizzle with the dressing. Season with freshly ground black pepper and flaky sea salt.

Ceci con Olio Infuso
Chickpeas with Infused Oil

These amazing chickpeas can be used as a vegetarian secondo (what Americans would call the main course) or as a great antipasto (appetizer). Serve with focaccia or ciabatta to soak up the luscious broth and olive oil.

Metric Measure	Ingredient	American Measure
200 grams	Dried chickpeas	7 ounces
3 cloves	Garlic, thinly sliced	3 cloves
3	Bay leaves, preferably fresh	3
1 teaspoon	Crushed red pepper, preferably Calabrian peperoncino	1 teaspoon
135 milliliters	Extra-virgin olive oil	½ cup plus 1 tablespoon
1½ teaspoons	Salt, preferably fine sea salt	1½ teaspoons
70 grams	Finely diced onion	2½ ounces
To taste	Freshly ground black pepper	To taste

1. Rinse and drain the chickpeas. Cover with water and refrigerate overnight.

2. Meanwhile, make the infused oil. Combine the garlic, bay leaves, crushed red pepper, and 90 milliliters (6 tablespoons) of the olive oil in a small pot. Heat until the garlic is just beginning to sizzle. Remove from the heat and allow to cool. Repeat the heating and cooling process two more times. After the last time, strain the oil, pressing on the solids to extract as much oil as possible.

3. The next day, drain the chickpeas, cover with fresh water 2½ centimeters (1 inch) over the chickpeas. Cook at a gentle boil for 15 minutes.

4. Add the salt and cook until almost tender, approximately 15 minutes longer. Cool in the cooking liquid and then drain, reserving the cooking liquid.

5. Combine the cooled chickpeas, onion, and 45 milliliters (3 tablespoons) of the olive oil in a heavy-bottomed saucepan. Sauté over medium heat until there are lots of brown bits in the pan and some of the chickpeas have brown spots.

6. Add the reserved cooking liquid to the chickpeas and simmer 15 minutes, seasoning with black pepper to taste. At the end, the broth should just cover the chickpeas.

7. Portion the chickpeas into small bowls. Top each portion with some of the infused oil.

Maltagliati con Ragù di Code di Bue
Maltagliati Pasta with Oxtail Ragù

This rustic sauce is especially good with thicker pasta shapes. If you're feeling ambitious, make Fresh Egg Pasta (page 45), roll it out to approximately #5 on your pasta machine, and then cut it into irregular triangles or squares, called *maltagliati*. Otherwise, consider a sturdy artisanal pasta such as busiati, fileja, calamarata, or fusilloni, among others. This makes enough sauce for 1 kilogram (2¼ pounds) of dry pasta or 3 recipes (1.2 kilograms or 2⅔ pounds) of fresh egg pasta.

Oxtail Ragù

Metric Measure	Ingredient	American Measure
1 (1-kilogram) can	Canned peeled tomatoes	1 (35-ounce) can
1 kilogram	Oxtail, cut crosswise	2¼ pounds
75 milliliters	Extra-virgin olive oil	2½ tablespoons
100 grams	Minced carrot	3½ ounces
100 grams	Minced onion	3½ ounces
100 grams	Minced celery	3½ ounces
4 cloves	Garlic, minced	4 cloves
100 grams	Tomato paste	3½ ounces
200 milliliters	Dry red wine	¾ cup plus 1 tablespoon
500 milliliters	Beef broth, Chicken Broth (page 15), or Vegetable Broth (page 161)	2 cups plus 1 tablespoon
1	Bay leaf, preferably fresh	1
1 teaspoon	Minced fresh thyme	1 teaspoon
1 teaspoon	Dried oregano	1 teaspoon
To taste	Salt, preferably fine sea salt	To taste
To taste	Freshly ground black pepper	To taste

1. Pass the tomatoes through a food mill. Reserve the resulting puree.

2. In a heavy-bottomed Dutch oven, brown the oxtail in the olive oil. Remove and reserve the oxtail.

3. Using the same pot and oil, sauté the carrot, onion, celery, and garlic until soft. Do not brown the vegetables.

4. Add the tomato paste to the vegetables and sauté, stirring frequently, until it is slightly darker and sweet-smelling, 1 to 2 minutes.

5. Add the wine and boil gently to evaporate.

6. Add the broth, pureed tomatoes, and browned oxtail with any collected juices from the oxtail. Bring to a boil. Reduce to a simmer.

7. Add the bay leaf, thyme, oregano, salt, and pepper. Simmer, partially covered, for approximately 3 to 4 hours, adding water as needed.

8. Allow the ragù to cool. Remove the oxtail and separate the meat from the bone, gristle, and fat. Shred the meat and return to the ragù.

PASTA AND ASSEMBLY

Metric Measure	Ingredient	American Measure
½ recipe	Oxtail Ragù (page 159)	½ recipe
500 grams dry or 600 grams fresh	Dry or fresh pasta	~1 pound dry or 20 ounces fresh
To taste	Salt, preferably fine sea salt	To taste
To taste	Freshly ground black pepper	To taste
45 grams	Freshly grated Parmigiano Reggiano cheese	1½ ounces
To taste	Rosemary Oil (page 262)	To taste
To garnish	Basil chiffonade	To garnish

1. Bring 3 liters (3 quarts) of water seasoned with 75 grams (¼ cup) of salt to a rolling boil.

2. Meanwhile, heat the Oxtail Ragù in a large sauté pan.

3. Add the pasta to the boiling salted water and cook at a rapid boil for approximately 2 minutes less than the minimum cooking time on the package for al dente pasta, stirring frequently to prevent sticking.

4. Drain the pasta, reserving the pasta-cooking water.

5. Add the par-cooked pasta to the ragù in the sauté pan and finish cooking at a moderate boil, adding the reserved pasta-cooking water 1 ladle at a time, shaking the pan and stirring the pasta, until the pasta is al dente, leaving the sauce liquid enough to just coat the pasta. Adjust the salt and pepper while finishing the pasta.

6. Off the heat, add the cheese and rosemary oil and then flip and stir the pasta to emulsify the cheese and sauce. Add a bit more cooking water if the sauce is too thick.

7. Garnish each serving with basil chiffonade.

BRODO DI VERDURE
Vegetable Broth

This vegetable broth is quick to make. It packs a lot of flavor. If you are making the broth for a specific dish, rather than to have on hand, feel free to add other mild-tasting vegetables that would compliment the dish, such as mushrooms.

Metric Measure	Ingredient	American Measure
85 grams	Shredded carrot	3 ounces
85 grams	Shredded celery	3 ounces
50 grams	Thinly sliced onion	1¾ ounces
1	Garlic clove, thinly sliced	1
1 teaspoon	Tomato paste	1 teaspoon
3	Whole black peppercorns	3
700 milliliters	Water	3 cups

1. Peel the carrots. Shred the carrot and celery using the teardrop holes of a box grater or finely chop.

2. Combine all ingredients in a stockpot.

3. Boil gently, partially covered, for 25 minutes. Strain and discard solids.

Italy Is Blessed with Poor Distribution

MARCH 3

Sommelier Week ended on February 26 with a morning tasting! Got that? Alcohol for breakfast!

To be sure, one reads lots about wine experts swishing and spitting when tasting wine, and I suspect they do much of the time. I've always found that a bit curious, though. Granted, without swishing and spitting, the accuracy and reliability of the tasting would decrease as the event went on (which, based on some recently written critiques, isn't worth much in the first place). Nonetheless, there is a whole sensory experience that happens when you actually swallow the wine that cannot be achieved by swishing and spitting. At least that's been my experience.

I was pleased then, when, on the first day of Sommelier Week, Chef Mark suggested that we actually swallow the wine, at least once for each wine tasted. I can truthfully report that everyone swallowed every time. There was no swishing and spitting among members of our group.

Orlando's coffee helped me get through sommelier week, during which Orlando started decorating my cappuccino with chocolate syrup.

The morning tasting started with a very small pour of each of two different vintages of a Lebanese white wine. The vintages were 2003 and 2001. Each wine could still age for another ten years. That is amazing for white wine! And, when you consider everything Lebanon has been through, it is nothing short of miraculous that wines like this are still produced.

We had a quick taste of a 1997 Riesling before moving on to beer.

Think about it. Beer is made from grain and yeast. It's really just liquid bread, right? Not so bad for breakfast after all!

Okay, okay, so I exaggerated a bit. We spent a few hours in the kitchen preparing for the evening meal before starting our morning wine and beer tasting with Chef Mark.

That evening was a new experience. We've had a pizza night, where each of us made a pizza of our choice in the wood-fired oven to share with everyone. We had a menu execution for which, as a group, we had to create and execute a multi-course menu. We had a pizza and cocktail night where, in teams of two, we had to devise a cocktail and a pizza that paired together and execute both in ten minutes!

The lineup of pasta dishes for pasta night. We were not told of the order of service until immediately before we had to go into the kitchen.

On the last day of Sommelier Week, however, we each had to make a first course for eighteen people. These were executed in succession. One student made soup, another risotto. The rest of us made pasta—starting by making the pasta by hand that morning.

In the lead-up to Pasta Night (which should rightfully be called Primo Piatto Night), each of us had to submit three different options for what we wanted to make. The chefs then decided which dish each of us would make. We were informed of our dishes in the morning, when we then set about preparing everything for that evening's dinner.

I got to make pasta alla chitarra with mussels in tomato sauce with peperoncino. My other options were linguine with clams in white sauce and lasagne alla Bolognese. I have become enamored of the chitarra.

Chitarra is the Italian word for guitar. It is also the word for a device that is used to cut pasta using guitar strings. It fascinates me far more than cutting pasta using a pasta machine. Apparently, the chitarra cuts the edges of the pasta more sharply, causing a different reaction with the sauce than is obtained using a pasta machine. (Italians are truly food-obsessed, and discussions like this are not uncommon, even among non-chefs.)

After each of us made and served our primo piatto (first course, which can be pasta, risotto, or soup), the chefs also each created a primo piatto. Each chef, that is, except Chef John (who

My pasta alla chitarra with mussels and spicy tomato sauce.

164 Dispatches from Calabria

runs the school) and Chef Chris, who was planning on making a barley risotto (orzotto) that got shelved until Saturday dinner due to time constraints. Chef Juan made a chocolate dessert.

Pizzo and Tropea Adventure

It was a lazy few days after Pasta Night. We had two days off followed by a slow Friday followed by another day off.

A view of the sea in Tropea. The church on top of the hill was also closed, like seemingly nearly every other attraction in Tropea and Pizzo.

On Wednesday, the day after Pasta Night, eight of us hired a driver to take us to Pizzo and Tropea. They are wonderful towns on the west coast of Calabria. Both are also largely closed this time of year.

Pizzo is known for its Grotto Church, carved into the rock. It was closed, though we did manage to snap a few pictures through the metal bars before leaving.

We stopped for gelato across the street, but that place was closed too. The proprietor offered to call the manager of the church to see if he would open for the Americans. Oh, we were told, if we had only come two days later when there would be different opening hours it might have been possible to get in. (Possible only in the sense that the official schedule said the hours were longer starting March 1, not necessarily that the official schedule would be adhered to.)

After gelato, we reconnected with our driver who, before taking us to Tropea, asked us if we wanted to stop at the castle in Pizzo, telling us that it was open. We agreed. The castle, however, was not open even though the signage indicated that it should have been (see the discussion of the church earlier). The benefit, though, was that the castle, unlike the church, is near the piazza, which we otherwise might have missed, and where we had a wonderful al fresco lunch before heading to Tropea. (I had fileja—a local pasta not unlike strozzapreti, but thicker—with a sauce of 'nduja and tomato.)

Tropea was also largely closed. There is a small alimentari (food shop) that several members of our group had been to on a prior visit, but it was shuttered when we arrived. Because most businesses in Calabria (except restaurants) close from 1 p.m. to 4 or 5 p.m., it wasn't clear whether the shop was closed for the season or for the afternoon.

Lucky for us, the alimentari was just closed for the afternoon. After padding around Tropea and finding a crumbing building perched on a bluff overlooking the sea that needed to be purchased and rehabbed, we discovered that the shop was open. I bought two 'nduja salami and a big package of peperoncino.

Our luck did not hold out with the restaurant where we wanted to have dinner, so around 5 p.m., we headed back to the school where we had dinner prepared by Chef Chris.

Enjoying Some Free Time

Thursday was another free day. The chefs made us an amazing brunch. Mariana started us off with mimosas made from freshly squeezed blood oranges. This was followed by eggs benedict on homemade English muffins accompanied by home fries. Next came waffles with market-fresh strawberries and whipped cream.

I opted for a two hour and forty-five minute walk in the afternoon that included the exploration of the hypermarket, Paoletti, in the nearby seaside town of Montepaone Lido.

Friday morning included a shopping trip followed by a free afternoon. After the mercatino in Soverato, we went to a kitchen and restaurant supply store in Catanzaro Lido and then to the Guglielmo store.

Mariana's wonderful blood orange mimosas.

Guglielmo is a local coffee roaster, the fourth largest in Italy. Between the restaurant supply store and the Guglielmo store, I made quite a shopping haul. Frank had taken back to the States my previous purchases (two very large sauté pans for pasta, five cookbooks, silicone molds, plastic drying racks for pasta and cheese, and four jars of spicy condiments), leaving me with more free space in my suitcase.

On Friday, I bought a chitarra for pasta (see earlier); a press for fruits and vegetables (but that is also used at the school for octopus and terrines); a specially coated twine used for cured meats (which is much better than the butcher's twine available in the States); plastic inserts for canning jars to keep the contents submerged under brine, vinegar, or oil; and porcelain espresso cups with the Guglielmo logo made to look like the flimsy disposable plastic cups used throughout Italy.

Saturday was another free day. I was in the kitchen, however, experimenting on a focaccia recipe and making a batch of carne adovada (pork shoulder braised in a bold chile-based sauce), thanks to Frank, who brought New Mexico red chiles on his recent visit.

Whenever we discuss the high quality of raw ingredients available in Italy, Chef John often points to the poor distribution system, which means that most food is hyperlocal. International foods are in very short supply, but if you can content yourself with Italian food, the hyperlocal nature of the food supply means that meals are based on super-good and largely fresh ingredients.

Sitting on my kitchen table is part of my shopping haul from two days ago: a press for fruit and vegetables...oh, and that octopus carpaccio!

Seasonality is a way of life. Italians eat what is in season. Not only is it better, it is cheaper. For example, artichokes are now 10 for €4, less than half of what they were just a couple of weeks ago.

As Chef John says, "Italy is blessed with poor distribution."

Focaccia
Focaccia

This focaccia reheats well, even if frozen. I often make a double batch and cut each loaf in quarters to freeze. A few minutes in a warm oven and you'll have wonderful, fluffy focaccia to accompany your meal. If you live in a dry climate, as I do in Palm Springs, increase the water from 450 grams to 480 grams (from $1^{7}/_{8}$ cup to 2 cups). Don't be shocked by dousing the dough with water and oil. The water creates steam for a fluffy loaf. Antimo Caputo Chef's Flour has the correct W-value.

Dough

Metric Measure	Ingredient	American Measure
750 grams	Italian 00 flour W-320	5½ cups plus 2 tablespoons
7.5 grams	Active dry yeast	¼ ounce
450 grams	Water	1⅞ cups
15 grams	Granulated sugar	1¼ tablespoons
22.5 grams	Salt, preferably fine sea salt	4 teaspoons
75 grams	Lard, room temperature	5 tablespoons plus 1 teaspoon
3 tablespoons plus more for bowl	Extra-virgin olive oil	3 tablespoons plus more for bowl

Salamoia (Brine)

Metric Measure	Ingredient	American Measure
150 grams	Water	⅔ cup
100 grams	Extra-virgin olive oil	½ cup less 2 teaspoons

1. In the bowl of a stand mixer fitted with a dough hook, combine the flour and yeast. Begin to mix on low. Slowly pour about ¾ of the water into the bowl.

2. Add the sugar slowly. Mix well. Add the remaining water.

3. When all the water is incorporated, add the salt. After the salt is incorporated, turn up the speed to develop gluten.

4. After there is good gluten development, reduce the speed and add the lard a little at a time, incorporating each addition. After the lard is incorporated, add the olive oil a little at a time.

5. After the olive oil is incorporated, increase the speed and mix until the dough makes a slapping sound against the bowl and the dough completely cleans the bowl. Pinch a bit of the dough and pull. You should see strands that resemble string in the dough. If not, mix a few minutes longer.

6. Lightly oil a large bowl with extra-virgin olive oil. Remove the dough from the mixer and shape into a smooth ball by repeatedly stretching the dough under itself. Put the dough seam-side down in the oiled bowl. Cover the bowl completely with plastic wrap. Allow the dough to rest at room temperature until it has at least doubled (or tripled) in size, approximately 2½ hours.

7. Lightly oil a 30 x 40 x 5–centimeter (12 x 16 x 2–inch) rectangular pan. Slide the dough into the middle of the pan. Without stretching, press the dough with your fingertips to dimple it and completely fill the pan. You may need to let the dough rest a few times during this process so that the gluten can relax.

8. Whisk together the ingredients for the salamoia. Pour the salamoia over the top of the dough. Allow the dough to proof in a moist environment at about 37°C (99°F) until it reaches the top of the pan, approximately 1 hour.

9. Gently transfer the dough to a preheated 220°C (425°F) oven with convection. Bake approximately 15 minutes and then reduce the heat to 190°C (375°F) and bake about 5 to 10 minutes longer, or until the top is light brown.

10. Remove the focaccia from the oven to a rack. Let the focaccia cool in the pan, covered with a cloth to retain moisture.

Tip: For rosemary focaccia, replace the 3 tablespoons of extra-virgin olive oil in the dough with Rosemary Oil (page 262), and replace 80 grams of the extra-virgin olive oil in the salamoia with rosemary oil. If desired, sprinkle the top with fresh, coarsely chopped rosemary just before putting the focaccia in the oven.

PASTA ALLE VONGOLE
Pasta with Clams

Linguine or bavette pasta are good choices for this dish. However, I really like using calamarati, a large-diameter pasta tube that resembles the cut body of calamari (squid), hence its name. You can remove the clams from their shells if you want a less rustic presentation. Even so, putting 1 clam still in its shell on top of each dish of pasta is a nice touch. A cayenne or serrano chile makes a good stand-in for an Italian peperoncino. You can use extra-virgin olive oil in place of garlic oil to garnish the finished dish.

Metric Measure	Ingredient	American Measure
24–36 as desired	Fresh clams	24–36 as desired
3 tablespoons	Coarse breadcrumbs	3 tablespoons
80 milliliters plus more	Extra-virgin olive oil	1/3 cup plus more
4 cloves	Garlic, bruised with a chef's knife	4 cloves
1	Fresh peperoncino, split, optional	1
250 milliliters	Dry white wine	1 cup
½ teaspoon plus more	Salt, preferably fine sea salt	½ teaspoon plus more
To taste	Freshly ground black pepper	To taste
500 grams	Dry pasta	~1 pound
3 tablespoons	Parsley or basil chiffonade	3 tablespoons
To garnish	Garlic Oil (page 57)	To garnish

1. Rinse the clams in several changes of fresh water.

2. Sauté the breadcrumbs in 2 teaspoons of olive oil until golden and crispy. Remove from heat and reserve.

3. In a heavy-bottomed Dutch oven, sauté the garlic and peperoncino, if using, in the olive oil until the garlic is golden.

4. Add the wine, ½ teaspoon of salt, and black pepper to taste. Boil lightly until reduced by half. Remove the garlic and peperoncino.

5. Add the clams, turn the heat to medium-high, cover the pot, and cook until the clams have opened, approximately 5 to 7 minutes, shaking the pot periodically.

6. As soon as the clams have all opened, pour the contents through a sieve, reserving the cooking liquid separately from the clams. Remove the clams from their shells, if desired.

7. Bring 3 liters (3 quarts) of water seasoned with 75 grams (¼ cup) of salt to a rolling boil.

8. Meanwhile, put the clam-cooking liquid in a large sauté pan and heat gently.

9. Add the pasta to the boiling salted water and cook at a rapid boil for approximately 2 minutes less than the minimum cooking time on the package for al dente pasta, stirring frequently to prevent sticking.

10. Drain the pasta, reserving the pasta-cooking water.

11. Add the par-cooked pasta to the clam-cooking liquid in the sauté pan and finish cooking at a moderate boil, adding the reserved pasta-cooking water 1 ladle at a time, shaking the pan and stirring the pasta, until the pasta is al dente, leaving the sauce liquid enough to just coat the pasta. Adjust the salt and pepper while finishing the pasta.

12. Add the clams to the pasta during the last 30 to 60 seconds of cooking to warm them.

13. Serve immediately, garnishing each portion with the sautéed breadcrumbs, parsley or basil chiffonade, and a drizzle of garlic oil.

Polpo alla Sous-Vide
Octopus Sous-Vide

If you've never had octopus, I encourage you to try this recipe. It is exceptionally easy—and delicious. Fresh octopus is best, but frozen will work. I suggest getting an octopus that weighs about 1 kilogram (2¼ pounds), plus or minus. This cooking method is very forgiving, so don't be too concerned if the octopus you find is a different weight. A well-seasoned puree of white beans is a wonderful accompaniment.

Metric Measure	Ingredient	American Measure
1 kilogram	Whole octopus	2 ¼ pounds
To taste	Salt, preferably fine sea salt	To taste
To taste	Freshly ground black pepper	To taste
3 tablespoons	Extra-virgin olive oil	3 tablespoons

1. Clean the octopus under running water. Squeeze out any dark, hard bits that might be lodged in the suckers.

2. Cut the octopus below the eyes. That will leave the eight tentacles attached to each other, separated from the head.

3. Remove the head above the eyes. Discard the middle portion with the eyes. (Note: The head is edible, but I wouldn't use it for this dish since it won't have the same visual appeal. To clean the head, however, squeeze out everything from inside and rinse well in running water. Reserve for another use.)

4. Use your fingers to press out the hard beak where the tentacles come together.

5. With the beak gone, separate the tentacles by cutting between each tentacle to the center.

6. Season the tentacles generously with salt and pepper.

7. Put the tentacles into a sous vide bag. I suggest using two large bags with four tentacles in each one. Arrange the tentacles so that they do not touch and are as straight as possible.

8. Vacuum-seal the bags, taking care to keep the tentacles separate as the air is removed.

9. Cook the tentacles at 82.2°C (180°F) for 6 hours.

10. Remove the bags from the sous vide, allow to cool to room temperature, and then refrigerate.

11. When you are ready to serve the octopus, open the bags. Sear the tentacles in a nonstick pan in a small amount of extra-virgin olive oil.

12. Serve immediately. This dish does not reheat well.

CARPACCIO DI POLPO
Octopus Carpaccio

Unlike the usual use of the term *carpaccio*, the octopus in this dish is cooked. This is a visually stunning way to serve octopus. I suggest putting very thin slices of octopus carpaccio on top of a salad of interesting greens such as valerian and watercress dressed with a bright lemon vinaigrette made from lemon juice, extra-virgin olive oil, salt, and pepper. Drizzle more dressing on the octopus slices and sprinkle with flaky sea salt and freshly grated lemon zest.

Metric Measure	Ingredient	American Measure
1 kilogram	Whole octopus	2¼ pounds

1. Prepare the octopus as for Octopus Sous-Vide (page 171) through step 4. Do not cut the tentacles apart.

2. Bring 3 liters (3 quarts) of water seasoned with 75 grams (¼ cup) of salt to a rolling boil.

3. Holding the octopus tentacles with tongs, dip them into the boiling water for a few seconds and remove. Repeat a few more times and the tentacles should have curled up nicely, after which, just drop the octopus into the water and boil gently until it is very tender, usually about 90 minutes, but it could be up to 2¼ hours, depending on the size of the octopus.

4. Remove the octopus and cut the tentacles apart.

5. Arrange the tentacles in a small vegetable press, preferably one where the chaser screws down, leaving as little air space as possible.

6. Pour some of the cooking water over the octopus in the press. Most of it will run out, but you want the octopus to be completely moistened with the cooking liquid before compressing it.

7. Screw down the chaser until tight. Refrigerate the entire apparatus for 24 hours. I suggest putting it into a large plastic bag to keep it from drying out.

8. When you remove the octopus, it should be a single block tightly stuck together.

9. Slice the block of octopus very thinly using a rotary meat slicer or a very sharp knife and a very steady hand.

Tip: If you don't have a vegetable press, you can use a potato ricer, but you won't be able to put all the tentacles in it at the same time. After arranging the tentacles in the ricer and squeezing the handles to apply pressure, wrap the handles together with some plastic wrap to maintain the pressure.

Tip: You cannot use sous-vide octopus for carpaccio, as the low cooking temperature does not generate enough gelatin to hold the octopus pieces together.

Pasta alla Chitarra con Cozze e Pomodorini
Pasta Cut on the "Chitarra" with Mussels and Cherry Tomatoes

I adore pasta alla chitarra. Chitarra means guitar in Italian. A chitarra for pasta is a wooden device strung with guitar strings over which a sheet of pasta is placed, and a rolling pin is rolled over the sheet to cut it. Typically, a chitarra is strung to cut wider on one side than the other. For this recipe, I use the narrow side. I roll out the pasta to a thickness that is as close as I can get it to the width the chitarra will cut. On my vintage pasta machine, that is setting #5. If you are not going to make your own pasta, I suggest using 350 grams of bavette or linguine instead.

Metric Measure	Ingredient	American Measure
1 recipe	Fresh Egg Pasta (page 45)	1 recipe
60	Fresh mussels	60
80 milliliters	Extra-virgin olive oil	1/3 cup
3 cloves	Garlic, bruised with a chef's knife	3 cloves
375 milliliters	Vegetable Broth (page 161) or water, divided	1½ cups
150 grams	Grape tomatoes	5 ounces
To taste	Cayenne pepper	To taste
To taste	Salt, preferably fine sea salt	To taste
To taste	Freshly ground black pepper	To taste
To garnish	Basil chiffonade	To garnish

1. Roll the pasta using setting #5 on a pasta machine, or whatever setting is closest to the width of the narrow side of the chitarra. Cut each sheet to a length of 25 centimeters (10 inches).

Italy Is Blessed with Poor Distribution

2. Place a pasta sheet on the narrow side of a chitarra. Roll over the pasta with a rolling pin, being careful not to move the pasta, until the strings have cut through it. As you cut each pasta sheet, sprinkle the strands with a little semola rimacinata (fine semolina) and form them into loose nests.

3. Allow the pasta to dry for a few hours, tossing it every now and then to be sure that it does not stick together.

4. Quickly wash the mussels in cold water. Remove any beards.

5. In a heavy-bottomed Dutch oven, combine the olive oil and garlic. Cook over low heat, stirring occasionally until the garlic is golden.

6. Add 250 milliliters (1 cup) of vegetable broth and bring to a boil.

7. Add the cleaned mussels to the boiling broth, cover the pot, and cook at a medium boil until the mussels are all open, approximately 3 minutes.

8. As soon as the mussels have all opened, pour the contents through a sieve, reserving the cooking liquid separately from the mussels. Discard the garlic and any mussels that do not open.

9. In a large sauté pan, sauté the tomatoes over medium-high heat until they just begin to blister, approximately 2 minutes. Add 125 milliliters (½ cup) of broth and the cayenne, if using. Boil briefly, gently pressing on the tomatoes to burst the skin. Reserve.

10. Bring 3 liters (3 quarts) of water seasoned with 75 grams (¼ cup) of salt to a rolling boil.

11. Meanwhile, add the liquid from the mussels to the sauté pan used for the tomatoes (no need to wash the pan) and heat gently.

12. Add the pasta to the boiling salted water and cook at a rapid boil for 2 to 3 minutes, stirring frequently to prevent sticking. The pasta should be firm in the center. If using dry pasta, boil for approximately 2 minutes less than the minimum cooking time on the package for al dente pasta, stirring frequently to prevent sticking.

13. Drain the pasta, reserving the pasta-cooking water.

14. Add the par-cooked pasta to the liquid in the sauté pan and finish cooking at a moderate boil, adding the reserved pasta-cooking water 1 ladle at a time, shaking the pan and stirring the pasta, until the pasta is al dente leaving the sauce liquid enough to just coat the pasta.

15. With the last ladle of liquid, add the mussels and grape tomatoes to the pasta. Taste and adjust the salt and pepper.

16. Garnish each serving with basil chiffonade.

Tip: If you are making your own pasta, you can add the grated zest of several oranges to the flour to create a citrus-perfumed pasta that will pair amazingly well with the sauce.

 ZUPPA DI POMODORO
Tomato Soup

I was never much for tomato soup but this version from the Italian Culinary Institute completely changed my opinion!

Metric Measure	Ingredient	American Measure
215 grams	Onion, diced	7 ounces
65 grams	Unsalted butter	4½ tablespoons
700 grams	Passata (tomato puree)	24½ ounces
200 milliliters	Water	¾ cup plus 1 tablespoon
To taste	Salt, preferably fine sea salt	To taste
To taste	Freshly ground black pepper	To taste
To taste	Freshly grated Parmigiano Reggiano cheese, optional	To taste

1. Using a heavy-bottomed saucepan, gently sweat the onion in butter until soft and golden but not at all brown.

2. Add the passata and water, using the water to rinse the last bits of passata out of the jar. Simmer, partially covered, for approximately 20 minutes.

3. Adjust the salt and pepper.

4. Puree the soup using an immersion blender or counter-top blender. If desired, add Parmigiano Reggiano cheese when blending.

5. Gently reheat the soup, if necessary.

GELATO AND MEATBALLS

MARCH 11

Forget Fellini, he's small fry. (See Dispatch #12.)

This past week was Gelato Week.

We started out gently on Sunday the third, belying what was to come next. We had a free morning and then had lunch of risotto followed by rolled stuffed pork with mashed potatoes and broccoli followed by an orange marmalade crostata (from marmalade we made during conserves week) in individual butter crusts that Ryan spent the better part of a day making.

In the afternoon, we went to three *gelaterie* (plural of gelateria) to taste and critique gelati. Chef Juan suggested that we sample the same gelati at each shop so that we had a consistent point of comparison. He further suggested that the two gelati be *fiordilatte* and *nocciola* (hazelnut).

Fiordilatte is absolute simplicity, consisting of milk, cream, and sugar. There's not even any vanilla. There's no hiding poor quality when making fiordilatte. In addition, fiordilatte is the base for many different gelati, so tasting that one gives a strong clue to the quality of many others, including many fruit gelati.

Nocciola is flavored with hazelnut paste, a very expensive nut paste if it's made with hazelnuts—and only hazelnuts—of the highest quality. (Nut pastes in Italy are truly amazing—and very expensive. They are basically nuts, and nuts only, ground under heavy rollers until they produce the most ethereal and wildly flavorful creamy pastes.)

Nut-based gelati are very popular in Southern Italy and cost almost twice as much to make as fiordilatte due to the cost of the nut pastes. Tasting a nut-based gelato is a good way to see if a gelateria is cutting corners, either in quantity or quality of nut paste.

We were, in fact, allowed to order as many different gelati at each shop as we wanted. Most of us just ordered two, with one or two people also ordering an extra pistachio gelato to share.

Pasta e fagioli, part of Monday's lunch. (See page 187 for a recipe.)

We got back to school late afternoon and had a few free hours before dinner.

More Gelato Exploration

Monday started with several hours of lecture about gelato, including topics such as serving temperature; ideal qualities (sweetness, creaminess, fluffiness, yumminess, and stability); the ideal ranges for each of the major compounds in gelato (fat, sugar, protein, solids, and so on); the anti-freezing power of different ingredients in gelato; basic gelato equipment; the major indicators of poor-quality gelato; gelato "pre-mixes" (the gelato equivalent of a boxed cake mix…you can guess how Chef John feels about these!); and the differences between sorbetto, cremolata, and gelato.

Around 11 a.m., we had a brief pause for a "grilled cheese" sandwich of house-made porchetta and fontal cheese on house-made rolls cooked in truffle butter! Truffle butter here is made from whole fresh truffles smooshed with butter—none of the (fake) "truffle" oil. This was just to tide us over until lunch at 1 p.m., which consisted of a caprese salad and focaccia followed by pasta e fagioli.

The afternoon was taken up by the production of a number of different gelato bases that were pasteurized and then refrigerated. The texture and flavor of the gelato improves if the mixture (called the base) is refrigerated for twenty-four hours before gelling. We made the following bases:

- Fiordilatte gelato (milk, cream, sugar)
- Caramel gelato
- Nut base (to be mixed with various nut pastes for an array of gelati)
- Strawberry sorbetto (a sorbetto is a gelato without dairy products)
- Lemon sorbetto
- Savory peanut gelato
- Orange cream gelato
- Coffee gelato
- Rum gelato

Almost all the bases include small amounts of ground carob (locust bean) and guar bean. Don't freak out about the guar and carob. Both are really agricultural products that have been eaten for hundreds of years. The alternative is using egg yolks, which are used in some gelati and which are more common in Northern Italian versions, rather than those from Southern Italy. The disadvantage of egg yolks is that they can introduce an eggy taste. They also complicate the pasteurization process.

On Tuesday, Chef John made the base for a chocolate sorbetto. Remember, sorbetto has no dairy products. When it was frozen it was absolutely delicious. If you didn't know, you would never imagine in your lifetime that it had no milk or cream! It did, however, have a tremendous quantity of excellent dark chocolate.

Chef John also made a "yellow base" using egg yolks and mascarpone, which was ultimately turned into vanilla gelato, as well as a strawberry coulis that was later swiped into a simple fiordilatte gelato.

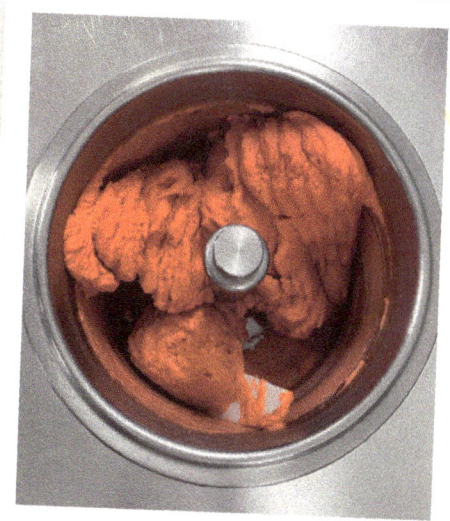

Strawberry sorbetto in the gelato batch freezer.

As the day progressed, many of the gelato bases from the previous day were frozen and then, of course, eaten. When I say many, I mean many.

Because Tuesday was Fat Tuesday—and this being Italy—we ate well. In between various gelati, lunch consisted of three meatball creations. The first was meatballs put onto a very large ring-shaped bread with lots of tomato sugo and cheese. The second was meatballs cooked with sweet peppers that were also made into sandwiches. The third was meatballs and sauce on ciabatta.

Most of the afternoon was devoted to making gelato bases. We each were tasked with coming up with a flavor of gelato with swipe-ins and toppings, if desired, and executing it.

Gelato Math

Executing gelato means math. There are ideal proportions for each component of gelato and we had to create our formulas to achieve these proportions. For example, milk is not just milk; it is water, sugar, fat, and protein.

The optimum proportions of each ingredient, according to Chef John are:

* 6 to 12 percent fat (less fat than premium ice cream)

Meatballs and sweet peppers ready to be put into another sandwich. (See page 185 for a recipe for meatballs and sweet peppers.)

Gelato and Meatballs

- ★ 16 to 22 percent sugar, of which glucose is not more than 20 percent (more sugar than most ice cream)
- ★ 8 to 12 percent non-fat milk solids
- ★ 0 to 4 percent other solids
- ★ 58 to 68 percent water
- ★ 32 to 42 percent dry residual

This adds up to more than 100 percent because the dry residual is not a separate category but the combination of anything in the gelato mix that remains behind if it is dried out, for example, milk solids, sugar, and so on.

Coming up with a new gelato formula, then, means determining which ingredients in which proportions will produce a mix of the desired qualities. Of course, this is only the beginning. The gelato has to taste yummy, too. But getting the numbers correct is a step in the right direction.

Orange crostata made with orange marmalade from conserves week was Sunday's lunchtime dessert.

I chose to make tiramisù gelato for which I decided to come up with a mascarpone gelato base. I then needed to make tiny, tiny cakes flavored with espresso that were baked, dried, and rebaked until crisp before being soaked in rum syrup and dropped into the gelato while it was being extruded. On top was a drizzle of chocolate mixed with oil so that it would not get too hard.

Wednesday started with an explanation of how to make brioss (dialect for brioche). These are similar to French brioche. They are used for gelato sandwiches. Unlike American "ice cream sandwiches," these are truly sandwiches: fluffy, slightly sweet brioche filled with different flavors of gelato, often three of them.

Chef John gelled some of the fiordilatte base from the previous day and made stracciatella (ragged) gelato. Stracciatella gelato is basically fiordilatte on top of which is drizzled wisps of melted chocolate that are broken up and worked into the gelato when it is served. Chef also made frutti di bosco (literally, fruits of the forest) gelato (mixed berry gelato) after which he made masa chablon (a chocolate coating) using white chocolate.

Chef John then made his knock-off of Nutella. It is simply a mixture of about two parts melted high-quality milk chocolate and one part hazelnut paste with a pinch of sugar. Without a doubt I could sit and just eat tubs of this stuff.

I had a revelatory moment when Chef John made white chocolate crumble. This concoction is truly amazing. Just take a big bar of exceedingly high-quality white chocolate and put it in the oven at 180°C (about 350°F) until it turns light brown all over and the entire thing caramelizes. Let it cool, crumble it, and sprinkle it with a bit of salt. You will have no idea it is white chocolate and it is the most sublime crunchy crumble for an enormous array of desserts.

Chef John makes roasted Italian meringue "marshmallows" for gelato.

In the afternoon, we started gelling the gelati we mixed up the day before. As they were made, they were dished out for the entire class. Here's the rundown of what we ate:

- White chocolate gelato with caramelized white chocolate crumbles (see the previous paragraph)
- Coffee gelato with a toasted walnut swipe
- Almond milk tea gelato
- Almond gelato with milk chocolate stracciatella
- Chocolate sorbetto
- Spicy chocolate gelato (made with the addition of peperoncino syrup)
- Amaretto gelato with chocolate and chopped almonds
- Tiramisù gelato with rum-infused coffee-flavored cake and chocolate drizzle (mine)
- Strawberry gelato with zabaglione
- Savory peanut gelato with Italian meringue toasted "marshmallows"
- Orange gelato with chocolate-dipped candied orange peel
- Pineapple, ginger, turmeric, and basil gelato with a honey drizzle
- Red wine gelato with a pecorino cream swipe and candied pancetta

We stopped there and continued the next day with:

- Vanilla gelato topped with cubes of pandoro (a sweet bread similar to panettone but [usually] without the fruit)
- Earl Grey tea gelato with a dried fig swipe
- Gorgonzola gelato with a pear coulis and chopped walnuts

We didn't make it to the last one: bourbon brown sugar gelato, so we had it the next night after dinner. It was wonderful. It was just a fiordilatte base with bourbon poured in. I am definitely going to make this one! I offered, multiple times, to store it in the freezer in my apartment, but so far that hasn't happened.

On Friday, the last day of Gelato Week, we had an extended lecture about setting up a gelato business including the necessary equipment, the layout of an ideal gelato kitchen (or gelato lab, as it's called here), pricing models for gelato, showcasing and storing gelato, and some business ideas.

Gelato Week wrapped up with a pizza party—just a party this time, no contest—in the pizzeria with the wood-burning pizza oven. It was a relaxing end to a very educational, but exhausting, and overly caloric week.

Saturday was a free day. Sunday starts Pastry Week, for which three new students will join us. Stay tuned….

CROSTATA DI MARMELLATA
Jam Tart

Use a very high-quality jam for this tart. You can make a larger tart with a thinner crust and more jam, if you want. The crust-to-fruit ratio really changes the characteristics of the tart. Proceed exactly as described, except use a 28-centimeter (11-inch) tart pan and approximately 675 milliliters (scant 3 cups) of jam.

Metric Measure	Ingredient	American Measure
1 recipe	Pasta Frolla (page 149)	1 recipe
475 milliliters	Jam, preferably homemade	Scant 2 cups
1	Egg	1
1 tablespoon	Milk	1 tablespoon

1. Put the chilled pasta frolla between parchment or waxed paper and roll it into a circle large enough to line the bottom and sides of a 24-centimeter x 2½-centimeter (9½-inch x 1-inch) tart pan with a removable bottom, leaving some overhang.

2. Cut the pastry even with the top of the tart pan. Save and chill the scraps.

3. Prick the bottom of the pastry in multiple places with a fork. Put the pastry-lined pan in the refrigerator for 10 to 15 minutes.

4. Meanwhile, roll the scraps into a rectangle approximately 24 centimeters (9½ inches) long by 9 centimeters (3½ inches) wide.

5. Chill the pastry rectangle.

6. Fill the tart shell with the jam.

7. Cut the rectangle of pasta frolla into 7 strips approximately 1 centimeter (scant ½ inch) wide. Use the strips to put a diamond-shaped lattice on top of the tart, evenly spacing 4 strips in one direction and then putting 3 strips, evenly spaced, at a diagonal to the first strips.

8. Beat the egg and milk to make an egg wash.

9. Brust the lattice with the egg wash.

10. Bake at 180°C (350°F) until golden brown, approximately 30 minutes.

11. Cool on a rack for 10 minutes. Remove the sides of the pan and cool completely.

GELATO AL FIORDILATTE
Milk and Cream Gelato

Although I have published an entire book on artisan Italian gelato, I had to include at least one recipe in this book because Gelato Week was such a significant part of my time at the Italian Culinary Institute. There is no substitute for weighing every ingredient when making gelato. Some ingredients are included in such small quantities that measuring by volume can be so inaccurate as to negatively affect the gelato. I converted the metric weights to American weights, but I recommend that you just set your digital scale to metric and ignore the American.

Gelato and Meatballs

Metric Measure	Ingredient	American Measure
20 grams	Powdered dextrose	0.71 ounces
1.25 grams	Guar gum	0.044 ounces
1.25 grams	Locust bean gum	0.044 ounces
0.50 grams	Salt	0.176 ounces
525 grams	Milk, 2%	18.52 ounces
135 grams	Granulated sugar	4.76 ounces
20 grams	Powdered fructose	0.71 ounces
34 grams	Powdered skim milk	1.20 ounces
263 grams	Heavy cream, 36% fat	9.28 ounces

1. In a small bowl, combine the dextrose, guar gum, locust bean gum, and salt. Mix very well. Reserve.

2. Combine the milk, granulated sugar, and fructose in a stainless-steel pot. Heat to 35°C (95°F), whisking occasionally.

3. Add the skim milk powder and whisk to dissolve completely.

4. Continuing to heat the milk mixture, slowly sprinkle in the dextrose mixture, whisking constantly to avoid lumps and keeping the mixture below 45°C (113°F). After the dextrose mixture is incorporated, heat to 85°C (185°F), stirring constantly and scraping the bottom of the pot with a rubber spatula.

5. Add the cream. Mix well. Heat to 75°C (167°F), stirring constantly, and hold for 15 seconds.

6. Chill quickly still in the pot, preferably in an ice bath. Allow the mixture to mature overnight, covered and refrigerated at 4°C (39°F) or less.

7. Just before freezing the gelato, add water to return the base to the calculated batch weight of 1,000 grams (35.27 ounces). Blend with an immersion blender. Taste and adjust salt, if necessary.

8. Freeze in a batch freezer.

9. Transfer the gelato from the batch freezer to a tub of appropriate size.

10. Harden in a deep freezer for at least 12 hours.

11. To serve, bring the gelato to approximately −13°C (9°F) by putting the entire tub of gelato into a freezer set to that temperature 12 hours before serving or by portioning it into individual bowls and putting the bowls into the refrigerator for approximately 10 to 15 minutes.

Tip: A countertop ice cream maker (the kind that uses a tub that is chilled in the freezer) makes good gelato.

Tip: For ingredients used in quantities of less than 100 grams (3½ ounces), I suggest a scale that measures in increments of 0.01 grams. These are available online at modest cost.

Tip: Before putting ingredients into the stainless-steel pot in step 2, record the weight of the pot. Then in step 7, add water to reach the combined weight of the original batch (1,000 grams) plus the weight of the pot.

POLPETTE E PEPERONI DOLCI
Meatballs and Sweet Peppers

I recommend using 85 percent lean ground pork for these meatballs. Combined with the breadcrumbs, this amount of fat will make tender meatballs. Meatballs should never be hard, nor should they have the bouncy texture of a well-made sausage. In place of breadcrumbs, you can use 50 grams (1¾ ounces) of several-day-old Italian bread with the crusts removed.

Metric Measure	Ingredient	American Measure
45 grams	Breadcrumbs	1.7 ounces
100 milliliters	Water	6⅔ tablespoons
450 grams	Ground pork, 85% lean	1 pound
1 large	Egg	1 large
15 grams	Freshly grated Parmigiano Reggiano cheese	½ ounce
15 grams	Freshly grated Pecorino Romano cheese	½ ounce
1 clove	Garlic, finely minced	1 clove
8 grams	Finely minced parsley	2 tablespoons
1¼ teaspoon plus more to taste	Salt, preferably fine sea salt	1¼ teaspoons plus more to taste
To taste	Freshly ground black pepper	To taste
As needed	Neutral oil, such as corn or sunflower	As needed
3 medium	Bell peppers, green or yellow	3 medium
1 medium	Onion	1 medium
3 tablespoons	Extra-virgin olive oil	3 tablespoons
375 milliliters	Passata or Basic Tomato Sauce (page 131)	1⅓ cups

Gelato and Meatballs

1. Combine the breadcrumbs and water. Allow the breadcrumbs to completely absorb the water and become tender.

2. Combine the pork, breadcrumb-water mixture, egg, cheeses, garlic, parsley, salt, and pepper. Mix with your hand until the mixture is completely homogeneous.

3. Divide into portions of approximately 45 grams (1.6 ounces) each. A 33-milliliter portion scoop (#30) is a perfect size for this.

4. Roll each portion into a smooth ball, moistening your hands with water as needed.

5. Bring 7 centimeters (3 inches) of neutral oil to 175°C (350°F) in a deep fryer or heavy pot. Fry the meatballs until deeply browned.

6. Drain the meatballs on paper.

7. Cut the bell peppers into strips approximately 1 centimeter (scant ½ inch) thick.

8. Cut the onion into slices approximately 1 centimeter (scant ½ inch) thick.

9. Sauté the bell peppers in the olive oil over medium-high heat until lightly charred in a few places.

10. Add the onions, reduce the heat to medium. Season with salt. Sauté until the onions are golden but not at all brown, stirring frequently.

11. Add the passata (or tomato sauce). Season with salt and pepper. Simmer, partially covered, approximately 15 minutes.

12. Add the meatballs and simmer another 30 minutes, partially covered, stirring once or twice.

Tip: In Italy, these meatballs are typically served as a secondo piatto, after a course of pasta (or maybe rice). My Italian-American side, though, always wants to stuff them into hoagie rolls, douse them with Olio Santo (page 147), and eat them standing over the kitchen sink with sauce dripping down my chin.

PASTA E FAGIOLI
Pasta and Beans

There are more recipes for pasta e fagioli in Italy than there are cooks—many more! I personally have four that are in my regular rotation plus a handful of others that I fit in from time to time. Pasta e fagioli in any form is the penultimate Italian comfort food for me (second only to potato gnocchi). This is an adaptation of the recipe that my mother made most often. In terms of flavor, it is reminiscent of the first time I had pasta e fagioli prepared by Chef John at a dinner event in California several months before I attended the Italian Culinary Institute.

Metric Measure	Ingredient	American Measure
⅓ medium	Onion, finely diced	⅓ medium
125 milliliters, divided	Extra-virgin olive oil	½ cup, divided
½ teaspoon or to taste	Crushed red pepper	½ teaspoon or to taste
1 (175-gram) can	Tomato paste	1 (6-ounce) can
700 milliliters	Water	3 cups
¼ teaspoon	Dried oregano	¼ teaspoon
⅓ teaspoon	Dried basil	⅓ teaspoon
To taste	Salt, preferably fine sea salt	To taste
To taste	Freshly ground black pepper	To taste
3 cloves	Garlic, bruised with a chef's knife	3 cloves
700 milliliters	Cooked dried baby lima beans plus cooking liquid to cover	3 cups
450–500 grams	Ditalini or other short tubular pasta	~1 pound
30 grams	Freshly grated Parmigiano Reggiano cheese	Generous 1 ounce

1. In a heavy-bottomed Dutch oven, sauté the onion in 60 milliliters (¼ cup) of the olive oil until soft and golden. Add the red pepper and sauté another minute.

2. Add the tomato paste and sauté, stirring frequently, until the tomato paste darkens slightly and smells sweet, approximately 2 to 3 minutes.

3. Add the water, oregano, basil, salt, and black pepper. Boil gently, partially covered, for 30 to 45 minutes, stirring occasionally. Adjust the seasoning as the sauce cooks.

4. Meanwhile, sauté the garlic in the remaining olive oil over low heat until browned. Remove from the heat. Discard the garlic and reserve the oil.

5. Bring 3 liters (3 quarts) of water seasoned with 75 grams (¼ cup) of salt to a rolling boil.

6. Meanwhile, add the beans and their cooking liquid to the tomato sauce and simmer, partially covered, until the pasta is ready.

7. Add the pasta to the boiling salted water and cook at a rapid boil for approximately 2 minutes less than the minimum cooking time on the package for al dente pasta, stirring frequently to prevent sticking.

8. Drain the pasta, reserving the pasta-cooking water.

9. Add the par-cooked pasta to the bean and tomato sauce mixture in the Dutch oven along with the garlic-flavored oil and finish cooking at a moderate boil, adding the reserved pasta-cooking water 1 ladle at a time, shaking the pan and stirring the pasta, until the pasta is al dente. Adjust the salt and pepper while finishing the pasta.

10. Off the heat, add the cheese and then flip and stir the pasta to emulsify the cheese and sauce. Add a bit more cooking water if the sauce is too thick.

Tip: Cook the beans as described for Beans and Greens (page 143) or use 2 cans (approximately 400 grams or 15 ounces) of baby lima beans.

SBRICIOLATA AL CIOCCOLATO BIANCO CARAMELLATO
Caramelized White Chocolate Crumble

Use very high-quality white chocolate for this creation, preferably one that only contains cocoa butter, sugar, and an emulsifier. Avoid bars that contain fats other than cocoa butter, as the taste and texture will be inferior. Sometimes vanilla is added, but I prefer white chocolate without vanilla, as the vanilla often overpowers the subtle flavor of white chocolate.

Metric Measure	Ingredient	American Measure
~125 grams	White chocolate bar	~4½ ounces

1. Put the chocolate bar on a silicone-lined quarter- or half-sheet pan.

2. Bake at 180°C (350°F) until golden brown. (Note: the edges will brown more than the center so be cautious not to overcook the bar.)

3. Cool the bar on the baking sheet.

4. Break it into small pieces and add salt to taste.

Gelato week ended with a pizza party.

Butter and Sugar and Lard, Oh My!

MARCH 24

We've done a bit of bread and pastry throughout the course, but for a week starting on March 11, that was our (nearly) exclusive focus. We had four additional students join us for Pastry Week, including Annie, a pastry chef from the Philippines who was also with us for Gelato Week. Additionally, three Air Force personnel came for Pastry Week. Each was a personal assistant working for one high-ranking Air Force officer.

Air Force personal assistants do all the tasks of an executive assistant, like maintaining schedules and organizing their bosses' activities, but they also maintain their bosses' uniforms (and business suits if they are required to wear civilian business attire as part of their Air Force duties); keep all areas of their bosses' houses that could be seen by guests in perfect shape; cook meals; and plan, execute, and serve dinner parties. They were a nice addition to our group. Their dedication and precision were awe-inspiring.

Pane Carasau puffs up as it bakes. Immediately upon taking it from the oven it is split in half, cooled, and rebaked until crispy. (See page 220 for a recipe.)

They were always the first to volunteer to try out anything, and they were meticulous to the point of near perfection—even with tasks they had never attempted before (like laminating puff pastry and rolling it into a perfect rectangle). Apparently, when they go through culinary training in the Air Force, the accuracy of their dice is tested by passing diced vegetables through screens of various sizes to confirm that they are able to consistently create perfectly diced vegetables. They were all really excited about incorporating Italian techniques and foods into their cooking.

We had a crazy day of demonstrations and hands-on work on the eleventh, including:

- Pane carasau, a crispy flat bread from Sardinia that I love and now know how to make
- "Italian" muffins (Chef John's take on "English" muffins, which are not Italian at all but fun to make nonetheless and in a strange way are not too dissimilar from Tuscan testaroli, of which there are several versions)
- Piadina, a flat bread (which we never finished because Chef Juan didn't like the way the dough turned out)
- Rosette (Roman bread rolls incised with a "rose" design on top)
- Hot dog and hamburger buns (obviously also not Italian)
- Mantovane
- Pane arabo

Chef John also demonstrated, and then we ate for lunch, a Piemontese pasta called tajarin (dialect for tagliolini) made with an absurd amount of egg yolk. It's something like forty egg yolks for 1 kilogram (2¼ pounds) of flour. (It makes you wonder what all the whites were being used for. I vaguely remember from early in the course that a long time ago, the whites were used for clarifying wine.) He also made candereli, potato dumplings from Alto Adige that are basically the dough for a potato gnocchi stuffed with a meat filling.

Pastry Wisdom

Maestro Paolo Caridi, one of Italy's top pastry chefs, joined us for two absolutely amazing days during which he demonstrated how to make an incredible array of Italian pastries, sweet breads, and confections, some pan-Italian and some local Calabrian treats.

I was pleased to discover that my cannoli recipe was very similar to his (smile), though he has the advantage of being able to fill his cannoli with sweetened sheep's milk ricotta, which is unavailable in my town. I've even tried to buy sheep's milk in order to make my own ricotta, but I can't find a source.

Maestro Caridi made egg-shaped confections (*uovo sodo goloso*) consisting of a "yolk" of marzipan surrounded by a "white" of white chocolate and pistachio paste. Using almond paste would have produced a more appropriate color for the "white," but he likes pistachios and they are a typical Calabrian product. (They also add an amazing flavor contrast to the marzipan center.) It was topped with

Three possible ways to fill colomba molds, clockwise from top: three pieces of dough, two pieces of dough overlapped, one piece of dough down the middle which will fill the "wings" as it rises.

melted white chocolate. He made these treats by emptying out eggshells and filling them with the various mixtures.

Colomba di Pasqua, an Italian traditional Easter bread, was perhaps the highlight of the two days. Essentially (this is an approximation but not far off) it is panettone baked in the shape of a dove. Panettone is a very rich sweet bread with candied fruits and/or raisins that is traditionally served at Christmas. Colomba is the Easter equivalent. This recipe is a two-day project (mostly due to the multiple rises of the dough) that I feel I could execute were it not for the fact that I don't have *lievito madre* (mother yeast).

Mother yeast is a preferment made with natural yeast. It is similar to sourdough starter except that the final product isn't sour. Other types of preferment are made with commercial yeast. If all goes well, it takes about a month to make a respectable mother yeast. Maestro Caridi demonstrated how to create and maintain one. He has been keeping his going for twenty-five years with *daily*—yep, daily not weekly—feedings. Try that without a staff of workers! (You'd have to take it on vacation with you. Explain *that* to TSA!)

Apparently, there is no substitute for lievito madre in this particular product, and it's not allowed to be called *colomba* if commercial yeast is used. Nonetheless, I am going to totally hack this recipe and use commercial yeast for my first go-round. I'm going to do this mostly because the ratios of eggs and butter to flour are exceedingly high. It's possible that the whole dough might just separate. I don't want to have spent a month cultivating lievito madre only to have the bread dough turn into a disaster.

If the colomba, and by association panettone and pandoro (which is like panettone but without dried or candied fruit), works out, it might be what finally compels me to maintain my own natural yeast starter.

In addition, Maestro Caridi demonstrated the following:

* Cudduraci, which is a sweet shortcrust pastry filled with shell-on hardboiled eggs, covered with another layer of crust, and lavishly decorated. Apparently,

Butter and Sugar and Lard, Oh My!

it is a traditional Calabrian pastry that a woman makes for her fiancé. The size of the pastry and number of eggs is supposed to correlate with the degree of "amore"!

- La pitta 'mpigliata, which is a traditional Calabrian sweetbread stuffed with candied fruits and spices. It is very rich. Traditionally it is given by a man to his fiancé. You guessed it, the larger it is….
- Agnello al forno, which is an almond shortcrust pastry in the shape of a lamb that is filled with candied fruits and nuts.
- Agnello di marzapane, which is a lamb made out of marzipan. This is Italy near Easter after all, hence all the lamb shapes and Easter breads.
- Babà, which are small yeast-risen breads soaked in rum syrup.
- Bocconotto, which are small filled pastries. In this case, Masetro Caridi used a cream filling.
- Fraguni, which are open-faced pastries filled with ricotta and salame that were originally carried as lunch for workers in Calabria.
- Croccante, which is basically almond brittle.
- Torrone, which is similar to croccante but without the sugar being cooked as dark.
- Marzipan sweets, which are basically marzipan stabilized with a little flour, butter, and egg white then rolled and baked. Adding a little baking powder makes them crunchy.

After Maestro Caridi finished his two days, we spent a crazy day in the pastry kitchen with Chef John and Chef Juan doing a tag team performance…er, demonstration. They were simultaneously preparing dishes while shouting instructions between them like a yodel bouncing back from a facing hillside.

With Chef John cooking multiple dishes at the same time, it was almost impossible to keep my notes straight. I had to keep flipping back and forth between pages to get the instructions associated with the correct recipe. But after weeks of practice, I was able to adjust my note-taking technique to accommodate directions being shouted out almost simultaneously for two different recipes from two different chefs. Also, because Chef John hates down time, he would start yet another recipe while waiting for the previous one. I was often recording three or four recipes at the same time.

That day we got experience with:

- Pasta sfoglia (puff pastry)
- Italian meringue
- Italian buttercream in two flavors: one vanilla and one hazelnut
- Pizzette (tiny pizza to be served as a snack)
- A brownie-like creation with abundant nuts but no flour
- Cornetti, the Italian version of croissants but definitely different
- Pasta frolla, a shortcrust pastry for tarts

Wrapping Up the Week

Friday morning was a market day, as usual. The weekly open-air market in Soverato has really been picking up over the past few weeks: more vendors, a larger array of produce, more customers. I will definitely miss the array of foods available once I get home. I'm even enjoying the chaos of the market. Though I don't speak much Italian, and I can't understand a word of the local dialect, I know enough to make a purchase and occasionally trade a sentence or two with a vendor.

Friday afternoon there were a few demonstrations back at school: frollini (a sweet pastry that can be baked on its own or filled), chocolate mousse, chocolate ganache, and a range of mono-portion cakes (in this instance, thin sponge cakes cut into shapes and layered with buttercream and covered with glaze or not).

Afterward, we each had to make a batch of pasta sfoglia (puff pastry). I don't imagine that I'm likely to make it again, but I felt like I did a credible job, never having done it before. The first step is rolling butter into a perfect square, which I did by placing it on parchment paper and then folding the edges of the paper over to make a square. It was then pretty easy to roll the butter to the folded edges and create a perfect square.

Maestro Caridi makes pasta frolla using the technique taught to him by his grandmother.

The butter went into the refrigerator while I rolled out the dough into a much larger square.

The sides of the square of dough had to be the length of the butter measured from corner to corner so that when the butter was put on the dough and rotated forty-five degrees, the four corners of dough could be folded over to encase the butter but not overlap it.

It's then a matter of putting the butter on the dough, folding the dough over the butter, and then going through a series of successive folds of the whole thing, rolling and chilling between each, to achieve a block of pastry with 576 different layers after four successive folds. With one more fold, you'd end up with 2,304 layers, but by then there is a real risk of having each layer be so thin that the butter leaks out.

There were no further plans to use the pasta sfoglia. We were to just have the experience of making it. It all got put into the freezer while we took a one-day break. However, the pastry came in very handy during the menu execution that started the day after Pastry Week ended when Chef John made a last minute "suggestion" to improve one of our dishes.

Stay tuned….

BABÀ
Babà

These little liquor-soaked treats are a great end to a meal. They can be made in advance and soaked in syrup just a few hours before being served. Three syrup suggestions follow. Feel free to come up with your own ideas. Babà molds vary in size. For small ones, holding about 30 milliliters (2 tablespoons) of dough, bake at the lower temperature noted.

Metric Measure	Ingredient	American Measure
500 grams	Italian 0 flour W-350 to W-400	3¾ cups
6.3 grams	Active dry yeast	2 teaspoons
500 grams	Whole eggs, lightly beaten	2 cups
25 grams	Honey	3½ teaspoons
50 grams	Granulated sugar	¼ cup
75 grams	Unsalted butter, room temperature	5⅓ tablespoons
10 grams	Salt, preferably fine sea salt	1¾ teaspoon
As needed	Syrup to soak the babà (see suggestions that follow)	As needed

1. In the bowl of a stand mixer fitted with a dough hook, mix the flour and yeast. Gradually add the eggs until you have added approximately 75 percent of them. Set the rest aside.

2. Add the honey and sugar and mix until there is good gluten formation.

3. Mix in the butter, cut into pieces, and then the salt.

4. Cover the bowl with plastic wrap and proof the dough at room temperature until it has tripled in size.

5. Return the bowl to the mixer and add the remaining eggs a little at a time mixing at low speed.

6. Mix on high to more fully develop the gluten.

7. Portion into babà molds, filling each approximately ¾ full. Allow to proof until the dough reaches the top of the mold. Bake at 160°C (325°F) to 180°C (350°F) until brown.

8. Cool slightly and then remove the babà from the molds and cool on a rack.

9. Soak the babà in an alcohol-infused syrup for several hours before serving. See suggestions that follow.

SYRUPS FOR BABÀ

Make a simple syrup of 1 part granulated sugar and 2 parts water by weight, for example, 200 grams (1 cup) sugar and 400 grams (1⅔ cup) water. Heat gently, stirring frequently until the sugar dissolves. Do not boil or overheat. Cool completely.

- Rum syrup: Combine 250 grams (8 ounces by weight) simple syrup and 65 grams (2 ounces by weight) of rum.
- Amaretto syrup: Combine 250 grams (8 ounces by weight) simple syrup and 95 grams (3 ounces by weight) of Amaretto.
- Hazelnut Crème syrup: Combine 250 grams (8 ounces by weight) simple syrup and 100 grams (3.2 ounces by weight) of Hazelnut Crème liqueur.

Tip: I have successfully made babà without farina Manitoba by adding vital wheat gluten. Use 483 grams of W-320 flour and 17 grams of wheat gluten in step 1.

Fraguni
Savory Ricotta-Filled Tarts from Calabria

These pastries were a traditional worker's lunch in Lamezia, Calabria. They go well with cocktails or as part of an antipasto spread. I also happily eat them for lunch. Antimo Caputo Chef's Flour is W-300 to W-320, so it is perfect for this recipe. If you live in an arid region, you may need to add up to another 35 grams (2½ tablespoons) of milk. This recipe doubles well.

Dough

Metric Measure	Ingredient	American Measure
250 grams	Italian 00 flour W-300	1½ cups
50 grams	Semola rimacinata	⅓ cup
2.1 grams	Dry yeast	½ plus ⅛ teaspoon
145 grams	Milk	½ cup plus 2 tablespoons
25 grams	Egg, lightly beaten	⅞ ounce
25 grams	Honey	⅞ ounce
25 grams	Extra-virgin olive oil	⅞ ounce
2.5 grams	Salt, preferably fine sea salt	Scant ½ teaspoon

1. Using stand mixer fitted with a dough hook, mix the flour, semola, and yeast. Add the milk, then the egg, then the honey, and then the oil, mixing well after each addition. Add the salt last. Mix on medium speed until a smooth, elastic dough forms.

2. Form the dough into a ball and place it a dry bowl covered with plastic wrap. Allow the dough to rest at room temperature until it has doubled in size.

3. Divide the dough into 10 pieces. Roll each into a taut ball (see directions for shaping pizza dough on page 62). Place on a half-sheet pan, cover with plastic wrap, and allow the dough to rest 30 to 60 minutes. While the dough balls are resting, make the filling.

Filling and Assembly

Be sure to drain the ricotta well so the pastries are not soggy. Homemade ricotta works best if it is allowed to drain for 5 hours after just making it. Although you can drain ricotta (homemade or otherwise) at a later time, it will never lose as much moisture as it will with a lengthy draining immediately after it is prepared.

Metric Measure	Ingredient	American Measure
300 grams	Ricotta, preferably homemade (page 246)	10¾ ounces
1 large	Egg	1 large
37 grams	Finely diced soppressata or other spicy salame	1⅓ ounces
½ teaspoon	Salt, preferably fine sea salt	½ teaspoon
To taste	Freshly ground black pepper	To taste

1. Combine the ricotta and egg to loosen the ricotta, especially with well-drained homemade ricotta.

2. Mix in the soppressata, salt, and black pepper.

3. Pat each ball of dough into a circle about 10 centimeters (4 inches) in diameter. Top with 33 milliliters (2 generous tablespoons) of filling. I use a #30 portioning scoop. Press down on the filling to form a circle, leaving about 1 centimeter (just under ½ inch) of dough around the filling.

4. Pinch the dough together, making pleats in five places around the perimeter of the dough to create a star design and make the crust stand up a bit around the filling.

5. Bake at 180°C (350°F) for 10 to 12 minutes, or until golden brown on the bottom.

6. Remove the fraguni from the baking sheet and cool on a rack. Refrigerate if not using within a few hours. Serve at room temperature.

PANE ARABO

"Arab" Bread

These somewhat flat breads bear an obvious relationship to pita and other Middle Eastern breads. In Italy, you can find versions that are more like pizza and others that are more like fluffy pita. What they all have in common is being relatively flat. Split in half, these make a tasty vehicle for a sandwich.

BIGA FOR PANE ARABO

When cooking in Italy, I always use a biga that is 50 percent hydration—that is, the weight of the water is equal to 50 percent of the weight of the flour. In the dry climates of Palm Springs and Santa Fe, where I now do the majority of my cooking, I find that I need to add more water to get the same outcome because the flour contains less humidity. If you are making this in a dry climate, you should use 125 grams (½ cup plus 1 teaspoon) of water.

Metric Measure	Ingredient	American Measure
225 grams	Italian 00 flour W-300 to W-320	1¾ cups less 1 tablespoon
0.75 grams	Active dry yeast	¼ teaspoon
113 grams	Ice water	½ cup less 1 teaspoon

1. Follow the instructions for a 22-hour biga on page 213.

DOUGH AND BAKING

I know that creating a mixture of flours to achieve a desired W-value can seem daunting, but it's just not practical to keep an array of flours for every possible W-value you might need. For this recipe, you can combine 179 grams (1⅓ cups) of Antimo Caputo Chef's Flour (W-300 to W-320) with enough Paolo Mariani "dolci" flour (W-180) to make 500 grams (3¾ cups). In a dry climate you will probably need to increase the water to 325 grams (1⅓ cups)

Metric Measure	Ingredient	American Measure
500 grams	Italian 00 flour W-220	3¾ cups
7 grams	Active dry yeast	2¼ teaspoons
5 grams	Powdered skim milk	1¼ tablespoons
280 grams	Water	1 cup plus 2½ tablespoons
9 grams	Granulated sugar	2¼ teaspoons
1 recipe	Biga for Pane Arabo (immediately preceding)	1 recipe
17 grams	Salt, preferably fine sea salt	3 teaspoons
30 grams	Lard, room temperature	2⅓ tablespoons

1. In the bowl of a stand mixer fitted with a dough hook, combine the flour, yeast, and powdered skim milk. Mix on low and add the water in two additions.

2. Mix in the sugar.

3. After a homogeneous mixture is obtained, add the biga. Mix until fully incorporated.

4. Add the salt and mix well.

5. Add the lard in 4 or 5 additions, mostly incorporating the previous addition before adding the next.

6. Increase the speed to medium and mix for about 5 minutes, or until the dough is stretchy, soft, and very slightly sticky.

7. Put the dough into a dry bowl. Cover with plastic wrap and allow the dough to rest for about 30 minutes.

8. Divide the dough into 12 portions and form each into a taut ball (see directions for shaping pizza dough on page 62). Keep the dough under a damp towel when you are not working it.

9. Roll each ball into a circle, approximately 10 centimeters (4 inches) in diameter.

10. Put the circles of dough on half-sheet pans lined with silicone mats.

11. Put the pans in a proofer at 37°C (99°F) with a container of just-boiled water to create a humid environment until the dough has tripled in size, approximately 30 minutes.

12. Flatten the risen dough with your hand. If you want thinner bread, roll again with a rolling pin.

13. Bake immediately at 220°C (425°F) until lightly golden, approximately 15 minutes.

14. After removing the bread from the oven, cover each half-sheet pan of just-baked bread with a towel until the bread is cool.

PIADINA

Italian Flatbread

These flatbreads originally from the Romagna region are popular throughout Italy. They are often folded over cured meat, cheese, and maybe a bit of arugula, and are best when freshly made. They can, however, be gently reheated in a dry pan or microwave. I usually use Paolo Mariani flour for "dolci" to make this bread. Some versions use olive oil instead of lard. If you live in a dry desert area as I do, you will probably need to increase the milk to 165 grams (1⅓ cups).

Metric Measure	Ingredient	American Measure
335 grams	Italian 00 flour W-180	2½ cups
1.1 grams	Dry yeast	⅓ teaspoon
135 grams	Milk	½ cup plus 1½ tablespoons
4 grams	Salt, preferably fine sea salt	¾ teaspoon
50 grams	Lard, at room temperature	3¾ tablespoons

1. In the bowl of a stand mixer fitted with a dough hook, combine the flour and yeast. Add the milk a little at a time while mixing on low speed. Mix well, but note that the dough will not be fully cohesive at this time.

2. Add the salt and mix.

3. Add the lard in several additions, mixing on higher speed until it is blended in.

4. Finish kneading the dough by hand. All the shaggy bits should combine into a firm, rather dry dough. If necessary, add a bit more milk or water. It may feel a little lumpy but it will become smooth after resting.

5. Form the dough into a ball, wrap tightly in plastic wrap, and allow the dough to rest at room temperature for 30 minutes.

6. Divide the dough into 8 portions. Shape into smooth balls (see directions for shaping pizza dough on page 62). Cover and allow the balls to rest at room temperature for 60 minutes.

7. Roll the balls into 20-centimeter (8-inch) circles. Cover with plastic wrap and allow the balls rest at room temperature for 90 minutes.

8. Cook in a nonstick sauté pan over medium heat until brown in spots. Flip over and brown the second side.

9. Cover the cooked piadine with a towel while cooking the remaining dough.

Pizzette
"Cocktail" Pizza

I call these cocktail pizzas because they are perfect for serving with a cocktail or aperitivo. Many bars in Italy serve apericena, which is a combination of the words *aperitivo* (cocktail) and *cena* (dinner). During the apericena, one buys one's drinks and the bar brings out food in waves, frequently including pizzette such as these. This is a very nontraditional dough. It is designed to be reheated—perfect for making in advance and then popping into the oven for a few minutes right before being served.

Metric Measure	Ingredient	American Measure
425 grams	Italian 00 flour W-320	14 ounces
7 grams	Dry yeast	¼ ounce
15 grams	Powdered skim milk	½ ounce
12 grams	Diastatic malt powder	4 teaspoons
30 grams	Sugar	1 ounce
110 grams	Milk	3⅔ ounces
105 grams	Lightly beaten whole egg	3½ ounces
105 grams	Lightly beaten egg yolk	3½ ounces
10 grams	Salt, preferably fine sea salt	Scant 2 teaspoons
100 grams	Butter, room temperature	6⅔ tablespoons
As needed	Pizza Sauce (page 62)	As needed
To taste	Dried oregano	To taste
To taste	Freshly grated Pecorino or Parmigiano cheese	To taste
To taste	Shredded mozzarella cheese	To taste

1. In the bowl of a stand mixer fitted with a dough hook, combine the flour, yeast, powdered skim milk, diastatic malt powder, and sugar. Mix to combine.

2. Add the milk all at once. After mixing, add the whole egg and then the egg yolks, mixing well after each addition.

3. Add the salt and then the butter.

4. Mix on medium speed, scraping the bowl several times, until a soft, elastic dough is formed. The dough should be tacky but not sticky.

5. Form the dough into a ball. Put the dough in a dry bowl. Cover with plastic wrap and refrigerate for approximately 1 hour.

6. On a lightly floured surface, roll the dough into a sheet 4 millimeters (1/16 inch) thick, dusting the dough and a rolling pin with flour as needed. Cut into 5½-centimeter (2½-inch) rounds. Remove the excess dough and reserve.

7. Place the dough circles on silicone-lined half-sheet pans. Top each with a spoonful of pizza sauce, a sprinkling of oregano, and a large pinch of grated cheese. Allow to proof, covered with inverted half-sheet pans, for approximately 30 minutes.

8. The remaining dough can be rerolled.

9. Bake at 160°C (325°F) with convection, until the dough is cooked, approximately 17 to 20 minutes.

10. Cool the pizzette.

11. When ready to serve, top each pizzetta with a large pinch of shredded mozzarella cheese and bake at 160°C (325°F) with convection until the cheese is melted. Serve immediately.

12. Cooled pizzette can be refrigerated or frozen.

Maestro Caridi's Fraguni, worker's pastry, filled with ricotta cheese and salame. (See page 198 for a recipe.)

An Execution at the Italian Culinary Institute

MARCH 28

After making our pasta sfoglia on Friday afternoon, March 15, at the end of Pastry Week (see the previous dispatch), we got together for a pizza party. This was a no-pressure pizza party—no competition, no judging—we just made and ate pizza and drank wine and beer. Well, there might have been a little bit of bourbon beforehand, but if there was, I'm not telling, or I don't remember, or something.

About pizza parties: Chef John feels there are certain foods that are so fundamental to Italian regional cuisine that we absolutely need to nail them perfectly by the time we finish this course. This includes pizza, focaccia, handmade pasta, and ciabatta, just to name a few. Pizza parties are fun, but they're also a way to keep practicing pizza-making to solidify our skills. It's a way to be in class without being in class.

Although the previous Pastry Week wasn't a particularly stressful period, we all seemed to let loose a bit more than we had at our previous pizza parties. Maybe it was the anticipation of the stress that we knew would accompany the upcoming execution…menu execution, that is!

The next day, Saturday, was nominally a free day. It was also beautiful. The chefs packed picnic lunches for us and we had an al fresco lunch on the beach. There was one little bit of business before lunches were distributed, however. We needed to divide ourselves

Pizza toppings prepared and ready for pizza night.

The menu card for Team B, my team.

into two groups for our next menu execution, for which preparation started the next day.

Each group also had to randomly pick ten slips of paper out of a box (well, this is a cooking school so it was really a plastic food container, not a box). Each of the twenty total slips of paper in the box contained the name of one of the twenty regions of Italy. Each team had to come up with a menu that reflected each of the regions it chose.

My group was assigned dinner so we didn't have a meeting to discuss our menu ideas with the chefs until noon the next day. The other group, assigned to prepare a luncheon, had a 9 a.m. muster. We took the afternoon off completely and planned to convene early the next morning to come up with menu ideas.

Some of us, and not just myself, were not in favor of squandering the extra time that we were afforded by not having to present our menu until noon the next day. We wanted to get at least a few hours of work in on the menu, but other members of the group were more laid back and wanted to drink and relax and drink and…. So a few of us did some research in the evening to identify the most characteristic raw ingredients and classic dishes of each of our regions. This proved to be a valuable head start the next day.

Coming up with a complex menu is stressful. Coming up with a complex menu that meets Chef John's criterion that it would be worthy of a €250 price tag is even more stressful. Chef John likes complicated menus. He also likes complicated dishes. Sometimes a complicated dish becomes even more complicated during the days of preparation as Chef John gets a new idea that he "suggests" we consider. He gets a certain gleam in his eye when an idea excites him, and suggestion or not, you know you've got to try it when he gets that look. (Remember the pasta sfoglia from the end of Pastry Week? It became one such complication.)

Fregola allo Scoglio. (See page 219 for a recipe for fregola with clams and cherry tomatoes.)

We blew by our noon presentation time the next day without a formed menu. It took us all day, and I mean all day, to come up with a menu that met his approval. We also had to pair four wines with our meal. We didn't actually work on the pairing until the day before service, but I've noted the wines along with the dishes with which they were paired. Here's where our menu ended up:

Antipasto Tris
Caponata with Marinated Anchovy Crudo
Baby Octopus Salad Perfumed with Citrus in a Puff Pastry Shell
Small Arancini Filled with Cuttlefish and Peas on Spicy Tomato Sauce
Pane Carasau (Sardinian Crispy Flatbread)
Wine: Prosecco
Table bread: Ciabatta

Primo Piatto #1
Risotto with Peas and Pea Cream Garnished with Mint Oil, Fried Peas, Parmigiano Chips, and a Fried Mint Leaf

Primo Piatto #2
Fregola allo Scoglio (Sardinian Toasted Pasta with Seafood)
Wine: Falanghina

Primo Piatto #3
Cannolo alla Norma

Secondo Tris
Rabbit Involtini with Prosciutto San Daniele and Sage, Porcini Mushroom Trifolata
Rabbit alla Ligure (Braised Rabbit with Olives, Artichokes, and Pine Nuts)
Pan-Seared Rabbit Loin with Balsamic Onion Sauce and Potato Puree
Spring Vegetables
Focaccia with Parmigiano-Reggiano and Black Pepper
Wine: Aglianico

Dolce Tris
Babà, Rum Syrup, Pistachio and White Chocolate Sauce, Candied Pistachio
Babà, Hazelnut Liqueur Syrup, Hazelnut and Milk Chocolate Sauce, Candied Hazelnut
Babà, Amaretto Syrup, Almond and Dark Chocolate Sauce, Candied Almond
Vin Santo Gelato
Cantucci
Wine: Vin Santo

Chef Juan made this beautiful pan de jamón (bread filled with ham) for the Venezuelan dinner.

With our menu finally settled just before dinner on Sunday, we put together a spreadsheet of all the ingredients we needed, as our shopper would depart at 8 a.m. the next day. We all went to bed early. But before that, Chef Juan and Mariana (also a culinary school graduate) treated us to a wonderful traditional Venezuelan dinner on Sunday. The hard work was to begin on Monday and this was a very welcome treat.

Mariana made this amazing polvorosa de cerdo (savory stuffed pastry) accompanied by a salad of valerian for the first course of the Venezuelan dinner.

SHOWTIME

We were allotted kitchen time starting at 2 p.m. on Monday. We met early in the day to plan out all the tasks, day by day, working toward serving our meal at 6 p.m. on Wednesday. We then made the initial assignment of tasks for the first day.

As the focaccia recipe was mine, I was asked to make it. Of the remaining dishes I particularly wanted to make the babà and the risotto. I wanted to make the babà because I'd never made babà before and Maestro Caridi had just taught us how, and the risotto because I love making risotto. Because I was making the focaccia and the babà, it was logical that I should make everything that needed to be prepared in the pastry lab. That still left the risotto as an option for me to prepare on the night of service, as all the component parts would be prepared by the other members of our group.

I spent three calm afternoons in the pastry lab (well, other than witnessing one meltdown by a kitchen assistant on the last day). I made:

- Biga (a preferment for ciabatta)
- Ciabatta
- Focaccia
- Pane carasau
- Cannoli shells
- Cantucci
- Babà
- Three different liquor syrups for the babà
- Chocolate-free sauces for each of the babà for a guest who did not eat chocolate (one of the other students made the chocolate-based sauces)

Cannolo alla Norma is really a Frankenstein. We took two classic Sicilian dishes, one sweet (cannoli) and one savory (pasta alla Norma), and combined them. I made savory cannoli shells. The filling was eggplant and three types of ricotta (fresca, salata, and infornata). The whole thing rested on a puddle of tomato sauce. This was one of the ideas that captivated Chef John after we had proposed a much more traditional pasta. (Gleam…suggestion…execution.)

As for the pasta sfoglia (puff pastry), we thought our antipasto was a done deal after Sunday's meeting but somewhere around Tuesday, Chef John thought it was too plain. He suggested (gleam…) that we make puff pastry shells to hold the baby octopus salad. As we were nearing execution time, one of the other students in our group was in the pastry lab rolling out, cutting, and baking the best of the puff pastry we had made on the last day of Pastry Week to make shells for the octopus salad!

The group asked if I would cover front of the house for the dinner. Everyone agreed that I could still make the risotto and that they would cover my position, but it just seemed too complicated and stressful, as well as disruptive for the guests, so I opted to just work front of the house. I had to introduce each dish, describe where it came from (if traditional) or how we created it using ingredients characteristic of one or more of our regions, and describe each of the wines and explain why they paired well with the dishes. I also added a bit of patter here and there to keep the evening light with anecdotes about the possible origin of the name "vin santo" and a story about Pasquale Caputo, aka Pat Cooper, the Italian-American comedian.

When the meal was over, the chefs marched into the kitchen to give us a bit of feedback (the positive feedback…the more critical feedback would wait until after break). As they were leaving, I asked Chef John if we could open a bottle of wine in the kitchen (a violation of school rules). He said we could do *anything* we wanted. The emphasis was his. I knew the criticism, when it came, would likely be sharp, as it should be (you can't justify a €250 dinner without perfection), but I also knew that his response was an indication that we had done a good job. It was a positive end to a taxing week.

The Final Day

Unlike our first menu execution where classes ended on the day we cooked and served our meals, we had one day of class left.

It was a pretty low-key day, though. We left at 8:45 in the morning on Thursday, March 21, for a "cultural excursion" to Azienda Statti. The Statti Company (azienda

= company) is located on an estate that has been in the hands of the baronial Statti family since the late 1700s. The company is currently managed by two brothers, Alberto and Antonio Statti.

The estate originally produced olive oil. It has been producing wine since the 1960s, but only in the last few decades have the brothers endeavored to market wine under their own name. The estate also has citrus groves, a range of other crops, eight hundred cows, and forage for the cows.

The organic waste created from crushing grapes for wine and pressing olives for oil, as well as the organic waste from the cows, is used to produce methane. Much of the methane is used to generate electricity. The olive pits are not used for methane but instead are dried and coarsely ground to produce fuel for pellet stoves that are used to heat the buildings. The estate is energy self-sufficient, and even sells electricity back to the local utility.

After a tour of the grounds and winery we had a tasting of eight wines, four white and four red. The group consensus was that the wines were quite good. Remember, we had a whole week of wine tasting with a sommelier as well as the occasional guided tasting, so we've tasted a fair amount of wine.

Other than Cirò in northeast Calabria, Calabrian wines aren't well known outside of Calabria. Statti is trying to break into a crowded market. One of its strategies is to price its wines aggressively low to try to gain market share. Good wines at great prices equals a winning strategy for consumers.

Following the wine tasting we were served an array of locally produced cheeses and salumi with bread and olive oil from Statti, of course. Statti olive oil is really good, too!

We got back to school minutes before lunch was served at 2 p.m. After lunch we were free. A five-day break was looming and the atmosphere was relaxed.

The next day, I planned on boarding a plane to Pisa to spend a few days with Zia Fidalma and cousin Massimo in Benabbio.

BIGA
Italian "Pre-Dough"

Biga is a pre-dough that is used in an array of Italian breads. Unlike lievito madre (mother yeast), which is a starter made from wild yeast similar to sourdough, biga is made with commercial yeast. Biga adds complexity to baked goods. I always start my biga the day before, so I make a 22-hour biga. If you need to make biga in less time, refer to the chart that follows and use flour of the correct W-value.

Metric Measure	Ingredient	American Measure
500 grams	Italian 00 flour (see below for W value)	3¾ cups
1.5 grams	Active dry yeast	½ teaspoon
250 grams	Ice water (see Tip)	1 cup

1. In the bowl of a stand mixer fitted with a dough hook, combine the flour and yeast.

2. Add the water and mix until thoroughly combined. (Note: There is no need to knead the dough to develop gluten. This will happen from the long hydration time coupled with the kneading of the final product.)

3. Put the dough into an ungreased bowl. Cover with plastic wrap (see Tip) and allow the dough to rest for the appropriate amount of time.

Tip: When baking professionally in Italy, biga is made in large quantities and covered with a cloth during the fermentation period. The dry crust is removed and the required amount of biga is portioned from the moist middle. I find that with the smaller quantities I make in my home kitchen, coupled with the minimal humidity where I live, I need to cover the biga with plastic wrap or it becomes too dry. With this method, you can make the appropriate amount of biga for the recipe without needing to account for discard.

Tip: The science behind biga indicates that the temperature of the flour plus the temperature of the room plus the temperature of the water should equal 55°C. This only works in degrees Celsius. There have been times that I have ignored this rule. I can't really say that I've noticed a significant difference. If you don't want to do the calculations, use ice water and I promise the results will be fine.

Tip: Use flour of the appropriate W-value based on how long the biga will rest before use:

W-Value	Rest Time (hours)
W-180	6–8
W-220	8–12
W-240	12–16
W-260	16–20
W-300	20–22
W-320	22–24

CANTUCCI
Tuscan Almond Biscotti

Cantucci are the Tuscan version of biscotti and are traditionally made with bitter almonds. Bitter almonds have the flavor that we associate with almonds, but they are unavailable in the United States. Stateside, I add almond extract (which is made from bitter almonds) to the almonds when toasting them to add the characteristic flavor. There is no leavening agent in this recipe. Also, I have successfully made these with American all-purpose flour instead of Italian 00 flour.

Metric Measure	Ingredient	American Measure
125 grams	Whole almonds, blanched, if desired (see Tip)	4½ ounces
1 teaspoon	Almond extract	1 teaspoon
2 large	Eggs	2 large
160 grams	Sugar	¾ cup plus ¾ tablespoon
½ pinch	Salt, preferably fine sea salt	½ pinch
50 grams	Unsalted butter, melted and cooled slightly	3½ tablespoons
250 grams	Italian 00 flour W-180 (see headnote)	1 cup less 1 tablespoon
1	Beaten egg for brushing	1
1 tablespoon	Milk	1 tablespoon

1. Toss the almonds with the almond extract. Put on a half-sheet pan and toast in the oven at 190°C (375°F) for about 5 minutes, during which time the almonds should become aromatic but not take on much color. Remove from the sheet pan and cool to room temperature.

2. In the bowl of a stand mixer fitted with a paddle, beat the eggs, sugar, and salt until creamy and light.

3. Mix in the melted butter. Add the flour and mix until just blended.

4. Add the almonds and allow the mixer to make just a few turns so as not to break the almonds. Finish mixing by hand.

5. Divide the dough into three or four portions. Form each portion into a log on half-sheet pans lined with silicone mats. The initial shaping can be done with a bench scraper, but the final shaping is best done with wet hands to get a smooth surface.

6. Beat the egg and milk. Brush the top of each log with the egg wash.

7. Bake at 180°C (350°F) until lightly browned on top. The length of time will vary depending on how thick the logs are (see Tip).

8. After the logs have cooled for about 10 minutes on the sheet pans, put them on a rack to cool completely.

9. When cool, slice the logs diagonally about 8 millimeters ($1/3$ inch) thick, or more or less to taste.

10. Lay the slices on a half-sheet pan, cut side up. Bake at 160°C (325°F) until dry and lightly golden, approximately 15 minutes. Turn the cantucci over and continue to bake until the second side is golden, about 5 minutes more. Cool on a rack.

Tip: If you use whole, unblanched almonds you will have visual contrast from the almond skin. Alternatively, blanched almonds will create a more elegant look but with less visual effect.

Tip: The cantucci will spread as they bake. If you want small cantucci, the logs should be no more than 2½ centimeters (1 inch) in diameter. Logs that are 5 centimeters (2 inches) in diameter will yield much larger cantucci.

CAPONATA
Caponata

This is one of the ways I use up eggplant from our garden. The vinegar allows it to be safely canned in a boiling water bath. If you don't want to can it, the caponata will keep in the refrigerator for several weeks. Caponata frequently appears on antipasto plates in our house in the months after harvest time.

Metric Measure	Ingredient	American Measure
180 grams	Diced red bell pepper	6⅓ ounces
180 grams	Diced celery	6⅓ ounces
360 grams	Diced onion	12⅔ ounces
320 milliliters	Extra-virgin olive oil	11 fluid ounces
1400 grams	Unpeeled eggplant cut in 1-centimeter (½-inch) cubes	3 pounds
600 milliliters	Water	20 fluid ounces
To taste	Salt, preferably fine sea salt	To taste
To taste	Freshly ground black pepper	To taste
70 grams	Turbinado sugar	5½ tablespoons
120 milliliters	Red wine vinegar	½ cup
120 milliliters	Vinegar-packed capers, drained	½ cup
140 grams	Chopped green olives	5 ounces
700 grams	Passata (tomato puree)	24½ ounces

1. Sauté the peppers, celery, and onions in olive oil until the onions become translucent. Add the eggplant and sauté, stirring frequently, until most of the eggplant has become translucent. This will only take a few minutes. Do not allow the eggplant to become mushy.

2. Add the water and salt and pepper to taste. Cover and cook until just tender, approximately 5 minutes.

3. Remove the cover. Quickly evaporate any remaining liquid.

4. Add the turbinado sugar and vinegar. Cook until almost dry.

5. Add the capers, olives, and passata. Bring to a simmer. Adjust the salt and pepper.

6. Pack into 250 milliliter (1 cup) Mason jars, leaving ½ centimeter (¼ inch) headroom and process in a boiling water bath for 10 minutes.

7. Store in a cool, dark place. Serve at room temperature.

CIABATTA
Ciabatta

The word *ciabatta* means slipper in Italian, and many loaves of ciabatta vaguely resemble a slipper. Ciabatta is a soft bread with lots of irregular holes. This recipe freezes particularly well. After thawing, the loaves can be reheated in a 180°C (350°F) oven for a few minutes to regain that just-baked softness.

BIGA FOR CIABATTA

I generally make a 22-hour biga using Antimo Caputo Chef's Flour or another W-320 Italian 00 flour. As with all of my baking recipes, I encourage you to measure ingredients by weight, not volume. If you want to make a biga with a different resting time, the instructions can be found on page 213.

Metric Measure	Ingredient	American Measure
800 grams	Italian 00 flour	6 cups
2.4 grams	Active dry yeast	¾ teaspoon
400 grams	Ice water	1⅔ cups

1. Make the biga following the process on page 213.

DOUGH AND BAKING

Semolina is flour made from durum wheat, a hard-grain wheat. Three grinds are commonly available in Italy: coarse, medium, and fine. So-called semola rimacinata (remilled), which is used in this recipe, is twice-ground semolina flour, a fine grind. You can buy Italian semola rimacinata online. If you are buying semolina packaged for the American market, be sure to get a very fine grind, as much of what is sold on the American market is a coarse grind.

Metric Measure	Ingredient	American Measure
500 grams plus more to shape the dough	Semola rimacinata	3¾ cups plus more to shape the dough
7 grams	Active dry yeast	¼ ounce
470 grams	Water	2 cups less 1 tablespoon

An Execution at the Italian Culinary Institute

1 recipe	Biga (immediately preceding)	1 recipe
3 grams	Granulated sugar	¾ teaspoon
34 grams	Salt, preferably fine sea salt	2 tablespoons
30 grams	Lard, room temperature	2⅓ tablespoons
30 grams plus more to oil the dough	Extra-virgin olive oil	2⅓ tablespoons plus more to oil the dough

1. In the bowl of a stand mixer fitted with a dough hook, combine the semola and yeast. Begin to mix on low.

2. Add half the water and then continue to add the water a little at a time, allowing it to mix in.

3. After a uniform mixture is obtained, add the biga. Mix on low until the mixture is homogeneous.

4. When well combined, add the sugar.

5. Add the salt and mix on higher speed to develop gluten.

6. Turn the mixer to low and add the lard a small amount at a time.

7. After all the lard in incorporated, drizzle in the olive oil.

8. When fully incorporated, increase the speed and mix until the gluten has fully developed.

9. Form the dough into a smooth ball and put it in a well-oiled bowl. Gently rub olive oil over the top of the dough. Cover the bowl with plastic wrap and allow the dough to rest for 30 minutes at room temperature, or until the gluten relaxes. It is ready when it does not spring back when depressed lightly with a finger.

10. Slide the dough out of bowl onto a surface dusted with semola. Slide the dough as much as possible; don't pull at it so as to not deflate it. You can very gently shape the dough into a rough rectangle, if desired, by sliding your hands under a corner and gently sliding them outward.

11. Cut the dough into three pieces. If desired, cut each piece in half.

12. Using a very wide bench scraper, again so as to not deflate the dough, put the pieces on half-sheet pans lined with parchment paper that has been dusted with semola.

13. Put the pans in a proofer at 37°C (99°F) with a container of just-boiled water to create a humid environment until the loaves have tripled in size.

14. Bake at 200°C (400°F) for approximately 20 minutes, using convection, until lightly golden.

15. Cool the loaves on the sheet pans, covered with a cloth to retain moisture.

16. The loaves may be frozen. Defrost and then heat in a 180°C (350°F) oven for about 5 minutes just before serving.

 Fregola con Vongole e Pomodorini
Fregola Pasta with Clams and Cherry Tomatoes

Fregola is small spherical pasta from Sardinia that is toasted. Each batch includes different degrees of toasting, which creates gustatory and textural interest. Cooking the clams in a dry pot produces a very concentrated liquid that is used to finish the pasta. In place of the crushed red pepper, you can use minced fresh red chile pepper to taste.

Metric Measure	Ingredient	American Measure
36	Littleneck clams	36
60 milliliters plus more	Extra-virgin olive oil, divided	¼ cup plus more
200 grams	Cherry tomatoes	7 ounces
150 milliliters	Dry white wine, divided	⅔ cup
1	Bay leaf, preferably fresh	1
1 teaspoon	Dried oregano	1 teaspoon
4 cloves	Garlic, thinly sliced	4 cloves
1 teaspoon or to taste	Crushed red pepper	1 teaspoon or to taste
450–500 grams	Fregola pasta	~1 pound
To taste	Salt, preferably fine sea salt	To taste
To taste	Freshly grated black pepper	To taste
3 tablespoons	Minced fresh parsley	3 tablespoons

1. Wash the clams in several changes of cold water. Put the clams in a dry heavy-bottomed Dutch oven. Cover and cook on medium-high heat until all the clams have opened, approximately 5 to 7 minutes. Pour the clams into a sieve, reserving the clams and cooking liquid separately.

2. In a sauté pan, heat 1 tablespoon of olive oil. Add the tomatoes and sauté until the tomatoes blister and begin to split, approximately 2 minutes. Add half the wine, the bay leaf, and the oregano and boil rapidly until most of the wine has evaporated. Transfer to a bowl and reserve.

3. Bring 3 liters (3 quarts) of water seasoned with 75 grams (¼ cup) of salt to a rolling boil.

4. Meanwhile, put the remaining 3 tablespoons of olive oil, garlic, and crushed red pepper into a large sauté pan. Sauté on medium heat until the garlic is golden. Add the remaining wine and immediately remove from the heat.

5. Add the pasta to the boiling salted water and cook at a rapid boil for approximately 2 minutes less than the minimum cooking time on the package for al dente pasta, stirring frequently to prevent sticking.

6. Drain the pasta, reserving the pasta-cooking water.

7. Add the par-cooked pasta to the garlic-wine mixture in the sauté pan and finish cooking at a moderate boil, adding the reserved clam-cooking liquid and then the pasta-cooking water 1 ladle at a time, shaking the pan and stirring the pasta, until the pasta is al dente, leaving the sauce liquid enough to just coat the pasta. Adjust the salt and pepper while finishing the pasta.

8. Add the tomatoes and clams along with the last ladle of pasta-cooking water.

9. Garnish each serving with a sprinkling of minced parsley and a drizzle of extra-virgin olive oil.

PANE CARASAU
Crispy Sardinian Flatbread

Semola rimacinata is twice-ground semolina. It is quite fine. Italian semola rimacinata is available online and in some specialty stores. If you are buying semola that is labeled "semolina" in the United States, be sure that it is a very fine grind. If you live in an arid climate, as I currently do, you may need to add up to 15 grams (1 tablespoon) more water to create a workable dough. I tested this recipe in a domestic oven that reaches 500°F. If you have a pizza oven or access to a commercial oven that can hold a higher temperature, set it at 350°C (660°F) for the initial bake.

Metric Measure	Ingredient	American Measure
500 grams	Semola rimacinata	4½ cups
3 grams	Dry yeast	1 teaspoon
250 grams	Water	1 cup plus 1 tablespoon
5 grams	Salt, preferably fine sea salt	Scant 1 teaspoon

1. Combine the semola and yeast in bowl of a stand mixer fitted with a dough hook. Begin to mix and then add the water a little at a time. After the water is incorporated, add the salt.

2. The dough is rather dry, but you should be able to incorporate all the flour by using your hands. If not, add a bit more water. Finish kneading by hand to form a firm, smooth dough.

3. Form the dough into a smooth ball. Put the dough in a dry bowl, cover with plastic wrap, and allow it to rest for 60 to 90 minutes, or until the gluten relaxes.

4. Divide the dough into 10 portions and roll into taut balls (see directions for shaping pizza dough on page 62).

5. Place the dough on a half-sheet pan lined with a silicone mat or parchment. Put the pan in a proofer at 37°C (99°F) with a container of just-boiled water to create a humid environment until the dough has doubled or tripled in size. This will take several hours.

6. Using a rolling pin on a semola-dusted surface, roll each ball into thin rounds approximately 20 centimeters (8 inches) in diameter.

7. Put the rounds on parchment-lined half-sheet pans. Two circles of dough will fit on each pan. Allow the circles of dough to rest for 10 to 15 minutes.

8. Bake at 260°C (500°F) (or higher, see headnote) until the dough is puffed and just beginning to brown around the edges.

9. Immediately remove from the oven and using a sharp, thin knife that will reach from the edge to the middle of each round, separate the top and bottom halves. Put rounds with the inside facing up on a rack while baking the rest of the dough.

10. When all the rounds have been cut, reduce the oven temperature to 180°C (350°F) and bake the rounds, inside up, until crispy and brown in spots.

A Cat Named Pancetta and a Pizza Called Amnesia

APRIL 2

Friday, March 22, was the first day of a five-day break at school. I headed for the airport in Lamezia Terme and boarded a Ryanair jet bound for Pisa. Cousin Massimo was meeting me at the airport and taking me to Benabbio to spend a few days with him and Zia Fidalma.

The flight was uneventful, but boarding was a bit chaotic. Though it seems to vary on different routes, Ryanair basically has three classes: Cattle Call, Priority, and Priority with Expedited Check-In. Priority sounds like a good thing since you get priority boarding (there's no such thing as boarding by row or group number in Italy) until you realize that more than half the plane has bought Priority, mostly so that they can bring more than a toothbrush on board.

Before the announcements start at the gate, passengers start forming into a mob—polite, mind you, but still a mob—stretching from the gate agent outward, filling any possible space in the boarding area. Apparently, this is Priority, but unless you've flown Ryanair before, you wouldn't know. Until I figured out what was going on (which really taxed my minimal Italian), I was only a few passengers from the end of the mob.

The Cattle Call passengers actually stay seated in the gate area. They can only bring on one bag that weighs a

Cavoletto, a wild green that Massimo and I picked from the garden plot that also contains their olive trees.

maximum of seven kilograms (just under fifteen and a half pounds), and it must fit under their seat, which is likely to be a middle seat since they don't get to select their own seats. They don't really need to try to sneak on the plane early, as happens in the States, because they don't need to struggle for bin space because they can't bring more than one small bag with them.

There was a small group of Priority Plus passengers queuing tranquilly at the gate. None of them was Italian. It's not clear why they've paid more than the cost of Priority to get expedited security screening. The airport in Lamezia Terme is small and there's not much time to be saved. Also, the Italians don't make you take off your shoes or remove your liquids or laptop from your bag! Getting through security is pretty easy.

It turns out that being at the end of the Priority mob isn't a big deal. After we clear the gate, we head down the ramp to form another mob near a set of sliding-glass doors. There's lots of empty space and I get a spot near the doors, as people congregate leisurely in this much bigger space.

Once all the Priority passengers are in the new holding area, the doors open and we walk across the tarmac to the waiting plane. This is not a regimented, walk-in-a-line-on-the-striped-area-toward-the-plane walk. This is more like the running of the bulls in Pamplona, just slower. (Italians never seem to be in a hurry.) I head toward the stairs at the back of the plane because my boarding pass says that's where I should enter. It turns out, I'm pretty much in the middle of the plane (row eighteen out of thirty-six).

Italians never seem to be in a hurry. (I just said that, right?) They stand in the aisle having conversations, taking off their jackets, neatly folding their jackets, putting their folded jackets on top of their bags in the overhead bins, having more conversations, thinking about getting out of the aisle and sitting. I'm convinced they'd stand there and have coffee if they could!

I finally make it to my seat, still uncrowded and with open overhead bins, but not before a slight, soft-spoken older man with a nice smile tries to have a conversation with me…in dialect. I had no idea what he was saying and smiled and nodded as I found my way to my seat, hoping I wasn't being socially inappropriate.

Massimo picked me up at the Pisa Airport and we drove about an hour to Benabbio where Zia Fidalma, and lunch, were waiting. Lunch was Zia's wonderful minestra di fagioli made with borlotti beans, cooked and pureed, with a bit of pasta (lumacone, specifically) added.

The house in which my father-in-law grew up along the River Lima at Viale Papa Giovanni XXIII (Pope John Paul XXIII Avenue) #1 in Fornoli. It's on the market for 150,000 euros!

I heard about this soup when Zia Fidalma, Massimo, and Francesca visited Calabria in February. It definitely lived up to the hype. At the table we drizzled it with unfiltered olive oil made from their own olive trees and added a bit of black pepper. Red wine accompanied the soup. Bread allowed me to sop up every bit of soup from my bowl before proceeding to cheese and fruit.

After lunch, Massimo and I walked to their garden plot full of olive trees. In years past, vegetables would have been planted among the trees, but no longer. We picked a wild green called *cavoletto*, which accompanied our dinner later that day.

After lunch, Massimo and I took a drive, first to Fornoli to see the house in which my father-in-law grew up, dubbed Casa Pieri by Zia Fidalma and Massimo. At ninety square meters (less than 970 square feet), the house is for sale for €150,000—a steep price.

Afterward, we went to Barga, a picturesque town where my husband's grandfather was born. We made a short stop at a wine shop in Bagni di Lucca owned by one of Massimo's friends before getting to Benabbio just after 7 p.m. for dinner.

Bourbon is difficult to come by in Italy. After a bit of Russian vodka, we settled down to the meal: fettine di manzo in umido (thinly sliced beef cooked in a small amount of tomato sauce with olives—and sometimes capers), purè di patate, cavoletto briefly boiled and dressed with olive oil, and bread. The olives were from their trees and cured by Zia Fidalma. The olive oil was also their own production. Fruit and cheese rounded out the meal for me, though there was also a homemade torta de mele (apple tart).

Spring flowers at the local garden center.

The next morning, we did a grocery run to the big hypermarket in Gallicano, a nearby town, before stopping at the open-air mercatino in Bagni di Lucca. Back at home we stood around the stove while Zia Fidalma made focaccette rimpiturite, which we ate hot from the griddle with stracchino.

Focaccette are thin savory pancake-like affairs made from a batter of flour and cornmeal with a slice of pancetta in the middle. The whole thing is cooked between two cast iron griddles. I declined dessert, but Zia Fidalma was prepared to make necci, a thin cake made of chestnut flour.

We did a bit of walking around Benabbio, including looking at the outside of houses for sale. The house adjacent to Massimo and Zia Fidalma is for sale. It has a kitchen, large salon, two bedrooms, and a bath on the first floor. There is an additional room on the second floor. On the ground floor is a workroom, a large cellar, and a garage. I also got to meet Pancetta, a cat that belongs to Massimo's cousin.

That afternoon we went for another drive, this time to Castelnuovo, and hit a few garden centers as well. In the evening, after another nip of vodka, we met Francesca for pizza at Es Vedra in Fornoli, where Casa Pieri is located. In fact, Casa Pieri and Es Vedra are on the same street: Viale Papa Giovanni XXIII (Pope John Paul XXIII Avenue). Casa Pieri is at #1. Es Vedra is at #94.

I'm happy to say that 'nduja has invaded Tuscany. I had a really wonderful pizza with 'nduja plus the better part of half a liter of wine. Francesca assisted me by drinking a glassful after finishing her beer. The pizza with 'nduja was listed on the menu as Pizza Amnesia. I can assure you that I don't want to forget it! I now think of Es Vedra as our neighborhood pizzeria even though we don't own Casa Pieri...yet!

Dinner prepared by Zia Fidalma: Fettine di Manzo in Umido, Pure di Patate, Cavoletto. The olives were cured by Zia Fidalma and came from their own trees as did the olive oil. (See page 114 for a recipe for fettine di manzo in umido.)

BACK TO CALABRIA

On Sunday, I flew back to Calabria. This time I knew the drill with Priority and managed to get in the right line at the gate. After an uneventful flight, I was met outside of baggage claim by my driver. As we were walking out of the airport at 1:45 p.m., he told me that he needed to be back at 3 p.m. to pick up some other people. Normally, the drive from the airport to the school is about forty-five minutes, not counting parking. I assumed he might be a bit late for his next trip. Not so! We made it back to the school in twenty-three minutes! Never once did I care to look at the speedometer as we were hurtling down the autostrada!

There were still two more days left to the break. Other than a three-hour walk on Monday that was prompted by a bourbon run, I spent the two days relaxing. The rest of the week was low-key as well.

We had cultural visits on Wednesday and Thursday. The Wednesday visit was to an agriturismo, where almost everything we ate, including all the cured meats, were made in-house. The Thursday visit was centered around a visit to Squillace to see the castle, visit a small shop that produces handmade and hand-painted terracotta, and have lunch prepared by someone's nonna in the style of a shepherd's lunch.

Despite the rain, we did the first two. Unfortunately, Nonna had been hospitalized and was unable to make lunch. Instead, we went to a restaurant where we were served a dizzying array of antipasti followed by a revelatory pasta of thick hand-made noodles (fileja, I believe) in a minimalistic but delicious tomato sauce with just the barest amount of porcini and shrimp. It was truly a perfect example of how less can be more.

Friday was a day off, though there was a run to the open-air market for those of us who wanted to go. I managed to buy a large quantity of peperoncino picante, which I plan to use to make cured meats, as well as two dozen babà molds.

Saturday was the last day before Cheese Week and the addition of new students to our group. It had been several weeks since we last sat in the kitchen and watched Chef John demonstrate the preparation of various dishes. It brought back a comfortable feeling, which several of us discussed later, to sit there and have Chef John demonstrate how to make pasta all'arrabbiata; fegato di coniglio con porri (rabbit liver with leeks); gnocchi, spade, e melanzane (gnocchi with swordfish and eggplant); and pasta alla carbonara—all of which we ate before lunch.

A wonderful antipasto platter of all housemade ingredients at Agriturismo La Sena in Santa Caterina dello Ionio.

After lunch, Chef Juan demonstrated a technique for making a frittata, which we of course ate with bread and roasted garlic aioli that Chef Juan also made to accompany the frittata.

In the afternoon, we joined Chef Juan in the pastry lab to make limoncello, arancello, and liquore di melograno (pomegranate liqueur). Chef John sent in afternoon snacks. First was rigatoni with a sauce of pureed fresh green peas, the sauce for which he had demonstrated that morning. Later we got white chocolate orange spuma (mousse) with panettone browned in butter and dotted with whipped cream!

With Cheese Week about to start the next day, for which four additional students would join us, followed by our final menu execution the following week, Saturday was really the last day we would be together ourselves as a group. When all the work was done, Chef Juan sliced a beautiful jamón ibérico de bellota that he had brought back from Spain before we began the master's program in January. He also served an amazing morcilla (blood sausage) from Spain that was made with fat from jamón ibérico. A few bottles of wine rounded out the afternoon.

At 7:45 p.m. we headed out for pizza with the new students who were joining us for Cheese Week. Our new adventure was about to begin.

Fileja con Gamberi e Funghi
Fileja Pasta with Shrimp and Mushrooms

I reconstructed this dish from a similar one that I had at a restaurant in Calabria. It is an example of how very few ingredients can create an amazing combination. I always have mushroom broth in the freezer to enrich an array of dishes. If you don't have any, take the stems from the mushrooms used in this recipe and chop them. Add 5 grams (⅙ ounce) dried porcini and 750 milliliters (3 cups) water. Bring to a boil and boil gently until reduced to 500 milliliters (2 cups). Strain and proceed with the recipe. If you have Garlic Oil (page 57) on hand, you can sauté the mushroom caps in a mixture of half garlic oil and half extra-virgin olive oil and eliminate the garlic cloves.

Metric Measure	Ingredient	American Measure
130 grams	Mushroom caps	4½ ounces
2 cloves	Garlic, bruised with a chef's knife	2 cloves
60 milliliters	Extra-virgin olive oil	4 tablespoons
To taste	Salt, preferably fine sea salt	To taste
500 milliliters	Mushroom Broth (page 118)	2 cups
To taste	Freshly ground black pepper	To taste
200 grams	Headless, unpeeled shrimp, U 31–40	7 ounces
250 milliliters	Passata (tomato puree)	1 cup
500 grams	Fileja or other rustic medium-length pasta	~1 pound
2 tablespoons	Basil chiffonade	2 tablespoons
As needed	Extra-virgin olive oil	As needed

1. Slice the mushroom caps 4 millimeters (1/6 inch) thick.

2. In a sauté pan, brown the garlic in olive oil over gentle heat until golden brown. Discard the garlic. Turn the heat to medium-high and add the sliced mushroom caps. Toss to coat with oil. Season with salt.

3. After the mushrooms have absorbed all the oil, reduce the heat to low until they start to release liquid. Return the heat to medium-high and sauté until some of the mushrooms become golden and a few get brown spots. Add 1/3 of the broth. Season with black pepper. Boil gently until the liquid has evaporated. Add another 1/3 of the broth and boil until evaporated. Add the remaining broth, adjust the salt and pepper, and boil until reduced to 125 milliliters (½ cup). Remove from the heat and reserve.

4. Meanwhile, bring a pot of salted water to a boil. Add the shrimp. As soon as the water returns to a boil, remove the pot from the heat and cover it. After 1 minute, drain the shrimp and plunge them in ice water to stop cooking. When cool, peel and devein the shrimp and cut them in half lengthwise. Reserve.

5. Bring 3 liters (3 quarts) of water seasoned with 75 grams (¼ cup) of salt to a rolling boil.

6. Meanwhile, combine the passata and cooked mushrooms with their liquid in a large sauté pan. Bring to a simmer.

7. Add the pasta to the boiling salted water and cook at a rapid boil for approximately 2 minutes less than the minimum cooking time on the package for al dente pasta, stirring frequently to prevent sticking.

8. Drain the pasta, reserving the pasta-cooking water.

9. Add the par-cooked pasta to the sauce in the sauté pan and finish cooking at a moderate boil, adding the reserved pasta-cooking water 1 ladle at a time, shaking the pan and stirring the pasta, until the pasta is al dente, leaving the sauce liquid enough to just coat the pasta. Adjust the salt and pepper while finishing the pasta.

10. Add the cooked shrimp during the last minute.

11. Garnish each serving with basil chiffonade and a drizzle of extra-virgin olive oil.

Frittata di Pasta
Pasta Frittata

A frittata is not an "Italian omelet"! A frittata and an omelet both contain eggs, and that's where the similarity ends. What you put into a frittata is (mostly) only limited by your imagination. I'm going to suggest you make a frittata di pasta, where the "filling" is leftover pasta. I particularly like a frittata made with leftover pasta aglio e olio (pasta with garlic and olive oil), pasta con acciughe, aglio e olio (pasta with anchovies, garlic, and olive oil), or pasta with a simple red sauce. Any shape pasta will work, but I am partial to spaghetti. About 100 grams (¼ pound) of pasta, precooked weight, works well, but use what you have.

Metric Measure	Ingredient	American Measure
3 tablespoons	Extra-virgin olive oil	3 tablespoons
1–2 cloves	Garlic, minced (optional)	1–2 cloves
~100 grams	Leftover pasta with sauce (precooked weight)	~¼ pound
8 large	Eggs	8 large
To taste	Salt, preferably fine sea salt	To taste
To taste	Freshly ground black pepper	To taste

1. In a 14-inch nonstick skillet (see Tip), gently sauté the garlic, if desired, in olive oil. If you are not using garlic, just heat the oil.

2. When the garlic is just turning golden, add the pasta and cook over gentle heat to completely warm it.

3. Meanwhile, using a whisk, beat the eggs. Season with salt and pepper.

4. After the pasta is warm, rearrange it in an even layer in the skillet. If you do not see a good slick of olive oil over the bottom of the pan, drizzle in some more and gently shake the pan to allow the oil to work its way to the bottom.

5. Pour in the eggs, turn the heat to very low, and cover the pan. If you don't have a lid that fits, try a pizza pan or a half-sheet pan.

6. Cook until the top of the frittata is just set and there is no liquid egg. This will take about 15 minutes, or more, if the heat is low enough. During this time, move the pan all around the burner (side-to-side and front-to-back) every couple of minutes so that the heat is not just concentrated in the middle of the pan, which can cause the frittata to burn.

7. When the frittata is just set, shake the pan to see if it is loose enough to slide out. If not, loosen the edges with a silicone spatula. (Note: If there was enough oil in the bottom of the pan it should not stick, but sometimes the sides of the frittata need a bit of loosening with a spatula.)

8. Slide the frittata onto a pizza pan. Do not flip the frittata. The side of the frittata that was facing up while in the pan should be facing up after you slide it into the pizza pan.

9. Invert the skillet over the frittata. Hold the pizza pan and skillet together with a hand on each side and flip the frittata over in one quick motion.

10. Return the skillet to the stove, uncovered. Cook for just a few more minutes to gently brown the (now) bottom (the previous top) of the frittata.

11. Slide the frittata back into the pizza pan or onto a large serving platter. Cut into wedges and serve immediately.

Tip: I rarely use nonstick cookware, but this is one of the few instances where it is truly helpful.

Tip: A couple of handfuls of thawed, frozen peas are a welcome addition to most types of pasta when making a frittata. Stir them into the pasta just before forming it into a uniform layer.

Tip: If desired, you can sprinkle the eggs with grated Parmigiano Reggiano or Pecorino Romano cheese once you've added them to the skillet.

LIMONCELLO
Limoncello

In Italy, limoncello is made with 190-proof (95 percent) alcohol. Many states in the United States do not allow the sale of 190-proof alcohol. The highest you may be able to find is 151-proof (75.5 percent alcohol). The higher the alcohol content, the more reliable the extraction of the lemon oils. Use the freshest lemons you can find, preferably ones with a thicker zest (the yellow part) so that it is easier to peel off without getting the bitter white pith. I provided the proportions for both 190-proof and 151-proof alcohol. The directions are identical.

USING 190-PROOF ALCOHOL

Metric Measure	Ingredient	American Measure
375 grams	Lemon zest (yellow part only)	13.23 ounces
600 milliliters	190-proof alcohol (such as Everclear)	20.29 fluid ounces
900 milliliters	Water	30.44 fluid ounces
675 grams	Granulated sugar	23.81 ounces

USING 151-PROOF ALCOHOL

Metric Measure	Ingredient	American Measure
375 grams	Lemon zest (yellow part only)	13.23 ounces
750 milliliters	151-proof alcohol (such as Everclear)	25.36 fluid ounces
750 milliliters	Water	25.36 fluid ounces
675 grams	Granulated sugar	23.81 ounces

1. Using a very sharp vegetable peeler, carefully pare the zest from the lemons without including any of the white pith. It will take about 27 to 30 large lemons to get enough zest.

2. In a large (4-liter or 1-gallon) glass jar, combine the lemon zest and alcohol. Swirl to moisten all the zest.

3. Store the jar in a cool, dark place for 7 days, swirling it at least once per day.

4. On the sixth day after combining the zest and the alcohol, combine the water and sugar in a different, well-sealed, nonreactive container. Swirl several times per day until the sugar is fully dissolved and the liquid is clear.

5. On the seventh day, pour the sugar syrup into the lemon zest–alcohol mixture. The mixture will become cloudy. Allow the mixture to mellow for 3 to 4 days, swirling once or twice daily. It will turn mostly clear after a few days.

6. Strain through a sieve, discarding the solids. Put the limoncello into bottles with tight-fitting caps. Allow the limoncello to rest for about a week at room temperature before drinking. It is best served frosty cold from the freezer or refrigerator.

7. This limoncello is best consumed within 1 year.

Minestra di Fagioli di Zia Fidalma
Aunt Fidalma's Bean Soup

This soup has legendary status in the family. If you can't find borlotti beans (I often bring them back from Italy), use cranberry or Roman beans. If you want a bit more texture, remove a ladle or so of beans from the soup before pureeing the soup and add them back with the pasta. Be sure to serve lots of bread so that everyone can wipe their bowls clean.

Metric Measure	Ingredient	American Measure
300 grams	Dried borlotti beans	10½ ounces
1 large	Carrot, peeled and cut in chunks	1 large
1 stalk	Celery, cut in chunks	1 stalk
1 large	Potato, peeled and cut in chunks	1 large
To taste	Salt, preferably fine sea salt	To taste
To taste	Freshly ground black pepper	To taste
1 medium	Onion, finely diced	1 medium
2 cloves	Garlic, minced	2 cloves
2 tablespoons	Extra-virgin olive oil	2 tablespoons
175 grams	Pasta, such as small shells	6 ounces

1. Rinse and drain the beans. Cover generously with water and refrigerate overnight. You can skip the soak, but the beans will take longer to cook.

2. If you have soaked the beans, drain and rinse. Combine the beans, carrot, celery, and potato in a saucepan. Cover generously with water (more generously if you did not soak the beans first) and boil gently, partially covered, until the beans are tender.

3. Puree the soup by putting it through a food mill (Zia Fidalma's method) or whizzing it in a blender (my method). Season with salt and pepper to taste.

4. Bring 2 liters (2 quarts) of boiling water seasoned with 50 grams (3 tablespoons) of salt to a rolling boil.

5. Meanwhile, sauté the onion and garlic in the olive oil until the onion is golden. Reserve.

6. Add the pasta to the boiling salted water and cook at a rapid boil for approximately 2 minutes less than the minimum cooking time on the package for al dente pasta, stirring frequently to prevent sticking.

7. Drain the pasta and add it to the soup along with the sautéed onion and garlic, being sure to scrape in every bit of the flavored olive oil. Finish cooking the pasta in the soup, adding a bit of boiling water or pasta-cooking water, as needed.

8. Serve immediately to prevent the pasta from overcooking.

9. Pass additional extra-virgin olive oil, freshly grated Parmigiano Reggiano cheese, and black pepper at the table.

 Rigatoni ai Piselli
Rigatoni with Peas

When fresh peas are at their peak at the farmers' market, this pasta is on the menu. But honestly, really good fresh peas are available for such a short time each year that I usually make this with frozen peas. If you want to garnish with mint oil, follow the recipe for Rosemary Oil on page 262 and substitute fresh mint. Basil chiffonade is another welcome garnish.

Metric Measure	Ingredient	American Measure
500 milliliters	Peas, frozen or shelled fresh	2¼ cups
To taste	Salt, preferably fine sea salt	To taste
To taste	Freshly grated black pepper	To taste
60 grams	Pancetta	2 ounces
100 grams	Finely diced onion	¾ cup
3 tablespoons	Dry white wine	3 tablespoons
500 grams	Dry rigatoni or other short pasta	~1 pound
55 grams	Freshly grated Parmigiano Reggiano cheese	2 ounces
To garnish	Mint oil or basil chiffonade	To garnish

1. Put the peas in a heavy-bottomed saucepan. If using fresh peas, add water to cover and boil until just tender. The time will vary based on the peas. If using frozen peas, add a few splashes of water and cook until just tender, 2 to 3 minutes.

2. If desired, reserve 1 ladle of whole peas to add to the pasta. Puree the cooked peas in a blender, adding water if needed to make a pourable puree. Season with salt and pepper. Leave the peas in the blender jar.

3. Cut the pancetta into matchsticks. In a large sauté pan, sauté the pancetta over medium-low heat until crisp. Remove the pancetta.

4. Sauté the onion in the rendered fat from the pancetta until soft. Add the wine and completely evaporate it, scraping up any browned bits.

5. Add the cooked onions and rendered fat to the peas and puree again. Do not clean the sauté pan.

6. Bring 3 liters (3 quarts) of water seasoned with 75 grams (¼ cup) of salt to a rolling boil.

7. Add the pasta to the boiling salted water and cook at a rapid boil for approximately 2 minutes less than the minimum cooking time on the package for al dente pasta, stirring frequently to prevent sticking.

8. Meanwhile, add the pea and onion puree to the sauté pan and heat gently.

9. Drain the pasta, reserving the pasta-cooking water.

10. Add the par-cooked pasta and reserved pancetta to the pureed peas in the sauté pan and finish cooking at a moderate boil, adding the reserved pasta-cooking water 1 ladle at a time, shaking the pan and stirring the pasta, until the pasta is al dente, leaving the sauce liquid enough to just coat the pasta. Adjust the salt and pepper while the pasta finishes cooking.

11. Off the heat, add the cheese and then flip and stir the pasta to emulsify the cheese and sauce. Add a bit more cooking water if the sauce is too thick.

12. Garnish each serving with a drizzle of mint oil or some basil chiffonade.

We Herd You Were Making Cheese

APRIL 8

Cheese Week started on Sunday, March 31. But first, as has become customary when new people join us for a week, we went out for pizza the evening before. The pizzeria is Il Ghittone in Montepaone Lido, a nearby town. It's the pizzeria that serves french fries and pizza…the one that has the automatic external defibrillator that I mentioned in Dispatch #1!

Pizza and french fries are child's play compared to the fat-and-cholesterol-laced week we were about to encounter.

Sunday started out slowly. It was a day devoted to tasting Italian cheeses. It was meant to be an introduction to the coming week. We tasted and discussed each of the following cheeses:

- Ricotta di pecora (sheep's milk ricotta) served with orange blossom honey
- Ricotta di vacca (cow's milk ricotta)
- Pasta filata (pizza cheese; in addition to being a cheese in itself, pasta filata is also the name of an entire family of cheeses that includes all the cheeses through burrata listed here)
- Fior di latte #1 (essentially mozzarella but made from cow's milk, so it's not called mozzarella in Italy)
- Fior di latte #2
- Provola (not as aged as provolone)
- Provolone dolce ("sweet" provolone; aged more than provola)
- Provolone piccante ("spicy" provolone; aged longer than provolone dolce)
- Burrata (fresh fior di latte or mozzarella surrounding a center of shredded, pasta filata [called stracciatella] mixed with heavy cream)

- Burrino (sheep's milk cheese surrounding a center of butter)
- Robiola di vacca (much like American cream cheese but a bit softer)
- Stracchino
- Taleggio
- Taleggio with mostarda (mostarda is a condiment made of candied fruit and a mustard-infused syrup)
- Formaggio di capra semistagionata (partially aged goat cheese)
- Grana Padano
- Pecorino Romano
- Pecorino Sardo
- Caciotta
- Gorgonzola dolce

Between the taleggio and taleggio with mostarda we were served a snack of *pizzette* (mini pizza) with truffled pasta filata and mozzarella—just to fend off hunger (right!). Midafternoon we had a cannoli-inspired "snack" made with sheep's milk gelato (in place of ricotta) topped with chocolate chips, an unbelievable slice of candied orange (not orange peel, but a whole orange!), and a cannolo shell.

After the last cheese, we had a few hours to recover before having a cheese-inflected dinner. After a couple of statins and some red wine for the resveratrol, it was time for bed.

A Memorable Polenta Concia

Monday was a day of lectures by Yi-Chern Lee, a milk scientist and product manager for Fonterra in New Zealand. But first, Chef John wanted to feed us! We moved from the dining room, which had been set up as a lecture hall, to the kitchen where we were served polenta concia.

Polenta concia as interpreted by Chef John.

Chef John's version of polenta concia was over the top, and it was exactly the reason I did not have breakfast before getting to class. I'm sure you've figured out by now that Chef John loves to feed people and loves to present them with new flavors. When Chef John is not teaching, as was the case on this day, he is more likely to use his time in the kitchen to whip up one dish after another for us. I figured we weren't going to get far through the morning before food arrived, so I skipped breakfast, though I did have an espresso doppio (double espresso).

Chef John's rendition of polenta concia consisted of polenta with milk added for smoothness. After cooking, it was mixed with Parmigiano Reggiano cheese and porcini trifolata (sautéed and braised porcini mushrooms) and put into individual terracotta bowls with a splash or three of extra-virgin olive oil on the bottom. An egg was put on each one, after which they were baked and then topped with lamb ragù.

Appropriately fortified until lunch, Yi-Chern started his lecture. He covered a lot of territory, starting with the basic chemical constituents of milk from different animals and factors that affect milk and milk quality. Much of the day was devoted to discussing each of the possible steps in cheesemaking. Not all steps are used for every cheese, but we covered all the possibilities. I have twelve pages of notes from his lecture.

Pecorino Calabrese coated in peperoncino and pecorino fossa coated in ash from the wood-burning pizza oven.

Cow's Milk Ricotta

The next day, Chef John demonstrated one of many possible ways to make cow's milk ricotta. It's called *direct ricotta* in that it is made directly from milk. The method is pretty much identical to the method I have been using, though I learned a few tricks about how to keep it creamy should one want it creamier rather than drier.

Traditionally ricotta is made from the whey left over from cheesemaking. The whey is acidified and heated, which causes that last bit of protein to coagulate to form ricotta. The yield is very low, so unless you are producing cheese on a very large scale and have huge amounts of whey, it is not practical to make ricotta using this method alone, hence the use of the direct method for small-scale production.

After the cow's milk ricotta, the rest of the day was devoted to making sheep's milk cheeses and other dairy products, including:

- Yogurt
- Buttermilk
- Tomini di pecora (an Italian soft cheese of the following varieties):
  - Calabrese

- Sardo
- Fossa
- Toscano
- Luinese

★ Pecorino Romano cheese

★ Pecorino tartufo (an Italian sheep's milk table cheese, dotted with small specks of truffle)

★ Piacentum ennese (with saffron)

★ Pecorino with oregano and peperoncino

★ Pecorino with green olives

★ Canestrato

★ Pecorino porcini

★ Pecorino with arugula, roasted black olives, and sun-dried tomato

Wednesday was devoted to learning to make ricotta and mozzarella from Maestro Salvatore Postella, who has been making mozzarella by hand for nearly fifty years. He says his largest production was a day when he made 6,000 balls of mozzarella…and not those tiny little things, either!

We started the process by heating 100 liters of fresh cow's milk. Technically, we are making *fior di latte*, not mozzarella, because we are using cow's milk instead of water buffalo's milk. To make the cheese, we need to heat the milk, add starter cultures, add rennet, cut the curds into large pieces, cut the curds into small pieces, mature the curds in the whey, drain and form the curds into a large block, cut the block of curds into small pieces, heat the curds with water to 90°C (194°F) to pasteurize them, and then work the curds until stretchy before forming them into mozzarella balls.

Tomini: plain, in rosemary oil, in peperoncino oil, and in garlic oil. (See page 247 for a recipe.)

Working mozzarella means putting your hands into water that is close to 90°C (194°F). At my house in Santa Fe, water boils at just about 92°C (198°F). Imagine putting your hands in that.

Chef John holds up the little provola that I made before hanging it in the cheese cave to age.

Now visualize making 6,000 balls of mozzarella on the same day!

In any case, Maestro Postella is amazing. There's beauty in his movement—with just a gentle flip, he almost caresses the curd and then gives it three small twists to form a ball of ethereal mozzarella. Ours, on the other hand, were like baseballs! But, hey, he's done this for fifty years. Besides, continuing to work the cheese takes it from mozzarella territory to pizza cheese to provola.

After doing a "play" mozzarella, when Maestro Postella invited us to try with the odd bit of curd, I decided to make provola when we were each given an actual portion of curd to work later in the day. The "play" mozzarella coupled with my experience trying to form mozzarella back at the beginning of the course (in January) convinced me that one or two more attempts wasn't likely to gain me appreciably more skill. I decided to try to make something where the extra working of the curd was actually a requirement. Getting some pointers on making provola could actually be helpful in the future if I decide to delve more into cheesemaking.

The next day, Chef John demonstrated the difference between mozzarella made by Maestro Postella and mozzarella made by us by breaking one of each open. Ours just couldn't compare. His was light, fluffy, and still oozing with liquid, just like good mozzarella should. Ours really was pizza cheese!

When Chef John pulled a provola out of the bowl of "our" cheese, he asked the kitchen staff (in Italian) who had made it. (I did.) The answer came back in Italian and was never uttered in English. He said that it was well formed and of the right texture. I felt pretty good about that!

But back to Wednesday. Maestro Postella made burrata, for which several of us shredded pasta filata to make stracciatella. He also made ricotta with the whey created when we made curd for mozzarella. As noted earlier, this is the traditional way to make ricotta, which means recooked. Maestro Postella used a hybrid method, using whey for acidification but adding milk to provide enough protein to make a reasonable quantity of ricotta.

Ricotta is made by taking whey (or whey and milk or milk or milk and cream), heating it, and then adding an acid such as lemon juice or vinegar to cause the proteins to coagulate. It squeezes the last little bit of cheese out of whey that has already been used to make a primary cheese. You could imagine then from this definition (and you would be right) that way back when, ricotta was the food of the poor. No longer…obviously!

We started on Thursday learning about different ways to salt cheese. The rest of the day was devoted to the making of cheese and other dairy products from cow's milk, including:

- Caciotta
- Stracchino
- Camoscio
- Mascarpone
- Taleggio
- Gorgonzola dolce
- Cream cheese (American)
- Ricotta salata
- Caprino (a fantasy cheese made from goat and sheep's milk)
- Grana (type)
- Fontal (type)
- Crème fraiche

One of three courses we had for lunch on Friday, all vegetarian, all cheese-inflected.

Cheese Week wound down on Friday with our last visit to the open-air market in Soverato, followed by a visit to an artisan producer of buffalo mozzarella and sheep's milk cheeses.

After lunch back at school, Chef John reviewed all the cheeses that had been made during the week and recapped the salting, aging, and conserving processes for each. Afterward, the four Cheese People went into the kitchen to make their own cheeses. The master's students were briefed on the details for our next menu execution, our last effort before graduation.

Pasta al Ragù Calabrese di Agnello
Pasta with Calabrian Lamb Ragù

Use a thick, rustic pasta for this dish. Strozzapreti or fileja would go well as would bucatini. This will make enough to sauce 1 kilogram (2¼ pounds) of dry pasta. Extra sauce freezes well.

Lamb Ragù

Metric Measure	Ingredient	American Measure
60 grams	Celery, very fine dice	2 ounces
75 grams	Carrot, very fine dice	2½ ounces
100 grams	Onion, very fine dice	3½ ounces
1	Hot red chile pepper, such as cayenne, split	1
2 cloves	Garlic, minced	2 cloves
75 milliliters	Extra-virgin olive oil, divided	5 tablespoons
500 grams	Lean lamb, such as leg or trimmed shoulder	~1 pound
30 grams	Tomato paste	2 tablespoons
500 milliliters	Dry red wine	2 cups
375 milliliters	Chicken Broth (page 15)	1½ cups
500 milliliters	Water	2 cups
2 teaspoons plus more	Salt, preferably fine sea salt	2 teaspoons plus more
To taste	Freshly ground black pepper	To taste
1½ teaspoons	Minced fresh rosemary	1½ teaspoons
2 grams	Juniper berries, crushed	1½ teaspoons
1 teaspoon	Dried oregano, preferably Calabrian oregano	1 teaspoon
½ teaspoon	Sugar	½ teaspoon
7 grams	Lightly chopped, loosely packed fresh basil	¼ cup

1. In a heavy-bottomed Dutch oven, sauté the celery, carrot, onion, chile pepper, and garlic in 3 tablespoons of extra-virgin olive oil until the onion is golden but nothing has browned. Remove and reserve.

2. In the same pot, add the remaining 2 tablespoons of extra-virgin olive oil and sauté the lamb until lots of brown bits develop.

3. Return the sautéed vegetables to the pot. Add the tomato paste and sauté briefly until the tomato paste just darkens slightly.

We Herd You Were Making Cheese

4. Add the red wine, broth, water, 2 teaspoons of salt, and freshly ground black pepper to taste. Bring to a boil, loosening all the brown bits.

5. Simmer 1 hour, partially covered. Add the rosemary, juniper berries, oregano, sugar, and fresh basil.

6. Simmer 3 more hours, adding water as needed to keep the meat barely covered. Adjust the seasoning while cooking.

7. At the end of the cooking time, there should be a minimal amount of liquid. Use a potato masher to shred the meat by pressing on it.

Pasta and Assembly

Metric Measure	Ingredient	American Measure
½ recipe	Lamb Ragù (immediately preceding)	½ recipe
500 grams	Dry pasta, rustic cut such as strozzapreti	~1 pound
40 gams	Freshly grated Pecorino Romano cheese	1½ ounces
3 grams	Basil chiffonade	2 tablespoons
To taste	Salt, preferably fine sea salt	To taste
To taste	Freshly ground black pepper	To taste

1. Bring 3 liters (3 quarts) of water seasoned with 75 grams (¼ cup) of salt to a rolling boil.

2. Meanwhile, bring the lamb ragù to a simmer in a large sauté pan.

3. Add the pasta to the boiling salted water and cook at a rapid boil for approximately 2 minutes less than the minimum cooking time on the package for al dente pasta, stirring frequently to prevent sticking.

4. Drain the pasta, reserving the pasta-cooking water.

5. Add the par-cooked pasta to the sauce in the sauté pan and finish cooking at a moderate boil, adding the reserved pasta-cooking water 1 ladle at a time, shaking the pan and stirring the pasta, until the pasta is al dente, leaving the sauce liquid enough to just coat the pasta.

6. Off the heat, stir in the cheese and basil chiffonade. Taste and adjust the salt and pepper.

Polenta Concia
Polenta with Cheese and Butter

I like the texture of this polenta made with a mixture of both coarse-grind and fine-grind cornmeal, but feel free to use one or the other if you prefer. Typical of many foods from Piedmont, this polenta is enriched with lots of dairy—cheese and butter in this case.

Metric Measure	Ingredient	American Measure
2 liters	Water	8½ cups
2½ teaspoons plus more	Salt, preferably fine sea salt	2½ teaspoons plus more
90 grams	Fine-grind cornmeal	½ cup
170 grams	Coarse-grind cornmeal	1 cup
200 grams	Fontina cheese, shredded	7 ounces
100 grams	Butter, room temperature	7 tablespoons
To taste	Freshly ground black pepper	To taste
If desired	Funghi Trifolati (page 248)	If desired

1. Bring the water and salt to a boil in a 4 liter (4 quart) heavy-bottomed saucepan.

2. Begin whisking the boiling water with a wire whisk. Sprinkle in the fine cornmeal and then then coarse cornmeal, whisking the entire time to avoid lumps.

3. Keep the polenta at a gentle boil, uncovered, and cook at least 45 minutes, or up to 1 hour, until it is thick but still pourable. Stir frequently with a silicone spatula to keep the polenta from sticking and burning.

4. Off the heat, stir in the shredded cheese and stir until melted.

5. Add the butter and stir until melted.

6. Adjust the salt and pepper to taste.

7. Pour into a large, shallow serving bowl. Top with funghi trifolati, if desired. Serve immediately.

RICOTTA DI VACCA
Ricotta

Much of the ricotta sold in Italy is made from sheep's milk. Sheep's milk ricotta is very difficult to find in the United States. In a pinch I'll buy ricotta, but I prefer to make my own. Buttermilk adds acidity to aid in the coagulation of the milk protein, but it also adds a flavor reminiscent of the whey from which ricotta is traditionally made. Drain the amount of liquid from the ricotta appropriate to the end use. For a creamy addition to pasta, drain for just a few minutes. For a drier texture, drain for a longer period. If you are using vinegar with 5 percent acidity, use 50 milliliters for the metric version and 3 tablespoons plus ½ teaspoon for the American version.

Metric Measure	Ingredient	American Measure
2 liters	Whole milk	2 quarts
250 milliliters	Heavy whipping cream (36% fat)	1 cup
250 milliliters	Buttermilk	1 cup
6.25 grams	Salt, preferably fine sea salt	1 teaspoon
3 tablespoons	White wine vinegar, 6% acidity	2½ tablespoons

1. Combine the milk, cream, buttermilk, and salt in a 4-liter (4-quart) heavy-bottomed Dutch oven.

2. Heat the milk mixture to 95°C (203°F), stirring frequently and scraping the bottom and sides of the pot with a silicone spatula. (Note: If you live at high elevation, plan on heating the milk mixture to 5°C [9°F] lower than the boiling point of water.)

3. When the milk mixture reaches temperature, remove from the heat and quickly stir in the vinegar.

4. Allow to sit for 10 minutes, by which time the milk solids should have coagulated on top. If not, add additional vinegar equal to ⅓ of the original amount, stir, and allow to sit for 10 minutes more.

5. Using a knife, cut through the curds making 5-centimeter (2-inch) parallel cuts. Repeat at a 90-degree angle.

6. Using a slotted spoon, lift the curds into a cheesecloth-lined sieve. Allow to drain for a few minutes to a few hours, depending on the intended use.

FORMAGGIO TOMINO
Tomino Cheese

Tomino, a cheese characteristic of the Piedmont region, is made from cow's or sheep's milk or a mixture. It is usually made in a small format that ages quickly. If desired, individual cheeses can be put into small jars and covered with Rosemary Oil (page 262), Garlic Oil (page 57), or Olio Santo (page 147). Tightly closed they will keep for up to 1 year at 10°C (50°F) to 12°C (54°F). If not preserved in oil, you can choose to roll individual cheeses in coarsely ground black pepper or a mix of finely ground hot and sweet red pepper.

Metric Measure	Ingredient	American Measure
3 liters	Non-homogenized, full-fat milk, cow or sheep	3 quarts plus 1/3 cup
125 grams	Full-fat Greek yogurt with active cultures	4½ ounces
Per manufacturer	Rennet (calf, goat, or sheep)	Per manufacturer
As calculated	Salt, preferably fine sea salt	As calculated

1. In a heavy-bottomed, nonreactive pot, heat the milk to 30°C (86°F). Add the yogurt and stir well. Allow the mixture to rest for 30 minutes.

2. Heat the milk to 36°C (96.8°F) and add the rennet, calculated as per the manufacturer's directions. Allow the mixture to rest for 1 hour.

3. Cut the curds at 2 centimeter (just under 1 inch) intervals, top to bottom and side to side. Allow the curds to rest for 10 minutes.

4. If you want a firmer cheese, make a second set of cuts at 2 millimeter (less than 1/8 inch) intervals top to bottom and side to side. Allow the curds to rest for 10 minutes. If you do not want a firmer cheese, skip this step. (I suggest skipping it the first time you try this recipe.)

5. Put the curds into 30- to 80-gram cylindrical cheese molds. After filling the molds, put an empty mold on top and press to remove air and excess moisture.

6. Place the molds on a nonreactive (such as plastic) rack and allow them to drain for 6 hours at a cool room temperature, 18°C to 25°C (64.4°F to 77°F).

7. Flip each mold over and gently tap against your hand to dislodge the cheese. Return each cheese to the rack, upside down. That is, the side that was at the bottom of the mold should be facing up. Note the time.

8. Weigh each cheese and record the weight.

9. Calculate the amount of salt needed for the first salting as 0.75 percent of the weight of the cheese. That is, the weight of the cheese x 0.0075 = amount of salt needed. This will be slightly different for each cheese.

10. Sprinkle the calculated amount of salt evenly on the top of the cheeses. When the salt has been absorbed (usually a few hours), flip each cheese over and add the same amount of salt to the other side.

11. Eighteen hours from the time noted in step 7, start to age the cheeses at 10°C (50°F) to 12°C (54°F) for 3 days.

12. At this point you can serve the cheese, wrap and refrigerate it, roll it in spices (see headnote), or submerge it in flavored olive oil (see headnote).

Tip: Calf rennet will make a milder cheese than goat or sheep rennet.

Tip: Instead of adding salt directly to the cheese after it is removed from the molds, you can dip each cheese into a saturated salt solution, that is, a solution where no more salt will dissolve in the water. At room temperature, water will dissolve approximately 26 percent of its weight in salt. To make a saturated solution, weigh out the amount of water desired and then add 30 percent of that weight in pure salt. Swirl the mixture several times per day for several days to be sure that the maximum amount of salt that can dissolve, has dissolved. There will be salt left on the bottom. Submerge each cheese in the saturated solution for 0.04 minutes for each gram of cheese. For example, a 50-gram cheese (just under 2 ounces) will be in the saturated salt solution for 50 grams x 0.04 minutes/gram = 2 minutes. If doing this, skip steps 9 and 10.

Funghi Trifolati
Braised Mushrooms

These braised mushrooms can be used as a side dish (contorno), as a sauce for pasta, as a topping for polenta, or as a component of risotto. Although the process is the same for all types of mushrooms, the cooking time will vary. Button mushrooms will braise in as little as 5 minutes, porcini will take around 15 minutes, and the king trumpet *(Pleurotus eryngii)* can take 2 hours or more. Obviously, the amount of liquid needed will vary based on cooking time but also based on intended use. As a side dish or topping for polenta, there should be minimal liquid remaining at the end of cooking; as a pasta sauce, more liquid; and as the broth for risotto, much more liquid.

Metric Measure	Ingredient	American Measure
500 grams	Mushrooms	1 pound
60 milliliters	Extra-virgin olive oil	¼ cup
To taste	Salt, preferably fine sea salt	To taste
1 to 2 cloves	Garlic, minced	1 to 2 cloves
60 milliliters	Dry white wine	¼ cup
As needed	Vegetable Broth (page 161) or water	As needed
1	Bay leaf, preferably fresh (optional)	1
To taste	Freshly ground black pepper	To taste

1. Wipe the mushrooms clean with a damp cloth.

2. Slice the mushrooms about ½ centimeter (1/5 inch) thick.

3. Heat the olive oil in a sauté pan over high heat. When shimmering, add the mushrooms. Stir frequently.

4. After the mushrooms have absorbed the oil, season generously with salt. Reduce the heat to low. Stir frequently until the mushrooms begin to release liquid.

5. Increase the heat to high and sauté until the mushrooms have turned golden and some are beginning to brown.

6. Add the garlic and stir until fragrant, about 1 minute.

7. Add the wine and allow it to evaporate.

8. Add broth or water, about 125 milliliters (½ cup) for button mushrooms, twice that for porcini, and enough to cover if using king trumpet mushrooms. If you are using the bay leaf, add it with the broth when cooking button or porcini mushrooms. For king trumpet mushrooms, add the bay leaf about 10 minutes before the end of cooking.

9 Simmer until the mushrooms are tender, adjusting the salt and pepper while the mushrooms cook.

Tip: You can add a few tablespoons of minced parsley after the mushrooms are off the heat.

Tip: If using these mushrooms for a pasta sauce, double the oil. If using them as the basis for a risotto, use at least ½ liter (2 cups) of broth. Use additional Vegetable Broth (page 161) or Chicken Broth (page 15) to finish the risotto.

Dispatch #19

And So It Ends (for Now!)

APRIL 14

The oven was ignited one last time for the master's program on April 9. On April 14, I flew home from Italy. The program officially ended on April 10 with a final dinner held in Catanzaro Lido. There were about thirty-six of us, counting students, family and friends, kitchen staff, and faculty.

Tuesday, April 9, was our final menu execution. We put on a dinner for about thirty guests. On Sunday the seventh, we submitted our suggestions to Chef John and he decided what we would make for the dinner. Mostly we got to make what we requested. We averaged about three dishes per student.

The dinner started with a cold antipasto buffet followed by *primi* (pasta and risotto dishes) that were plated in the kitchen and served to the guests. We had two waiters to assist us. There were a number of *secondi* (second plates, usually meat or fish) including Gerard's insane truffle porchetta. Gerard opined that the value of the porchetta, which was slathered with pureed truffles before it was rolled and slowly roasted, was more than his entire net worth!

I made three cheeses for the antipasto buffet, as well as lasagne alla Bolognese in individual ramekins. The cheeses I made were all tomini but flavored differently. My request to also make pecorino was not approved. Probably because there wasn't time to age it sufficiently.

The tomini were made from raw cow's milk, though in the future I would definitely pasteurize the milk. There are few cheeses that really benefit from being made of raw milk, otherwise the risk just isn't worth it. Tomini can be made from sheep's milk as well. Finding sheep's milk in New Mexico is difficult, so mine will likely be made with cow's milk. I'm also going to try a combination of cow's and goat's milk as soon as I can find a source of non-homogenized milk. (Homogenized milk is not ideal for cheesemaking.)

Fritters with simple tomato sauce.

Tomini are usually small cheeses, made in molds that hold 80 to 100 grams (about 3 ounces) when finished. One style contains a fuzzy (penicillium mold) exterior, like brie and camembert, but most, in my limited experience, do not. I opted for the latter. They can, and often are, aged briefly (just a few days) to create a mellow cheese. Longer aging is possible, but given their small size, two weeks is about the maximum.

Clockwise from top right my tomini flavored with peperoncino, tomini with garlic and oregano, tomini with crushed black pepper. Bruschetta made by another student. (See page 247 for a recipe for tomini.)

To make tomini, the milk is heated and inoculated with yogurt to begin to acidify it. Subsequently rennet is added. After the curds are cut, the proto-cheese is heated to firm up the curds before they are put into molds. After draining and salting, they are aged for a few days at 10°C (50°F) to 12°C (53.6°F), just a little cooler than a wine cellar. I am committed to having tomini in our wine cellar soon!

I rolled some of the tomini in coarsely ground black pepper before aging. Others I rolled in a mixture of sweet and hot peperoncino powder. To the last portion, I added minced fresh garlic and dried Calabrian oregano to the curds before putting them into molds. Tomini can also be aged in flavored oil such as garlic, rosemary, or peperoncino oil.

As I was coating the cheese with black pepper and peperoncino, Adriana, the dishwasher who is filling in for Maria (who recently had surgery), indicated that she rubbed her cheeses with olive oil before coating them with spices. I might give that a try. I have no idea what it might do to the cheese, but since these aren't cheeses that age long, there's no risk that the oil will go rancid as could happen with a long-aged cheese.

I made cheese for menu execution because a week or so before, Chef John told me he wanted to see me make cheese ("and not ricotta" were his words) for menu execution. It's similar to his comment earlier in the course about wanting to see me make pasta ai frutti di mare or pasta allo scoglio (or a similar a la minute pasta made with seafood). I think these are items that he's using to gauge skill level or techniques that he thinks I need to know if I'm going to teach cooking (which I plan on doing on my return).

In any case, without his urging I probably would not have made cheese. Now I'm hooked! The variety of cheeses that can be made without extensive aging times is incredible. I can use the wine cellar. If I start getting into aging for more than a month or so, I suspect I'll have to buy a refrigerated wine cave to sit next to my gelato batch freezer...wherever that ends up!

I got a big compliment from Chef Juan's mom, who is visiting from Venezuela, regarding my cheese. I also got lots of compliments about my lasagne alla Bolognese (which is going to appear on the table at Easter this year).

Step one was making the ragù Bolognese, the recipe for which Chef John pares down to the absolute essentials compared to many published recipes (though I added a bit of garlic, which he doesn't do). His recipe is packed with flavor from very few ingredients. Step two was making fresh pasta and cutting it into circles that just fit inside the individual ramekins. The pasta air-dried for a day. Step three was making the besciamella and refrigerating it overnight so that I could squeeze it out of a pastry bag. All of those steps happened on April 7 and 8.

Me making individual lasagne, the first plated dish of the evening.

One Last Menu for Graduation

The morning of April 9, my last menu execution day, was pretty mellow for me. My cheeses were aging without need of attention until it was time to cut them and plate them for the buffet. I layered twenty-nine ramekins (the total we had) with lasagne, hoping that one of our thirty guests didn't want lasagne!

It was a Zen-like meditative experience: a thin layer of ragù, a sheet of pasta, another thin layer of ragù, then besciamella piped in to cover, then Parmigiano Reggiano cheese, then pasta, followed by more ragù, besciamella, and Parmigiano followed by pasta, then ragù, Parmigiano, and a drizzle of melted butter. This brought each ramekin to just below the top.

I put them on a sheet tray, inverted another sheet try on top, and put them in the walk-in. My work was done. I spent the rest of my time in the kitchen helping others who had more last-minute work to do.

The lasagne ramekins were served as the first primo of the evening and, therefore, were the first plated dish after the serve-yourself antipasto buffet. I baked them and drizzled them with a tiny bit of house-made rosemary oil just before serving them.

Before we got to the primi, however, Chef John made a little speech and then gave us our certificates. A few hours earlier we had gotten our official Italian Culinary Institute chef's jackets, which we were all wearing. It was an emotional moment:

the culmination of three months of hard work and weight gain in the service of researching the flavors of Italy. (It sounds facetious but it's really true.)

I started drafting this dispatch on Thursday, April 11. All the students left that day, except for me. When planning my flights, I decided that I didn't want to be rushed with packing during the last days of the course, so I planned my departure for Saturday.

Today, Chef Juan and I spent a couple of leisurely hours inspecting all the salumi we made back in January and maintaining the large cuts, like prosciuttino and capocollo. Maintaining means checking weight loss. Each type of cured meat product has an ideal percentage of weight loss as part of the curing process. Maintaining also means cleaning off any mold with white wine vinegar.

Mold is a natural part of Italian salumi. Mold doesn't really penetrate the surface of the meat. As it appears, one just cleans it off. Ideally the meat is checked every few days. Sometimes one reapplies another coating of whatever seasoning was on the exterior. The seasoning doesn't really penetrate the meat any longer as the surface is dry, but it acts as another protective layer on the meat. Some of the cured meats that we made in January won't be ready until October.

On Friday, the staff was reorganizing the kitchen after our three-month marathon and taking inventory. I maintained all the salami and then vacuum-packed everything that didn't need more aging. My afternoon was spent packing for my departure.

Once I get home on April 14, I'll be in full cooking mode getting ready for Easter dinner on the twenty-first. I've taken my lessons to heart and plan on making the following, assuming I can get all the ingredients:

A selfie, from left to right, the author, Mary Margaret, and Ryan.

A final memory of the view from our terrace the day before leaving Calabria.

Antipasto
Ricotta Fresca Fatta in Casa, Condita con Olio d'Oliva
Melanzane Sott'olio
Tonno del Chianti
Fraguni
Salame con Pane di Formaggio alla Romana
Arancini con 'Nduja
Fave con Pecorino

Primi
(Served in sequence on individual plates)
Risotto ai Piselli, Crema di Piselli, Olio di Menta
Minestra di Fagioli Borlotti di Zia Fidalma
Lasagne alla Bolognese

Secondo
Abbacchio alla Romana
Carciofi e Patate
Focaccia

Dolci
Torta di Agnello di Sanguinamento (Bleeding Lamb Cake, a recent tradition in our house)
Babà con Sciroppo di Rum
Gelato di Crema di Arancia, Scorza d'Arancia Candita, Cioccolato Bianco Caramellato Sbriciolato

My plan for the summer is to go through my notes from the course and cook, cook, cook. I feel like I need to do that to integrate the information and truly make it mine.

I plan on making my way back to Italy at the beginning of August for about two months for guided independent study in regional Italian cuisine both at the Italian Culinary Institute and at venues in Northern and Southern Italy. Until then, I'll try to get back to a regular schedule of posting blogs with recipes and stories.

Bene, allora, e arrivederci a tutti!

A Last-Minute Update!

I'm spending the night before my trans-Atlantic flight at Il Picolo Bed and Breakfast, which is quite literally a five-minute drive from Leonardo da Vinci airport in Fiumicino. The owners suggested I have dinner at BioAgriola Traiano, a very short walk from the B&B.

The food was wonderful. The owner speaks five languages, and when she heard I was a chef, she brought out the kitchen staff (both in their twenties) to meet me. The food was superb! Now I have to make visits to the B&B and the agriturismo a regular part of my trips back to Italy. It won't be difficult given how close they are to the airport.

BESCIAMELLA
Béchamel Sauce

Americans typically use equal volumes of butter and flour when making besciamella. Europeans typically use equal weights. Due to the difference in the weight-to-volume characteristics of flour and butter, Americans use approximately twice as much butter per unit of flour as do Europeans. This can create an overly rich besciamella. Any of the recipes in this book that require besciamella specify the amounts of flour, butter, and milk. This is a recipe for a medium-thick besciamella. The process is the same for all variations, only the ratios of milk to butter and flour change. Note that all measurements for this recipe are by weight, not volume.

Metric Measure	Ingredient	American Measure
12.5 grams	Unsalted butter	½ ounce
12.5 grams	All-purpose flour	½ ounce
250 grams	Milk, 2% or whole	10 ounces
To taste	Salt, preferably fine sea salt	To taste
⅛ teaspoon or to taste	Freshly grated nutmeg, optional	⅛ teaspoon or to taste

1. Melt the butter in a small, heavy-bottomed pot over medium-low heat.

2. When the foam mostly subsides, add the flour and stir constantly with a silicone spatula for 1 to 2 minutes to eliminate the raw flour taste but without browning.

3. Add the milk, approximately 2 tablespoons at a time, mixing well after each addition with a silicone spatula to prevent the development of lumps.

4. After all the milk has been added, increase the heat slightly and bring to a boil, continuously scraping with the silicone spatula.

5. Boil for 1 minute. Remove from the heat. Add salt and nutmeg to taste.

6. If not using immediately, pour into a heat proof bowl and cover with plastic wrap, pressing the plastic onto the top of the besciamella to prevent the formation of a skin. Refrigerate.

Tip: if making larger quantities of besciamella, say 500 grams (17½ ounces) of milk or so, it is helpful to heat the milk in advance. Doing so will speed up the process of bringing the final mixture to a boil. For small quantities, there is really no advantage to this added step.

Lasagne alla Bolognese
Lasagne Bolognese

Italian-American lasagna (Americans use the singular form, lasagna, whereas Italians use the plural, lasagne) usually has much less pasta in proportion to the other ingredients than does lasagne in Italy. This lasagne Bolognese is one of the models for lasagne in Italy. Layers of pasta are dressed lightly with ragù and besciamella but there is no "filling" per se, as there often is in Italian-American lasagna (such as layers of ricotta and/or meat). There are a number of component parts that need to be prepared in order to make this lasagne, but the ragù and the besciamella can be done a day or two in advance. The lasagne itself can be assembled early in the day and refrigerated until an hour before baking.

Besciamella

Make a 25 percent besciamella. The besciamella will need to be piped into the lasagna with a pastry bag because it will not be pourable or spreadable, but the advantage is that it will not make the lasagna overly wet.

Metric Measure	Ingredient	American Measure
2 liters	Milk, 2% or whole	2 quarts plus ½ cup
250 grams	Unsalted butter	8¾ ounces
250 grams	All-purpose flour	2 cups less 2 tablespoons
To taste	Salt, preferably fine sea salt	To taste

1. Warm the milk but do not boil it.
2. Prepare the besciamella using the process described on page 256, but add about 60 milliliters (¼ cup) of milk with each addition.
3. Refrigerate the besciamella with plastic wrap on the surface.
4. Bring to room temperature and stir before using.

Assembly

Lasagne Bolognese is traditionally made with spinach pasta. Making pasta with fresh or frozen spinach can be challenging, so I recommend using spinach powder if you choose to go this route. (See the Tip for more information.) I have chosen not to provide a specific quantity of Parmigiano Reggiano cheese as this is a matter of personal preference, but I would use at least 400 grams (14 ounces) for this quantity of lasagne. Once baked and cooled, lasagne Bolognese freezes well. Reheat gently at 120°C (250°F), tightly covered.

Metric Measure	Ingredient	American Measure
Double recipe	Fresh Egg Pasta (page 45)	Double recipe
1 recipe	Ragù Bolognese (page 260), at room temperature	1 recipe
As needed	Freshly grated Parmigiano Reggiano cheese	As needed
As needed	Milk	As needed
100 grams	Unsalted butter, melted	3½ ounces
To taste	Rosemary Oil (page 262)	To taste

1. Make the pasta shortly before assembling the lasagne. Roll the pasta into thin sheets, approximately #7 on most "vintage" pasta machines. (Note: If your machine goes above this setting, it is likely a newer one that is designed to produce very thin pasta for dishes that are not traditionally Italian.)

2. Cut the pasta the correct length to fit into the lasagne pan. Save the irregular pieces.

3. Spread a thin layer of ragù on the bottom of a deep rectangular lasagne pan with straight sides that is approximately 25 x 35 centimeters (10 x 14 inches) in size. The layer of ragù should not be thick. You should be able to see the bottom of the pan in places.

4. Put a layer of uncooked pasta on the ragù, overlapping just enough to cover the bottom of the pan. For the first and last layers, I select pasta sheets that are the most regular. For the middle layers, I will cut and add in some of the irregular pieces as needed to make a complete layer.

5. Top the pasta with a thin layer of ragù.

6. Put the besciamella in a pastry bag with a medium-wide opening. Pipe parallel rows of besciamella on top of the ragù. Space the rows about as far apart as they are wide.

7. Sprinkle a generous amount of Parmigiano Reggiano cheese on the besciamella.

8. Add another layer of pasta and gently press to level the layer and spread the besciamella a bit.

9. Top the pasta with ragù, besciamella, and Parmigiano Reggiano cheese.

10. Repeat layers, gently pressing each new layer of pasta, until you have used up all the pasta.

11. Top the final layer of pasta with besciamella and Parmigiano Reggiano cheese only, no ragù. Because you want this layer of besciamella to be

spreadable, thin it with some milk until you reach an easily spreadable consistency. I usually make the final sprinkling of Parmigiano Reggiano cheese more generous than the ones in the middle.

12. Drizzle the melted butter over the top of the lasagne.

13. Drizzle with rosemary oil now or after baking, as desired.

14. Bake at 180°C (350°F) until completely heated through, approximately 1 hour. An instant-read thermometer should register 75°C (165°F) in the middle of the lasagne. By this time the top should be golden brown.

15. Allow the lasagne to rest at room temperature for 20 minutes before cutting.

Tip: After cutting the pasta sheets, calculate how many layers of pasta you will have for the pan. This will help you portion the besciamella.

Tip: If the lasagne is browning too quickly, put a half-sheet pan on top to cover. If it is not browning enough, move it near the top of the oven.

Tip: To make spinach pasta, replace 16 grams (0.56 ounces) of flour in the double batch of pasta with an equivalent amount of spinach powder. Mix thoroughly before adding the eggs.

CRESCIA DI FORMAGGIO PASQUALINA ALLA ROMANA
Roman Easter Cheese Bread

I use half Antimo Caputo Chef's Flour and half Paolo Mariani "dolci" flour to get the desired W-value. If you don't have access to Italian flour, I would opt for King Arthur bread flour. Although it will react slightly differently, it will still make a great loaf. If you want a cheesier loaf, increase the Pecorino Romano cheese to 200 grams (7 ounces).

Metric Measure	Ingredient	American Measure
400 grams	Italian 00 flour W-225	3 cups
7 grams	Active dry yeast	¼ ounce
125 milliliters	Milk, 2%	½ cup
6 large	Eggs	6 large
12.5 grams	Sugar	1 tablespoon
150 grams	Freshly grated Pecorino Romano cheese	5⅓ ounces
5 grams	Salt, preferably fine sea salt	Scant 1 teaspoon
60 grams plus more for the pans	Unsalted butter, room temperature	4⅓ tablespoons plus more for the pans

1. In the bowl of a stand mixer fitted with a dough hook, combine the flour and yeast. Mix on low, slowly streaming in the milk.

2. After the milk is incorporated, add the eggs one at a time, mixing well after each addition.

3. Add the sugar and Pecorino Romano cheese. Mix well.

4. Add the salt and knead with the dough hook until there is good gluten formation. The dough should be elastic and there should be visible stranding if a small piece is pulled.

5. Add the butter and continue to mix until fully incorporated.

6. Remove the bowl from the machine. Leave the dough hook in the bowl with the dough. Cover the bowl with plastic wrap and allow the dough to rise at warm room temperature until it has doubled in size.

7. Put the bowl back in the mixer and reattach the dough hook. Mix on low to deflate the dough.

8. Divide the dough between two buttered loaf pans that are 11 x 23 centimeters (4½ x 9 inches) in size. Put the dough in a proofer at approximately 37°C (99°F), with a bowl of just-boiled water to add moisture. Allow the dough to rise until it has doubled in size.

9. Bake at 180°C (350°F) until golden brown, approximately 35 minutes, rotating once.

10. Cool 10 minutes in the pans and then remove and cool completely on a rack.

 Ragù Bolognese
Ragù Bolognese

There are a number of points of contention regarding how to make ragù Bolognese. Pancetta or no pancetta? Beef and pork or just beef? Ratio of tomato to final sauce? Milk or no milk? This is a simple, but delicious, version that does not use pancetta or milk and skews toward a bit more tomato. If you do not have garlic oil, lightly brown a bruised clove of garlic in olive oil. Discard the garlic before adding the meat. Ragù Bolognese freezes well.

Metric Measure	Ingredient	American Measure
3 (1-kilogram) cans	Peeled canned tomatoes in tomato puree	3 (35-ounce) cans
100 grams	Finely diced carrot	3½ ounces
100 grams	Finely diced onion	3½ ounces
60 grams	Finely diced celery	2 ounces
60 grams	Unsalted butter	4 tablespoons
2 tablespoons	Garlic Oil (page 57)	2 tablespoons
500 grams	Ground beef, 15% fat	~1 pound
500 grams	Ground pork, 15% fat	~1 pound
500 milliliters	Dry, full-bodied red wine	2⅛ cups
1	Bay leaf, preferably fresh	1
To taste	Salt, preferably fine sea salt	To taste
To taste	Freshly ground black pepper	To taste

1. Pass the canned tomatoes through a food mill to remove the seeds and any bits of skin. Reserve.

2. Sauté the carrot, onion, and celery in the butter over medium-low heat until soft, approximately 10 to 12 minutes. Do not brown. Reserve.

3. Sauté the beef and pork in the garlic oil over medium-high heat until a lot of brown bits develop.

4. Add the wine, bring to a boil, scraping up all the brown bits, and completely evaporate the wine.

5. Add the sautéed vegetables, tomato puree, and bay leaf to the meat mixture. Season to taste with salt and pepper. Simmer 3 to 4 hours until reduced by 50 percent.

6. Taste occasionally to adjust the salt and pepper.

Olio Profumato al Rosmarino
Rosemary Oil

I keep a squeeze bottle of rosemary oil next to my stove at all times. I use it to add a burst of flavor to many dishes, both while cooking and afterward.

Metric Measure	Ingredient	American Measure
60 grams	Fresh rosemary sprigs	2 ounces
400 grams	Extra-virgin olive oil	1¾ cups

1. Cut the rosemary sprigs into pieces approximately 5 centimeters (2 inches) long.

2. Combine ⅓ of the rosemary with the olive oil in a small pot. Heat to 120°C (250°F). Immediately remove from the heat and allow the rosemary to steep in the oil until it reaches room temperature.

3. Pour the oil through a sieve and discard the rosemary.

4. Return the oil to the pot and repeat the process two more times, using ⅓ of the rosemary each time.

5. When cool, strain and bottle the oil. Store at room temperature, tightly covered.

The author receives his certificate from Chef John Nocita.

And So It Ends (for Now!)

Index

A

Air Force personnel, 191–192
alcohol, distilling, 126
Almond Biscotti, Tuscan, 214
anchovies
    Anchovy Garlic Paste, 29
    cleaning, 54–55
    Mafalde Pasta with Broccoli, 58–59
Anchovy Garlic Paste
    Burrata and Broccoli Rabe
      Antipasto, 157–158
    Pasta alla Puttanesca, 32–33
    recipe, 29
Aperol Spritz, 68, 71
"Arab" Bread, 199–201
Arancini, 71–73
arborio rice
    about, xviii
    Arancini, 71–73
    Mushroom Risotto, 120–122
    Parmesan Cheese Risotto, 64–65
    Roman Rice Balls, 21–22
Artichoke Lasagna, Lamb and, 44–45
Aunt Fidalma's Bean Soup, 233–234

B

Babà, 196–197
Bagni di Lucca open-air mercatino, 226
Baked Ricotta, 63
Basic Tomato Sauce
    Lupara, 30–31
    Meatballs with Pecorino Cheese, 18–19
    Meatballs with Sweet Peppers, 185–186
    Pasta alla Norma, 75
    Pasta alla Puttanesca, 32–33
    Pasta all'Amatriciana, 135–136
    recipe, 131–132
beans and legumes
    Arancini, 71–73
    Aunt Fidalma's Bean Soup, 233–234
    Beans and Greens, 143–145
    Chickpeas with Infused Oil, 158–159
    Cotechino Sausage with Lentils, 16–17
    Pasta and Beans, 187–188
    Rigatoni with Peas, 234–235
Béchamel Sauce, 256
beef
    Meatballs with Pecorino Cheese, 18–19
    Ragù Bolognese, 260–261
    Thinly Sliced Beef Braised in Tomato
      Sauce with Black Olives, 114–115
beer
Pizza Dough, 61–62
beverages
    Aperol Spritz, 68, 71
    Limoncello, 232–233
    mixology session, 128–129, 130
    sommelier training, 151–152, 153, 163
Biga
    "Arab" Bread, 199–201
    Little Bread Rolls, 84–85
    recipe, 213–214
bomba Calabrese, 127
Braised Mushrooms
    Polenta with Cheese and Butter, 245
    recipe, 248–249
Braised Rabbit
    Whole Wheat Pasta with
      Rabbit Ragù, 86–88
breads
    "Arab" Bread, 199–201
    Ciabatta, 217–219
    Crispy Sardinian Flatbread, 220–221
    Focaccia, 167–169
    Italian Flatbread, 201–202
    Italian "Pre-Dough," 213–214
    Little Bread Rolls, 84–85
    Pizza Dough, 61–62
    Roman Easter Cheese Bread, 259–260
brioss, 180
Broccoli, Mafalde Pasta with, 58–59

broccoli rabe
    Burrata and Broccoli Rabe
        Antipasto, 157–158
    Orecchiette Pasta with Broccoli
        Rabe and Sausage, 59–61
Burrata and Broccoli Rabe Antipasto, 157–158

C

Cacio e Pepe, 132–134
Calabrian Preserved Spicy Eggplant, 145–146
Calabrian Sausage, 103–104
calamari
    Mollusk Ragù, 50
Candied Orange Peel, 134
Cannoli, 73–74
capers
    Caponata, 216–217
    Pasta alla Puttanesca, 32–33
    Thinly Sliced Beef Braised in Tomato
        Sauce with Black Olives, 114–115
Caponata, 216–217
Caramelized White Chocolate Crumble, 188
carnaroli rice
    about, xviii
    Arancini, 71–73
    Mushroom Risotto, 120–122
    Parmesan Cheese Risotto, 64–65
    Roman Rice Balls, 21–22
carrots
    Aunt Fidalma's Bean Soup, 233–234
    Basic Tomato Sauce, 131–132
    Chicken Broth, 15–16
    Concentrated Chicken Stock, 83–84
    Cotechino Sausage with Lentils, 16–17
    Fusilloni Pasta with 'Nduja and
        Tomato Sauce, 116–118
    Lamb Ragù, 46–47
    Maltagliati Pasta with Oxtail Ragù, 159–161
    Pasta with Calabrian Lamb Ragù, 243–244
    "Priest-Strangler" Pasta with
        Veal Ragù, 19–21
    Ragù Bolognese, 260–261
    Vegetable Broth, 161
    Whole Wheat Pasta with
        Rabbit Ragù, 86–88
Catanzaro Lido market, 3, 152–153
Cauliflower with Bechamel, Roast, 5–6
celery
    Aunt Fidalma's Bean Soup, 233–234
    Basic Tomato Sauce, 131–132
    Caponata, 216–217
    Chicken Broth, 15–16
    Concentrated Chicken Stock, 83–84
    Fusilloni Pasta with 'Nduja and
        Tomato Sauce, 116–118
    Maltagliati Pasta with Oxtail Ragù, 159–161
    Pasta with Calabrian Lamb Ragù, 243–244
    Ragù Bolognese, 260–261
    Vegetable Broth, 161
    Whole Wheat Pasta with
        Rabbit Ragù, 86–88
cheeses
    author's, 251–253
    instruction on, 237–238, 239–242
    See also individual cheeses
chicken
    Chicken Broth, 15–16
    Concentrated Chicken Stock, 83–84
    Roast Chicken, 4
    Roman-Style Chicken, 33–34
Chicken Broth
    Cotechino Sausage with Lentils, 16–17
    Lupara, 30–31
    Maltagliati Pasta with Oxtail Ragù, 159–161
    Mushroom Risotto, 120–122
    Orecchiette Pasta with Broccoli
        Rabe and Sausage, 59–61
    Parmesan Cheese Risotto, 64–65
    Pasta with Calabrian Lamb Ragù, 243–244
    recipe, 15–16
    Roman-Style Chicken, 33–34
    Thinly Sliced Beef Braised in Tomato
        Sauce with Black Olives, 114–115
Chickpeas with Infused Oil, 158–159
Chile Peppers in Oil, 8–9
chitarra pasta cutters, 40–41, 164, 166
chocolate
    Caramelized White Chocolate
        Crumble, 188
    Tiramisù, 76–78
Ciabatta, 217–219
clams
    Fregola Pasta with Clams and
        Cherry Tomatoes, 219–220
    Pasta with Clams, 169–170
"Cocktail" Pizza, 202–204
cocoa powder
    Cannoli, 73–74
    Tiramisù, 76–78
colomba, 193
Concentrated Chicken Stock
    recipe, 83–84
    Whole Wheat Pasta with
        Rabbit Ragù, 86–88
cotechino

about, 11–12
    Cotechino Sausage with Lentils, 16–17
Crispy Sardinian Flatbread, 220–221
cured meats
    about, 11–13
    inspecting, 254
    instruction on, 95–99
    See also individual meats
cuttlefish
    Mollusk Ragù, 50

D

demi/demi-glace, 126–127
desserts and sweets
    Babà, 196–197
    Cannoli, 73–74
    Caramelized White Chocolate Crumble, 188
    instruction on, 192–195
    Jam Tart, 182–183
    Milk and Cream Gelato, 183–185
    Red-Wine Poached Pears, 119
    Ricotta Tart, 148–149
    Sponge Cake, 6–7
    Sponge Cake with Cream and Fruit, 7–8
    Tiramisù, 76–78
    Tuscan Almond Biscotti, 214
distillation process, 126
double zero (00) flour, xvi
durum, xvii

E

eggplant
    Calabrian Preserved Spicy Eggplant, 145–146
    Caponata, 216–217
    Pasta alla Norma, 75
    Pasta Frittata, 230–231
    pressing, 127
    Stuffed Eggplant Rolls, 146–147
equipment, about, xix–xx
espresso
    Tiramisù, 76–78
exams, 79–81
extra-virgin olive oil, about, xvii

F

fennel
    Cotechino Sausage with Lentils, 16–17
fermentation, 126–127
Fileja Pasta with Shrimp and Mushrooms, 228–230
fiordilatte, 177
fish soup, 154
Fish Stock
    "Perfume of the Sea" Pasta, 34–36
    recipe, 36–37
Flat Pancetta, 99–101
flour, about, xvi–xvii
focaccette, 226
Focaccia, 167–169
fontina cheese
    Polenta with Cheese and Butter, 245
Fregola Pasta with Clams and Cherry Tomatoes, 219–220
Fresh Egg Pasta
    Lamb and Artichoke Lasagna, 44–45
    Lasagne Bolognese, 257–259
    Pasta Cut on the "Chitarra" with Mussels and Cherry Tomatoes, 173–175
    recipe, 45–46
Fried Zucchini Blossoms, 115–116
frogs' legs, lollipopping, 55, 154–155
Fusilloni Pasta with 'Nduja and Tomato Sauce, 116–118

G

Gallicano market, 226
garlic
    Anchovy Garlic Paste, 29
    Beans and Greens, 143–145
    Fregola Pasta with Clams and Cherry Tomatoes, 219–220
    Garlic Oil, 57
    Linguine "from the Reef," 48–49
    Mafalde Pasta with Broccoli, 58–59
    Maltagliati Pasta with Oxtail Ragù, 159–161
    Pasta with Clams, 169–170
    "Perfume of the Sea" Pasta, 34–36
    Roman-Style Chicken, 33–34
    Slow-Roasted Pork, 101–103
    Spaghetti with Garlic and Oil, 89–90
    Thinly Sliced Beef Braised in Tomato Sauce with Black Olives, 114–115
    Tuna of Chianti (Pork Confit), 106–107
    Tuscan Sausage, 104–105
    Whole Wheat Pasta with Rabbit Ragù, 86–88
Garlic Oil
    Lupara, 30–31
    Orecchiette Pasta with Broccoli Rabe and Sausage, 59–61

  Pasta alla Puttanesca, 32–33
  Pasta with Clams, 169–170
  "Perfume of the Sea" Pasta, 34–36
  Ragù Bolognese, 260–261
  recipe, 57
gelato
  about, 177
  instruction on, 178–182
Gelato, Milk and Cream, 183–185
guanciale
  Pasta all Gricia, 136–137
  Pasta all'Amatriciana, 135–136
Guglielmo (coffee roaster), 113, 166–167

H

haircuts, 113–114
head cheese, 12, 98
hog casing, xviii–xix
honey
  Savory Ricotta-Filled Tarts from Calabria, 198–199
Hot Chile Oil, 147–148

I

ingredients, about, xvi–xix
Italian Flatbread, 201–202
Italian "Pre-Dough," 213–214

J

Jam Tart, 182–183

L

lamb
  Lamb and Artichoke Lasagna, 44–45
  Lamb Ragù, 46–47
  Pasta with Calabrian Lamb Ragù, 243–244
Lasagne Bolognese, 257–259
lemons
  "Perfume of the Sea" Pasta, 34–36
Lentils, Cotechino Sausage with, 16–17
lima beans
  Pasta and Beans, 187–188
Limoncello, 232–233
Linguine "from the Reef," 48–49
Little Bread Rolls, 84–85
Lucchese spice blend
  Tuscan Sausage, 104–105
Lupara, 30–31

M

Mafalde Pasta with Broccoli, 58–59
Maltagliati Pasta with Oxtail Ragù, 159–161
Manitoba flour, xvi
mascarpone
  Tiramisù, 76–78
Matera, trip to, 143
measurements, xv–xvi
Meatballs
  with Pecorino Cheese, 18–19
  with Sweet Peppers, 185–186
menu planning, 109–110, 112, 208–209, 255
Milk and Cream Gelato, 183–185
mixology, 128–129, 130
Mollusk Ragù
  Linguine "from the Reef," 48–49
  recipe, 50
mother yeast, 193
mozzarella
  "Cocktail" Pizza, 202–204
  instruction on, 240–241
  Roman Rice Balls, 21–22
  Stuffed Eggplant Rolls, 146–147
Mushroom Broth
  Fileja Pasta with Shrimp and Mushrooms, 228–230
recipe, 118
mushrooms
  Braised Mushrooms, 248–249
  Fileja Pasta with Shrimp and Mushrooms, 228–230
  Lupara, 30–31
  Mushroom Risotto, 120–122
  Polenta with Cheese and Butter, 245
mussels
  Linguine "from the Reef," 48–49
  Mushroom Broth, 118
  Pasta Cut on the "Chitarra" with Mussels and Cherry Tomatoes, 173–175

N

'nduja
  about, 2, 98
  Fusilloni Pasta with 'Nduja and Tomato Sauce, 116–118
nocciola, 177

O

octopus
  Octopus Carpaccio, 172–173

Octopus Sous-Vide, 171–172
Olio Santo
    Orecchiette Pasta with Broccoli Rabe and Sausage, 59–61
olive branches, smoking with, 12
olive oil, about, xvii, 212
olives
    Caponata, 216–217
    Pasta alla Puttanesca, 32–33
    "Perfume of the Sea" Pasta, 34–36
    Roasted Olives, 76
    Thinly Sliced Beef Braised in Tomato Sauce with Black Olives, 114–115
onions
    Aunt Fidalma's Bean Soup, 233–234
    Basic Tomato Sauce, 131–132
    Calabrian Preserved Spicy Eggplant, 145–146
    Caponata, 216–217
    Chicken Broth, 15–16
    Chickpeas with Infused Oil, 158–159
    Concentrated Chicken Stock, 83–84
    Cotechino Sausage with Lentils, 16–17
    Fish Stock, 36–37
    Fusilloni Pasta with 'Nduja and Tomato Sauce, 116–118
    Lamb Ragù, 46–47
    Maltagliati Pasta with Oxtail Ragù, 159–161
    Meatballs with Sweet Peppers, 185–186
    Mushroom Risotto, 120–122
    Parmesan Cheese Risotto, 64–65
    Pasta and Beans, 187–188
    Pasta with Calabrian Lamb Ragù, 243–244
    "Priest-Strangler" Pasta with Veal Ragù, 19–21
    Ragù Bolognese, 260–261
    Rigatoni with Peas, 234–235
    Tomato Soup, 175
    Tuna of Chianti (Pork Confit), 106–107
    Vegetable Broth, 161
    Whole Wheat Pasta with Rabbit Ragù, 86–88
oranges
    Aperol Spritz, 71
    Candied Orange Peel, 134
Orecchiette Pasta with Broccoli Rabe and Sausage, 59–61
Oxtail Ragù, Maltagliati Pasta with, 159–161

P

pancetta
    Flat Pancetta, 99–101
    Pasta all Gricia, 136–137
    Pasta all'Amatriciana, 135–136
    Rigatoni with Peas, 234–235
panettone, 193
Paoletti (hypermarket), 166
Parmesan Cheese Risotto, 64–65
Parmigiano Reggiano cheese
    Arancini, 71–73
    Chicken Broth, 15–16
    "Cocktail" Pizza, 202–204
    Lamb and Artichoke Lasagna, 44–45
    Lasagne Bolognese, 257–259
    Lupara, 30–31
    Mafalde Pasta with Broccoli, 58–59
    Maltagliati Pasta with Oxtail Ragù, 159–161
    Meatballs with Sweet Peppers, 185–186
    Mushroom Risotto, 120–122
    Parmesan Cheese Risotto, 64–65
    Pasta and Beans, 187–188
    "Priest-Strangler" Pasta with Veal Ragù, 19–21
    Rigatoni with Peas, 234–235
    Roman Rice Balls, 21–22
    Spaghetti with Garlic and Oil, 89–90
    Tomato Soup, 175
    Whole Wheat Pasta with Rabbit Ragù, 86–88
passport/visa process, 27–29
pasta
    about, xvii–xviii
    Aunt Fidalma's Bean Soup, 233–234
    Cacio e Pepe, 132–134
    Fileja Pasta with Shrimp and Mushrooms, 228–230
    Fregola Pasta with Clams and Cherry Tomatoes, 219–220
    Fresh Egg Pasta, 45–46
    Fusilloni Pasta with 'Nduja and Tomato Sauce, 116–118
    instruction on, 39–41
    Lamb and Artichoke Lasagna, 44–45
    Lasagne Bolognese, 257–259
    Linguine "from the Reef," 48–49
    Lupara, 30–31
    Mafalde Pasta with Broccoli, 58–59
    Maltagliati Pasta with Oxtail Ragù, 159–161
    Orecchiette Pasta with Broccoli Rabe and Sausage, 59–61
    Pasta all Gricia, 136–137
    Pasta alla Norma, 75
    Pasta alla Puttanesca, 32–33
    Pasta all'Amatriciana, 135–136
    Pasta and Beans, 187–188

Pasta Cut on the "Chitarra" with Mussels
    and Cherry Tomatoes, 173–175
Pasta Frittata, 230–231
Pasta with Calabrian Lamb Ragù, 243–244
Pasta with Clams, 169–170
"Perfume of the Sea" Pasta, 34–36
"Priest-Strangler" Pasta with
    Veal Ragù, 19–21
Rigatoni with Peas, 234–235
Spaghetti with Garlic and Oil, 89–90
Thinly Sliced Beef Braised in Tomato
    Sauce with Black Olives, 114–115
Whole Wheat Pasta, 90–91
Whole Wheat Pasta with
    Rabbit Ragù, 86–88
Pasta Frolla
    Jam Tart, 182–183
    recipe, 149
    Ricotta Tart, 148–149
pasta machines
    about, xx
    instruction on, 40–41
pasta sauté pans, xix–xx
Pears, Red-Wine Poached, 119
peas
    Arancini, 71–73
    Rigatoni with Peas, 234–235
Pecorino Romano cheese
    Arancini, 71–73
    Cacio e Pepe, 132–134
    "Cocktail" Pizza, 202–204
    Fusilloni Pasta with 'Nduja and
        Tomato Sauce, 116–118
    Lupara, 30–31
    Meatballs with Pecorino Cheese, 18–19
    Meatballs with Sweet Peppers, 185–186
    Orecchiette Pasta with Broccoli
        Rabe and Sausage, 59–61
    Pasta all Gricia, 136–137
    Pasta alla Puttanesca, 32–33
    Pasta all'Amatriciana, 135–136
    Pasta with Calabrian Lamb Ragù, 243–244
    Roman Easter Cheese Bread, 259–260
    Roman-Style Chicken, 33–34
    Stuffed Eggplant Rolls, 146–147
peppers, bell
    Calabrian Preserved Spicy
        Eggplant, 145–146
    Caponata, 216–217
    Meatballs with Sweet Peppers, 185–186
    Roman-Style Chicken, 33–34
peppers, chile
    Calabrian Preserved Spicy
        Eggplant, 145–146
    Chile Peppers in Oil, 8–9
    Hot Chile Oil, 147–148
    Pasta all'Amatriciana, 135–136
    Pasta with Calabrian Lamb Ragù, 243–244
"Perfume of the Sea" Pasta, 34–36
pici, 153–154
pigs, butchering, 93–96
Pisa, trip to, 223–226
pizza
    "Cocktail," 202–204
    contest involving, 139–141
    instruction on, 54, 56–57
Pizza Dough, 61–62
Pizza Sauce
    "Cocktail" Pizza, 202–204
    recipe, 62
Pizzo, trip to, 165
polenta concia, 238–239
Polenta with Cheese and Butter, 245
Porchetta
    about, 95
    recipe, 101–103
pork
    Calabrian Sausage, 103–104
    Meatballs with Sweet Peppers, 185–186
    Pork Cutlets with Marsala, 88–89
    Ragù Bolognese, 260–261
    Slow-Roasted Pork, 101–103
    Tuna of Chianti (Pork Confit), 106–107
    Tuscan Sausage, 104–105
pork belly
    Flat Pancetta, 99–101
potatoes
    Aunt Fidalma's Bean Soup, 233–234
preferments, 193
"Priest-Strangler" Pasta with Veal Ragù, 19–21
Prosecco
    Aperol Spritz, 71
provolone
    Stuffed Eggplant Rolls, 146–147
puff pastry, 195–196, 211

rabbit
    butchering, 81
    porchetta from, 95
    Whole Wheat Pasta with
        Rabbit Ragù, 86–88
Ragù Bolognese
    Arancini, 71–73
    Lasagne Bolognese, 257–259
    recipe, 260–261

raspberries
    Sponge Cake with Cream and Fruit, 7–8
Red-Wine Poached Pears, 119
rice
    about, xviii
    Arancini, 71–73
    Mushroom Risotto, 120–122
    Parmesan Cheese Risotto, 64–65
    Roman Rice Balls, 21–22
Ricotta
    Baked Ricotta, 63
    Cannoli, 73–74
    instruction on, 239–240, 241–242
    recipe, 246
    Ricotta Tart, 148–149
    Savory Ricotta-Filled Tarts from
        Calabria, 198–199
ricotta salata cheese
    Pasta alla Norma, 75
    "Perfume of the Sea" Pasta, 34–36
Rigatoni with Peas, 234–235
risotto
    Mushroom Risotto, 120–122
    Parmesan Cheese Risotto, 64–65
    rice for, xviii
    technique for, 56
Roast Cauliflower with Bechamel, 5–6
Roast Chicken, 4
Roasted Olives
    Pasta alla Puttanesca, 32–33
    recipe, 76
Roman Easter Cheese Bread, 259–260
Roman Rice Balls, 21–22
Roman-Style Chicken, 33–34
Rosemary Oil
    Lamb and Artichoke Lasagna, 44–45
    Lasagne Bolognese, 257–259
    Maltagliati Pasta with Oxtail Ragù, 159–161
    recipe, 262
    Whole Wheat Pasta with
        Rabbit Ragù, 86–88
rum, dark
    Tiramisù, 76–78

S

saffron
    Arancini, 71–73
salame
    Savory Ricotta-Filled Tarts from
        Calabria, 198–199
    Stuffed Eggplant Rolls, 146–147
salt, curing with, 12–13

sausage
    Calabrian Sausage, 103–104
    casing for, xviii–xix
    Cotechino Sausage with Lentils, 16–17
    instruction on, 98–99
    Lupara, 30–31
    Orecchiette Pasta with Broccoli
        Rabe and Sausage, 59–61
    stuffing, xix
    Tuscan Sausage, 104–105
savoiardi
    Tiramisù, 76–78
Savory Ricotta-Filled Tarts from
    Calabria, 198–199
scales, xix
scamorza
    Stuffed Eggplant Rolls, 146–147
schiacciata, about, 2
seafood
    Fileja Pasta with Shrimp and
        Mushrooms, 228–230
    Fregola Pasta with Clams and
        Cherry Tomatoes, 219–220
    Linguine "from the Reef," 48–49
    Mollusk Ragù, 50
    Octopus Sous-Vide, 171–172
    Pasta Cut on the "Chitarra" with Mussels
        and Cherry Tomatoes, 173–175
    Pasta with Clams, 169–170
    "Perfume of the Sea" Pasta, 34–36
semola rimacinata, xvii
Shortcrust Pastry
    Jam Tart, 182–183
    recipe, 149
    Ricotta Tart, 148–149
shrimp
    Fileja Pasta with Shrimp and
        Mushrooms, 228–230
    Linguine "from the Reef," 48–49
    "Perfume of the Sea" Pasta, 34–36
Sicily, trip to, 67–69
Slow-Roasted Pork, 101–103
smoking with olive branches, 12
Sogo di 'Ndjua
    Fusilloni Pasta with 'Nduja and
        Tomato Sauce, 116–118
sommelier training, 151–152, 153, 163
soppressata
    Savory Ricotta-Filled Tarts from
        Calabria, 198–199
    Stuffed Eggplant Rolls, 146–147
soups
    Aunt Fidalma's Bean Soup, 233–234

Chicken Broth, 15–16
Concentrated Chicken Stock, 83–84
fish, 154
Fish Stock, 36–37
Mushroom Broth, 118
Tomato Soup, 175
Vegetable Broth, 161
Soverato market, 53, 166, 195, 242
Spaghetti with Garlic and Oil, 89–90
spinach
    Beans and Greens, 143–145
Sponge Cake
    with Cream and Fruit, 7–8
    recipe, 6–7
Statti Company, 211–212
stone tools, 80–81
stracciatella gelato, 180
Stuffed Eggplant Rolls, 146–147
sugar syrups, 129

T

Thinly Sliced Beef Braised in Tomato Sauce with Black Olives, 114–115
Tiramisù, 76–78
tomato paste
    about, xviii
    Concentrated Chicken Stock, 83–84
    Maltagliati Pasta with Oxtail Ragù, 159–161
    Pasta and Beans, 187–188
    Pasta with Calabrian Lamb Ragù, 243–244
    "Priest-Strangler" Pasta with Veal Ragù, 19–21
    Thinly Sliced Beef Braised in Tomato Sauce with Black Olives, 114–115
tomato puree (passata)
    about, xviii
    Caponata, 216–217
    Fileja Pasta with Shrimp and Mushrooms, 228–230
    Fusilloni Pasta with 'Nduja and Tomato Sauce, 116–118
    Lamb Ragù, 46–47
    Meatballs with Sweet Peppers, 185–186
    "Priest-Strangler" Pasta with Veal Ragù, 19–21
    Roman-Style Chicken, 33–34
    Tomato Soup, 175
    Tomato Soup, 175
tomatoes
    about, xviii
    Basic Tomato Sauce, 131–132
    Fish Stock, 36–37
    Fregola Pasta with Clams and Cherry Tomatoes, 219–220
    Linguine "from the Reef," 48–49
    Maltagliati Pasta with Oxtail Ragù, 159–161
    Pasta Cut on the "Chitarra" with Mussels and Cherry Tomatoes, 173–175
    Pizza Dough, 62
    Ragù Bolognese, 260–261
tomini, 251–252
Tomino Cheese, 247–248
Tropea, trip to, 165–166
Tuna of Chianti (Pork Confit), 97–98, 106–107
tunnel-boning quail, 55
Tuscan Almond Biscotti, 214
Tuscan Sausage, 104–105
Tutto Calabria, trip to, 130

V

Veal Ragù, "Priest-Strangler" Pasta with, 19–21
Vegetable Broth
    Braised Mushrooms, 248–249
    Maltagliati Pasta with Oxtail Ragù, 159–161
    Mollusk Ragù, 50
    Pasta Cut on the "Chitarra" with Mussels and Cherry Tomatoes, 173–175
    recipe, 161
vegetable presses, xx
vialone, xviii

W

weight gain, 25, 67
white chocolate
    Caramelized White Chocolate Crumble, 188
    crumble made from, 181
Whole Wheat Pasta
    recipe, 90–91
    Whole Wheat Pasta with Rabbit Ragù, 86–88
wine, Marsala
    Pork Cutlets with Marsala, 88–89
wine, red
    Calabrian Sausage, 103–104
    Concentrated Chicken Stock, 83–84
    Fusilloni Pasta with 'Nduja and Tomato Sauce, 116–118
    Lamb Ragù, 46–47
    Lupara, 30–31
    Maltagliati Pasta with Oxtail Ragù, 159–161
    Pasta with Calabrian Lamb Ragù, 243–244

    "Priest-Strangler" Pasta with
        Veal Ragù, 19–21
    Ragù Bolognese, 260–261
    Red-Wine Poached Pears, 119
    Thinly Sliced Beef Braised in Tomato
        Sauce with Black Olives, 114–115
wine, white
    Braised Mushrooms, 248–249
    Chicken Broth, 15–16
    Cotechino Sausage with Lentils, 16–17
    Fish Stock, 36–37
    Fregola Pasta with Clams and
        Cherry Tomatoes, 219–220
    Linguine "from the Reef," 48–49
    Mafalde Pasta with Broccoli, 58–59
    Mushroom Risotto, 120–122
    Parmesan Cheese Risotto, 64–65
    Pasta all'Amatriciana, 135–136
    Pasta with Clams, 169–170
    "Priest-Strangler" Pasta with
        Veal Ragù, 19–21
    Rigatoni with Peas, 234–235
    Roast Chicken, 4
    Roman-Style Chicken, 33–34
    Slow-Roasted Pork, 101–103
    Thinly Sliced Beef Braised in Tomato
        Sauce with Black Olives, 114–115
    Tuscan Sausage, 104–105
    Whole Wheat Pasta with
        Rabbit Ragù, 86–88
W-value, xvi, 80

Y

yogurt
    Tomino Cheese, 247–248

Z

zampone, about, 12
Zucchini Blossoms, Fried, 115–116

www.ingramcontent.com/pod-product-compliance
Lightning Source LLC
Chambersburg PA
CBHW041409300426
44114CB00028B/2967